MANAGING THE
WORLD ECONOMY

MANAGING THE WORLD ECONOMY

The Consequences of Corporate Alliances

PETER F. COWHEY

JONATHAN D. ARONSON

COUNCIL ON FOREIGN RELATIONS PRESS

NEW YORK

COUNCIL ON FOREIGN RELATIONS BOOKS

The Council on Foreign Relations, Inc., is a nonprofit and nonpartisan organization devoted to promoting improved understanding of international affairs through the free exchange of ideas. The Council does not take any position on questions of foreign policy and has no affiliation with, and receives no funding from, the United States government.

From time to time, books and monographs written by members of the Council's research staff or visiting fellows, or commissioned by the Council, or written by an independent author with critical review contributed by a Council study or working group are published with the designation "Council on Foreign Relations Book." Any book or monograph bearing that designation is, in the judgment of the Committee on Studies of the Council's Board of Directors, a responsible treatment of a significant international topic worthy of presentation to the public. All statements of fact and expressions of opinion contained in Council books are, however, the sole responsibility of the author.

If you would like more information on Council publications, please write the Council on Foreign Relations, 58 East 68th Street, New York, NY 10021, or call the Publications Office at (212)734-0400.

Copyright © 1993 by the Council on Foreign Relations®, Inc.
All rights reserved.
Printed in the United States of America.

This book may not be reproduced, in whole or in part, in any form (beyond that copying permitted by Sections 107 and 108 of the U.S. Copyright Law and excerpts by reviewers for the public press), without written permission from the publishers. For information, write Publications Office, Council on Foreign Relations, 58 East 68th Street, New York, NY 10021.

Library of Congress Cataloging-in-Publication Data

Cowhey, Peter F., 1948–
    Managing the world economy : the consequences of corporate
alliances / Peter F. Cowhey and Jonathan D. Aronson.
        p.   cm.
    Includes bibliographical references and index.
    ISBN 0-87609-132-X : $16.95
    1. Strategic alliances (Business)   2. Automobile industry and trade.   3. Semiconductor industry.   4. Telecommunication.   5. International economic relations.   6. Commercial policy.   7. Competition, International.   I. Aronson, Jonathan David.   II. Title.
    HD69.S8C69   1993   92-42450
    338.8–dc20   CIP

93   94   95   96   97   EB   10   9   8   7   6   5   4   3   2   1

Cover Design: Michael Storrings

Alliances have consequences.
For Adam, Megan, and Zachary

"Who governs the life of men and, generally, the entire situation here on earth?"

"Man himself governs it." . . .

"Sorry," the stranger responded mildly. "But in order to govern, it is, after all, necessary to have a definite plan for at least a fairly decent period of time."

—Mikhail Bulgakov
The Master and Margarita

"Looking beyond the Uruguay Round to the *trade issues of the 1990s*, Ministers emphasize the need to address the new dimension of trade policy. This includes a whole range of issues which arise because of the increasing globalisation of the world economy and the closer relationship between trade policy and competition, investment, technology and innovation, and environment policies. The increasingly international scope of economic activity has seen the emergence of areas in which the needs of private agents and governments run ahead of the existing 'rules of the game.' There is a perceived need for better understanding of these issues and, where appropriate, convergence of policy approaches and considerations of fresh rules. Many issues, traditionally viewed largely from a domestic policy perspective, have taken on an international dimension, affecting the setting of trade and investment policies themselves. Hence, widening the consideration of trade policies in the 1990s to take account of new developments will go hand-in-hand with efforts to avoid conflict with other policy spheres."

—Communiqué of the
Council of the OECD
at Ministerial Level
Paris, June 5, 1991

CONTENTS

LIST OF TABLES

LIST OF ACRONYMS

AMD	Advanced Micro Devices (U.S. firm)
ANSI	American National Standards Institute
ASEAN	Association of Southeast Asian Nations
ASIC	Application-specific integrated circuit (customized chip)
BIS	Bank for International Settlements
BRITE	Basic Research in Industrial Technologies for Europe
CCITT	International Consultative Committee for Telephone and Telegraph (of ITU)
CMOS	Customized metal oxide on silicon (chips)
COS	Corporation for Open Systems
CSPP	Computer System Policy Project
DCA	Domestic corporate alliance
DRAM	Dynamic random-access memory (memory chip)
EC	European Community
ECU	European Currency Unit
EDI	Electronic data interchange
EPROM	Erasable programmable read-only memory (chips)
Esprit	European Strategic Programme for Research and Development in Information Technology
FOF	Foreign owned firm
GATT	General Agreement on Tariffs and Trade
GEIS	General Electric Information Services
GIMM	Global information movement and management
HDTV	High-definition television

ICA	International corporate alliance
ICL	International Computers Limited (U.K. firm)
IDC	International Digital Communications (Japanese telephone ICA)
IMF	International Monetary Fund
ISO	International Standards Organization
ITO	International Trade Organization
ITU	International Telecommunication Union
JESSI	Joint European Submicron Silicon Initiative (of the EC)
KDD	Kokusai Denshin Denwa (Japanese international telephone company)
LDP	Liberal Democratic Party (of Japan)
MCC	Microelectronics Computer Technology Corporation (U.S. DCA)
MFN	Most-favored nation
MITI	Ministry of International Trade and Industry (Japan)
MOSS	Market-Oriented Sectoral-Specific talks (between the U.S. and Japan)
MPT	Ministry of Posts and Telecommunications (Japan)
MTO	Multilateral Trade Organization (proposed December 1991)
NTBs	Nontariff barriers
NTT	Nippon Telegraph and Telephone Company
NAFTA	North American Free Trade Agreement
OECD	Organization for Economic Cooperation and Development
ONA	Open Network Architecture
RACE	Research for Advanced Communications in Europe
R&D	Research and development
RISC	Reduced instruction set chip
SIA	Semiconductor Industry Association
SII	Structural Impediments Initiative
SITA	Société Internationale de Telecommunications Aéronautiques
SRC	Semiconductor Research Corporation

SWIFT	Society for Worldwide Interbank Financial Telecommunications
TI	Texas Instruments (U.S. firm)
TNC	Transnational corporation
TRIMs	Trade-related investment measures
UAW	United Auto Workers
USTR	Office of the U.S. Trade Representative
VANs	Value-added networks
VERs	Voluntary Export Restraints
VLSI	Very Large Scale Integrated Circuit Association
VRAs	Voluntary export restraint agreements

ACKNOWLEDGMENTS

This book began as an effort to understand the significance of the veritable flood of international corporate alliances. It has turned into something much broader. In 1985 we worked with C. Michael Aho, senior economist at the Council on Foreign Relations, and Paul Kreisberg, director of studies at the Council, to develop a Council on Foreign Relations study group on international corporate alliances. (Nicholas X. Rizopoulos, director of studies at the end of the project, also was patient and supportive.) Lewis Young agreed to serve as chair of the study group. Insightful presentations for the study group were made by Thomas Atkinson, Albert Bressand, and Bruce Kogut. Barbara Jenkins and Sandra Peterson were the able reporters for the sessions. Kevin McKilly provided research assistance. Martha Little read and contributed valuable comments on the manuscript. Badi Foster, Harry Freeman, Denis Gilhooly, Leon Hollerman, Peter Pestillo, and Richard Solomon made useful comments as the manuscript approached completion. We are grateful to all of these individuals for their help and to all of those who attended one or more of these sessions: Claude Barfield, Stephen Blank, Timothy Curran, Wolfgang Danspeckgruber, William Diebold, Jr., Catherine Distler, Kempton Dunn, Wayne Edisis, Geza Feketekuty, Harry Freeman, Ellen Frost, Thomas Gardener, Richard Gardner, William Glasgall, David Gompert, John Guilfoyle, Jeffrey Hart, Michael Hodin, Suzanne Hooper, Merit Janow, Daniel Kasper, Abraham Katz, Steven Koltai, Simon Lazarus, Hakan Ledin, Edward Morse, David Mowery, Richard Nelson, Eli Noam, Kenneth Oye, Andrew Pierre, Alan Romberg, Oscar Ruebhausen, John Ruggie, Charles Schmitz, John Seigle, Daniel Sharp, Herbert Steinke, Jr., Paula Stern, Yoshindo Takahashi, Fred Tamalonis, Adrian Tschoegl, Brian Turner, Raymond Vernon, Penny Walker, Frank Weil, Oliver Williamson, and Ernest Wilson.

After five sessions between December 1985 and June 1986, we were inundated with information and promised to produce a book manuscript in short order. In truth, we were still uncertain about how to describe the wider significance of international corporate alliances. We procrastinated. We tackled other book projects. We each married and had children. Every so often someone from the Council would call us and gently ask when the manuscript could be expected. We gulped.

Five years, three children, and two books later, our ideas about international corporate alliances began to come together. Perhaps we were lucky: much of the literature cited here did not exist when we began. Ultimately we recognized that the book we were writing about international corporate alliances was actually about a broader topic—management of the world economy. Once we made this conceptual leap, we began to see international and domestic corporate alliances as indicators of important trends that are reorganizing the world economy. From there the manuscript began to take form. Michael Aho and the Council on Foreign Relations helped by organizing two review groups to comment on the very penultimate drafts of the book. We are grateful to participants in these two groups. In New York in November 1990 we received valuable input from Michael Aho, Steve Blank, William Diebold, Jr., Geza Feketekuty, Bruce Kogut, Suzanne Hooper, Marc Levinson, Nicholas X. Rizopoulos, and Allison von Klemperer. On March 1, 1991, the Berkeley Roundtable on the International Economy arranged a second review group for the book. Those involved were Michael Aho, Vinod Aggarwal, Stephen S. Cohen, Carol Evans, Bonnie Gold, David Mowery, Greg Noble, Joanne Oxley, Laura Tyson, Steve Weber, and John Zysman.

Several people and institutions deserve a final word of special thanks. We thank David Gompert (then of AT&T) and Geza

Feketekuty at the Office of the U.S. Trade Representative for serving as our mentors as Council fellows. The Rockefeller Foundation provided generous support to Peter Cowhey. The Berkeley Round-table on the International Economy and Promethee often assisted us. And both of us have profited from being researchers and teachers at schools dedicated to the study of international affairs— the Graduate School of International Relations and Pacific Studies at the University of California, San Diego, and the School of International Relations at the University of Southern California.

The World Economy in Transition

CHAPTER ONE

Organizing Global Economic Management

This book considers the relationship between the globalization of large private firms and the management of the world economy. It examines how changes in the world economy affect business firms, how firms respond to these changes, and how corporate strategies affect government management of the world economy.

The way the world economy works has changed dramatically during the past forty-five years. In general, firms have adapted faster than governments. Over time the gap between existing regulations and reality has grown so large that it interferes with effective management of global commerce, and discourages economic growth.

Government officials and business leaders are looking for answers to three questions. First, does the spread of activist government policies on international competition necessarily imply an end to an open and integrated world economy? Our answer is no: countries can open markets to foreign competition and embrace industrial policies simultaneously. We define *open industrial policy* as one that gives foreign firms the freedom to contest local markets, not one that removes all trade barriers. Some economists worry that new nontariff barriers and restrictions on foreign investment will undermine the integration of the world economy created by the post-1945 regime for free trade. We believe that they are confusing closure with interventionist responses to new economic challenges.[1]

Governments are beginning to regulate open, competitive markets in new ways. New global policy responses are needed, but the open world economy is not on the verge of collapse.

Since World War II the distinctive corporate management style, economic organization, and political relations of U.S. industry with Washington have been the standard for the world market. Global rules evolved in response to the agenda of competitive issues raised by firms rooted in U.S.-style approaches (which were themselves a variant of a century of British tradition). The second question is related to the structure and behavior of firms: can the implicit model of the relationship between firms and governments on which world trade rules has rested since 1945 be sustained? In short, what will be the fate of the U.S. model of industrial organization that has dominated global commerce in one form or another since the mid-nineteenth century? Can the U.S. model be revived, or must it be replaced? Our answer is that the old model of industrial organization is obsolete and needs to be replaced by a new one.

The redistribution of economic power from the United States to Japan and Europe means that new styles of industrial organization will share the strategic center. We contend that the old model for organizing international commerce is as out of date as American hegemony. The United States is still the greatest military power on the earth, the U.S. economy still eclipses Japanese and resurgent European economic might and could rebound in the 1990s, but the United States no longer can manage the world economy alone, and neither Japan nor Europe is able to or seeks to assume the mantle of hegemonic leadership. Therefore, countries and companies need to find new ways to manage global economic relations.[2]

New national rules for managing world commerce already have emerged. As new forms of government strategy for advancing economic growth (such as industrial targeting by Japan) have advanced to the forefront, corporations react and adapt, usually more rapidly than governments. The emergence of transnational corporations (TNCs) and later of international corporate alliances (ICAs) were logical reactions by private firms to changing circumstances.[3] ICAs were part of the problem for policymakers but part of the solution for private firms.

The U.S. model is being supplanted. For the international economic order to thrive, it must adapt and solve the problems posed by the globalization of the private sector. The process of developing and implementing a new model is already underway. It is significant that as governments and corporations struggle to make this transition, the nature of international economic relations is being transformed: free trade and investment were at the heart of the old model; market access, fair competition, and the internationalization of domestic regulations will be at the core of the emerging model of international commerce.

As firms change, they are making national economies more interdependent. Even if governments introduce new forms of oversight to manage competition, greater interdependence is likely. Governments may protect national firms, but the production and technology of many firms already are so global that world economic integration will proceed on a competitive basis. The third question follows from the other two: in the future will it be possible for governments to sustain the traditional tools for managing world commerce? In other words, will policymakers continue to rely mainly on multilateral trade agreements, emphasize trade as the leading edge of global commerce, and assume that domestic and international economic policies are separate and independent from each other? Again, our answer is no. New ordering principles are needed that redefine the boundaries separating global and regional, trade and investment, domestic and international, and goods and services.

THE EMERGENCE OF INTERNATIONAL CORPORATE ALLIANCES

The story of international relations until the 1960s was about the cumulative extension of the power of sovereign territorial states over political and economic affairs. One of the most dramatic changes of the past three decades is the growth of political and economic activity outside the traditional jurisdiction and organizing principles of states. The European Community is the most obvious example. An EC corporation may someday have an EC charter and have rights and duties defined by a blend of EC and national laws. The European Community is unlikely to replace the individual European states as the ultimate source of political authority, but U.S. officials recognize that a complaint against Airbus is already a complaint against the European Community as well as several member governments. Alliances are corporate responses to fundamental economic trends, to market imperfections created by government rules, and to global corporate missions that cannot easily be organized by traditional national rules and economic infrastructures.

Alliances between firms from different countries are not a new phenomenon. For decades, transnational corporations have operated joint ventures with local firms in host countries. Most commonly, joint ventures linked a large TNC from an industrial country with a small firm based in a developing country. Most of these joint ventures operated exclusively in the developing country. Usually they were formed to satisfy local rules concerning ownership and production, because the laws of many countries require that their citizens control a minimum percentage of any major business. Similarly, many countries insist that a portion of inputs into the production process be sourced locally. To meet such requirements, transnational corporations often entered into joint ventures with local firms. Typically, the foreign TNC retained majority ownership and management control over the local operation. To earn their minority shares, local investors generally provided the required local content.[4]

Partnership arrangements also linked firms from industrial countries. For example, NEC, one of Japan's most visible high-technology firms, was set up in 1899 as Japan's first joint venture with a U.S. company—Western Electric. ITT acquired Western Electric's interest in 1925, and NEC eventually "freed itself from this affiliation and began to grow as an independent company" in 1965. ITT remained NEC's largest stockholder until the early 1970s.[5] In many of these ventures the local partner supplied low-priority products or inputs that the TNC used throughout its global operations. Original-equipment manufacturing deals usually involved products that were considered to be outside the core business of the company that purchased them. Thus if Olivetti relied on Japanese suppliers for facsimile machines offered in its own consumer product line, then Olivetti almost certainly did not intend to build its strategic advantage in the electronic marketplace on this technology.

By the early 1980s a new type of joint venture emerged that focused more on strategic processes, products, and markets. Giant firms like AT&T, Philips, General Motors, and Toyota entered into international corporate alliances that joined leading strategic competitors from different countries.

We define *international corporate alliances* (ICAs) as ongoing relationships between companies from two or more countries that involve significant markets, products, R&D, and other important process technologies that shape the strategy of global market leaders. An international corporate alliance between General Motors and Toyota occurs if one or more vehicles important to the plans of both firms in key markets are jointly produced on an ongoing basis; the project by itself is so significant to both firms that we consider it an ICA. If Toyota enters a coproduction arrangement with a subsidiary of Tata Industries in India, however, this is not classified as an ICA; it is a traditional joint venture even though Tata is an important Indian industrial group. Finally, Ford and Mazda may have minority ownership positions in Kia Motors of Korea, which provides them with low-end vehicles for sale internationally. Kia is more than a provider of local content, the product is strategic for Ford, and although Kia is not now a strategic competitor to Ford, it could become one. The Ford alliance therefore is part of a pattern of relationships that is transforming Ford (and General Motors). No two or three alliances may equal the importance of Ford in the market, but Ford itself may rely on a dozen alliances to keep it competitive. Thus Kia is part of the ICAs of Ford because the company's central strategy relies directly on a group of ICAs for key products and processes.[6]

The proliferation and potential power of these alliances led to a fascination with ICAs. In the mid-1980s the business press proclaimed that these international corporate alliances were the wave of the future.[7] If U.S. firms could no longer dominate world markets, perhaps they could maintain much of their influence by leading consortia of companies from other countries.

By 1987 journalistic enthusiasm faded somewhat, and the business press began to warn of the dangers of cross-national corporate alliances. Would ICAs transfer technology from U.S. firms to their foreign partners without capturing any long-run benefit for the firm or the country in return? Would ICAs between U.S. and Japanese firms eventually lead to the triumph of Japanese firms over their American counterparts?[8] Perhaps lagging U.S. firms that tried to turn around their fortunes by entering into alliances were playing into the hands of their competitors.[9]

Even as criticism of ICAs mounted, U.S. firms began to experiment more actively with alliances among domestic firms to try to meet global competitive challenges. Domestic corporate alliances (DCAs) occur when strategic competitors from a single country work together to strengthen their position in a key market, share technology, or introduce new products. DCAs have long thrived in Japan. Japanese companies, with the encouragement of the Japanese Ministry of International Trade and Industry (MITI), often rely on domestic corporate alliances to enhance Japan's overall competitive potential in the world market. For example, in the early 1970s when Japanese banks began to venture overseas, they tested the waters by forming two new banks—Allied Bank International, owned by sixteen regional Japanese banks, and the Japan International Bank, owned by seven large Japanese banks. Once Japanese banks were convinced that they needed to venture abroad, they did so on their own, ultimately disbanding the domestic corporate alliances. Four Italian banks created the Italian International Bank for the same reasons.[10]

Responding to the perceived high-technology threat from Japan, U.S. firms have begun to explore DCAs. The Microelectronics Computer and Electronic Corporation (MCC) and Sematech are two examples. (During the same period, as part of its drive toward a single European market, the European Community created a hybrid of ICA and DCA. Leading national firms from Europe entered EC-wide consortia to respond collectively to competitive challenges from the United States and Japan. Eureka, for example, is an EC R&D consortia that focuses on advanced technologies.) By 1990, however, prominent critics such as Michael Porter were arguing that

DCAs were another false start because they weakened competition at home, thereby hurting international competitiveness.[11]

Corporate alliances can be approached from a different direction, however. Countries and international institutions can promote and facilitate economic prosperity and fairness in an increasingly complicated world. What are their options, and how might they be implemented? We examine the role, operation, and management of ICAs in the context of the postwar international economic system to understand their implications for managing the world economy and for making foreign economic policy. We view ICAs as private partnerships that may alter political dynamics and that may alter trade advantages. Trade diplomacy involving ICAs therefore may require new forms of international oversight that go beyond traditional powers exercised exclusively by national governments. We do not try to pinpoint the precise benefit or harm that ICAs cause to U.S. economic growth or business competitiveness. Although this book may have significant implications for corporate management, it is mainly concerned with international economic relations among nations.

Skeptics argue that ICAs are at best useful transitional devices to assist firms during the restructuring of global industries and are thus likely to be short-lived. This was, after all, the fate of steel and banking consortia in the 1970s and 1980s. We believe that many ICAs are important and will persist because they are part of the phenomenon restructuring economic processes in ways that defy traditional national governance. ICAs also are important to both governments and corporations during hard times and volatile periods. Economic collapse most often stems from the inability of economies to adjust to problems of transition, not because countries prefer a closed, anarchic world economy. During periods of transition, politicians try to reorder the system within which they live, not to decimate it. The new strategic policies implemented by private firms, particularly the globalization of the firm epitomized by ICAs, must be taken into account when seeking new ways to manage the world economy. At the same time, TNCs are becoming more national in character because they appreciate the advantages of a strongly competitive home base for manufacturing and services. IBM is a good example of this two-pronged evolution. Even as IBM is establishing a large number of significant ICAs, it is, for the first time, working to build domestic corporate alliances to reinforce its U.S. manufacturing base.

The emergence of international corporate alliances is an indicator of the deep changes currently transforming the world economy. ICAs are both a consequence and a cause of changes in today's world economy. They are a rational business response to problems arising from the new structure of international commerce. In the short run they permit companies to solve problems associated with operating on a global stage. Corporate strategies—such as relying on ICAs—can help firms cope with the imperfections of highly competitive markets. As they do so, global, U.S.-based TNCs rethink how to manage their internal activities, relate to other firms, and interact with governments. And they incorporate many innovations from the Japanese and pan-European models of industrial organization related to the restructuring of the private corporate order.

ICAs and DCAs are slowly reorganizing U.S. industry. Alliances influence the range of policy options available to governments and ultimately will lead to major innovations in the rules and policies that govern international commerce. But even as firms work with their international counterparts at private diplomatic efforts to resolve matters of dispute, their efforts are likely to be impeded by imperfect competitive markets. Firms do not have the resources or mission to resolutely follow unprofitable strategies simply to show mutual good faith over the long term. Governments have a much easier time making and upholding promises concerning long-term market policies. Thus, although ICAs can change the menu of demands and choices concerning the management of world commerce (see Chapter 8), their shortcomings suggest the need for new forms of government activism in selected markets.[12]

This book suggests how policymakers can adapt the rules and principles that govern international commerce to address the underlying causes that led to the emergence of ICAs and to respond to the consequences of these alliances. We describe how the world economy now works, how firms have contributed and responded to its recent changes, and, in the wake of these changes, what key strategic choices governments and international firms now face. By exploring these questions, we also explore how governments must alter their trade, investment, and industrial promotion policies to manage the world economy successfully.

STRUCTURE OF THE BOOK

The post-1945 international economic system has fallen apart, and like Humpty Dumpty, it is impossible to put it back together again. The challenge we face is to create a new order. Reform is possible, and in this book we suggest the kinds of new policies that are needed to manage the world economy successfully in the 1990s and beyond.

The book is organized in three parts. Our argument unfolds over the next nine chapters. The remainder of Part I, Chapters 2 through 4, concentrates on how the world economy has changed over the past four decades. Chapter 2 examines the six major pillars on which the postwar world economy was built—four that were related to the structure of governance and two that determined how it worked. Chapter 3 examines the changes that are transforming the late twentieth-century world political economy and the responses of firms to these changes, particularly their efforts to globalize their operations through alliances. We stress that the changes overtaking the global economic regime are about more than trade liberalization or protection and that ICAs provide novel ways to share competitive assets among firms. Chapter 4 then juxtaposes the deterioration of the pillars that supported the free-trade system and the emergence of new pillars necessary for the functioning of a market-access regime. Each pillar in the new market-access regime corresponds to one in the old free-trade regime.

Part II elaborates on our analysis and highlights the new choices facing globalized firms by examining the experiences of three important sectors: Chapter 5 examines the automobile sector; Chapter 6 focuses on the semiconductor industry; and Chapter 7 concentrates on international telecommunications services. Each sectoral chapter first examines the way one industry operated under the six pillars that made up the free-trade regime and then analyzes how companies in the sector responded to the erosion of the six pillars. Particular attention is paid to how firms used ICAs to deal with the changing global economic environment and to what extent each sector corresponds today to the emerging market-access pillars described in Chapter 4.

Finally, Part III considers how governments might best manage the twenty-first-century world economy. Chapter 8 presents a brief synopsis of the status of world trading arrangements as the Uruguay Round staggered to a close in late 1992, reviews the consequences of corporate alliances, and suggests some underlying principles that governments can adopt to try to manage the world economy today. Chapter 9 suggests how governments can reform the structure and governance of the world economy, showing in considerable detail how governments can implement the first four new pillars. The relative advantages of bilateral and multilateral negotiations as a means for managing the world economy receive special attention when we examine how governments can restructure negotiations and ultimately their relations with each other and with the private sector under a new market-access regime. Finally, Chapter 10 focuses on the kinds of rules that governments will need to develop as they struggle to manage a complex and inherently unmanageable world economy during the 1990s and beyond. Governments will continue to intervene in the economy, despite the objections of ardent free marketeers, but governments need to rethink how they do so and in which areas.

The world economy can and should remain open to trade and investment across national boundaries, but the terms on which a vigorous and open world economy will be managed need to change in fundamental ways. Bilateral and minilateral negotiations and industry-specific understandings are not the first blows in a global trade war: they are new tools and means for managing the world economy. By keeping markets open, governments can ensure that the losses incurred by bottom-up plurilateral negotiations and specialized industry codes will be offset by innovation from continuing globalization and a net increase in competition.

CHAPTER TWO

The Six Pillars of the Postwar World Economy

In the late 1940s the United States dominated the process of rebuilding the world trading regime. Free trade was always the U.S. goal even though the imperfect system that emerged overflowed with specialized arrangements for key sectors. The international economic order is changing in fundamental ways. We no longer are experiencing a highly publicized, incremental adjustment of the old system. Instead, the global economy is moving toward a new standard—one we call a market-access regime—built on open industrial policies at the national level.

A regime is the set of principles (theories about the way the system should operate), norms (underlying expectations about governing relations), rules (more explicit guidelines for behavior), and decision-making systems for governing international relations. Although most regime theorists do not consider the structure of firms to be part of the regime, regime theory is most useful if it analyzes the effective pattern and consequences of how a market is governed. Because regimes are premised on how the principles and rules will influence the conduct of firms, if there are significant changes in the nature of firms, the practical meaning of the formal principles of the regime will change. The main task of an international economic regime is to manage the interaction of the public sector with the private sector. It is defined by the mix of public norms and rules governing openness and private "governance" of the market by firms.[1] Regimes can be transformed if either the form of openness or the globalization of firms changes. We expect emerging market-access regimes will combine substantial openness to international competition, significant globalization of firms, and vigorous efforts by governments to promote industrial advantage.

To understand how the world economy has changed, it is necessary to review the postwar free-trade system for managing international commerce. Traditional free-trade regimes restrict the use of foreign economic policy instruments such as tariffs and quotas and ensure nondiscrimination among countries, thereby speeding the process of liberalization and reducing the temptation to cheat. Free-trade theory usually assumed that international rules did not cover domestic economic policies unless they conflicted with other key principles such as transparency and national treatment. Foreign investment was a secondary issue, in part because governments have disagreed on the rules for more than forty years. Although countries worried about protecting the property rights of their nationals overseas, investment itself was critical only in those sectors where there was a tacit agreement that liberalizing investment rules could be a full or partial substitute for liberalizing trade barriers. A free-trade regime is considered "open" if countries permit market competition at home and between countries.

The free-trade regime was not highly globalized because most firms within it were not highly globalized. Trade and foreign investment largely reflected the competitive advantages conferred on firms by their home countries. Globalization is a popular term today for describing changes in the world economy because it is suggestive but elastic. We use *globalization* to mean that the leading firms rely on foreign markets, on production and competitive assets (such as access to research and development) in other countries, and on global networks (such as the global payments network shared by the leading banks) to accomplish their fundamental business objectives. Globalization is related to how corporations organize themselves and how governments evaluate global competition. Globalization is ubiquitous but does not take the same form in each industry. A firm that earns a large share of its revenues from exporting is more global than a firm selling only at home. A company that relies on extensive international production and support facilities is more global than a firm that relies just on exporting. A firm that enjoys global competitive advantages because of special production advantages it has developed in other countries is even more global.[2]

The post-1945 version of free trade was a political invention of powerful countries. The United States, in collaboration with Great Britain and other countries, created new international institutions and rules to promote free trade with stable currencies. The United States proposed an international economic system that mirrored its own domestic policies and pattern of industrial organization. The system assumed that governments used macroeconomic policy tools to steer the domestic economy, but the goal was to minimize sectoral planning and government regulation except in service sectors. Antitrust policy was used to protect consumer welfare. Free trade was, in many ways, the global counterpart of antitrust policy. The precise form of global liberalization was shaped by the determination of U.S. policymakers to promote domestic employment and social welfare. The free-trade regime was consistent with numerous provisos to ensure that trade did not upset commitments to employment.[3] The United States recognized that in any international economic regime governments had to help each country balance international liberalization against domestic prosperity. The global system combined a commitment to market forces in the context of minimum social welfare goals. The International Monetary Fund (IMF) and the World Bank reflected U.S. efforts to establish new international institutions to improve global macroeconomic coordination and assistance. The United States conceived of the International Trade Organization (ITO) as the third leg of the postwar economic triad. When it proved impossible to gain approval of the ITO, the General Agreement on Tariffs and Trade (GATT) emerged as a second-best substitute.[4] The GATT reflected the assumption that most government policies influencing trade occurred at the border because governments could not effectively gain advantages through industrial policies. The GATT was intended to codify a set of rules and principles that would reduce regulation and planning hampering trade in individual sectors for goods. U.S. officials realized, of course, that absolute free trade was unobtainable, but to a large extent they embraced the ideas and political commitments of an earlier generation of British free traders—that comparative advantage is a product of history, geography, and accident, and that countries have certain comparative advantages (such as labor or capital endowments) and specialize in industries where they possess greater relative endowments than others.

THE FOUR PILLARS THAT DEFINE THE STRUCTURE OF THE WORLD ECONOMY

At its core U.S. postwar foreign economic policy and the free-trade system was based on six fundamental pillars—four pillars that defined the implicit structure of postwar world economy and two pillars that specified the rules.

The U.S. Model of Industrial Organization

The U.S. model of industrial organization served as the prototype for governments as they regulated competitive advantages. The architects of the postwar world assumed that U.S. companies would be the dominant players and that U.S. practices for managing public-sector and private-sector relationships would triumph. Although market-oriented Keynesian policies became a guide for industrial countries—for example, most countries made a larger effort to limit state monopolies than in the past—everyone acknowledged significant variations from the U.S. model would prevail in other countries.

Domestic politics set the initial agenda of what states seek from international economic regimes. Countries want economic regimes that reinforce domestic political bargains related to markets. This is what the United States did when it enshrined its model of industrial organization as the basis for the postwar economic regime. The same logic explains why the United States supports free trade for wheat and protection for textiles. Domestic political demands inevitably incorporate expectations about international factors. Government leaders and firms consider the international competitive and political environment when they decide which domestic and foreign economic policies to pursue. To illustrate, French high-technology firms want protection from Japan but do not want their actions to provide U.S. firms with a justification for excluding French products from the U.S. market.

To the extent that the United States dominated the world economy, the rules and practices used by the U.S. government and its firms for organizing competitive policies and industrial promotion defined the terms for global competition. Others might experiment with industrial policies or alternative ways of organizing firms, but they had little impact on the core competitive realities of the world market as long as the United States remained the pivotal supplier and marketplace.

Large U.S. firms provided the model of corporate efficiency and accountability. These professionally managed, multidivisional, multifunctional, often vertically integrated firms pioneered the formation of the modern transnational corporation.[5] TNCs favored large-scale, internally owned and operated production and distribution. Alliances among firms were the exception, not the rule. There was nothing on the American scene comparable to the Japanese keiretsu.

Just as critically, U.S. firms cared little whether they served foreign markets by exporting or by producing overseas. Although the United States was the world's largest exporter, policies were built around free-trade ideals, not around the concept of export-led growth. Indeed, American firms were far less attuned to and dependent on foreign markets than their European counterparts. Most U.S. exports were accounted for by a small number of large firms that had production, inventory, and distribution practices that could be replicated elsewhere. Moreover, American firms were willing to source components and products from foreign firms. Indeed, one of the major stimuli to Asian industrialization was sourcing to U.S. firms.

The U.S. model presumed that there was little hierarchical planning of sectoral development in the public or private sector. In short, it assumed a classically open national market—open to competition at home and from abroad according to the dictates of competitive markets. It assumed that individual firms usually maintained an arm's-length relationship with their home country governments and financial sectors but that they were subject to extensive antitrust supervision. The most important tools of government policy were consumer and R&D spending and the procurement policies associated with military and civilian science programs.[6] For many years these tools for steering the economy were not on the GATT agenda. Nonetheless, the U.S. economy was quite open. Nontariff barriers were relatively minor. Most foreign investment was welcome. The "leaky" quality of intellectual property in the United States meant that although other countries complained that U.S. firms did not transfer enough technology to their overseas operations, the overall pool of U.S. know-how was widely accessible through licensing and scientific journals.[7] There also was a substantial flow of technology via subcontracting of production for U.S. firms overseas. In addition, U.S. rules and the operation of U.S. firms were reasonably transparent. For example, the Administrative Procedures Act of 1946 forces the disclosure of enormous amounts of information about how U.S. economic rules are made and provides numerous points of access for lobbyists. Antitrust laws, Securities Exchange Commission (SEC) regulations, and the Uniform Commercial Code also require a great deal of disclosure by firms and work against closed systems of economic relations among groups of firms. Thus, the U.S. market, and the regulations that governed it, were understandable to America's economic partners.

A final consequence of U.S. dominance and the American style of industrial organization was that the governance of world trade could be relatively simple. U.S. dominance meant that U.S. domestic economic policies effectively governed many of the complexities of world markets. The U.S. predilection for reasonably open, arm's-length arrangements in markets meant that transaction costs were low. Although the major challenges to world commerce were never limited to quotas and tariffs, this situation was approximated during an era dominated by the U.S. approach to industrial organization. Low transaction costs (the costs of gathering information, bargaining, and enforcing agreements) also meant that global bargaining framed by a few elegant rules sufficed to anchor the world trade system.

Separate Systems of Governance

The second pillar of the postwar world economy was that separate systems of governance managed domestic economies and the international economy and that separate international institutions had jurisdiction over international trade, investment, and monetary systems. In essence, the domestic and international economies and their management were treated as separate and independent. Domestic regulatory and industrial promotion policies were not to spill over internationally, and local regulators operating at the level of states and municipalities in the United States and elsewhere were to be reasonably free from interference from trade authorities.

At home and abroad institutions responsible for pieces of economic policy engage in ongoing turf battles for political support to control issues and pull them away from other bureaucracies. In the United States separate government bureaucracies administer trade, monetary, investment, and even energy policies. All countries separate money from other bureaucracies, but many combine trade and industry under a single bureaucracy. In addition, the GATT, the IMF, the World Bank, and the International Energy Agency are separate, often competitive, institutions. Both at the national and international levels there is a distinct hierarchy of power and influence among the various institutions and bureaucracies. Finance ministers, who are responsible for monetary and fiscal policy, routinely outrank their counterparts responsible for trade policy, who in turn outrank officials who oversee areas such as communications. Similarly, the IMF and World Bank have many more employees and larger budgets than the GATT and are perceived to be more important. In 1983 and 1984 U.S. Trade Representative William Brock suggested that the link between trade and finance was critical, that trade ministers ought to be routinely invited to the annual IMF/World Bank meetings in Washington, and that if trade and finance ministers worked as partners, they could make headway on the LDC debt problem. He was rebuffed.[8] Institutions simultaneously protect their turf against poaching from others. This is in part because political leaders usually divide up administrative grants of authority in ways that promote turf wars. This helps them control the bureaucracy by ventilating issues more widely and promoting political leaders into the appeals court on jurisdiction. However, the free-trade regime was supposed to be insulated from domestic turf fighting. Located in Geneva, far from the bustle of the World Bank and the IMF in Washington, the GATT was allowed to oversee the trade realm by its more powerful brethren.

Although it was generally recognized that conflicting domestic economic policies could lead to subsidies and other trade-distorting measures, often it was assumed that these policies did not matter or did not matter enough to disrupt the politics of tariff and quota reduction. Sometimes officials did not act because they simply did not know what to do to resolve the clash between national employment policies and trade policy.[9] This meant that domestic economic policies evolved in bureaucratic settings unconcerned with the expectations of trade regimes. Just as critically, the implication of the U.S. model of industrial organization for the world economic regime was that most industrial promotion policies did not matter much. The few policies that were seen as important—such as R&D or procurement—were exempt from international oversight. Moreover, other countries found these exceptions less onerous because the U.S. industrial structure was open.

Separation of Goods and Services

The third pillar of the postwar world economy—that manufactured goods and commodities were traded internationally but that most services were produced and consumed nationally—in effect divided the world economy into two parts, one for goods and the other for services. Free trade and investment rules—including GATT rules—applied to goods and not to services. Raw materials, components, and finished goods were exchanged across national borders, whereas most services were supplied on a national basis. The basic delivery of services was usually accomplished by national monopolies or a limited number of national firms. To the extent that foreign firms were allowed to compete, they were strictly controlled and regulated. Indeed, foreign firms that wished to trade services generally had to establish themselves in the target country. To the extent that the international exchange of services occurred outside the transportation sector, it usually required foreign investment or took the form of jointly provided services. Telecommunications was the classic example of jointly provided services. Telecommunications monopolies in two countries would, in effect, hand off a communication to one another at the midpoint between the two countries. Thus, except for "cinematograph films," services are not mentioned in the GATT articles.[10] Even the GATT Codes for nontariff barriers negotiated during the Tokyo Round trade negotiations in the late 1970s only touched on services traded in conjunction with goods.[11] Under pressure from Congress and a few service-sector firms such as American Express and AIG, U.S. negotiators proposed addressing services directly during the Tokyo Round negotiations, but other nations balked. U.S. Trade Representative Robert Strauss decided not to go to the mat for services, but he promised service providers that services would be an important agenda item in the next round. Except for some general recommendations such as the Code of Liberalization of Current Invisible Operations, adopted by the Organization for Economic Cooperation and Development (OECD), international accords governing services usually were confined to seemingly narrow recommendations and technical agreements on standards administered by organizations such as the International Telecommunication Union and the International Civil Aviation Organization. However, these organizations often reinforced cartel-like behavior in their markets.

Universal Codes of Conduct

Everybody recognized that the trade order was imperfect and that the ideal of free trade never would be achieved. But for the most part policymakers were unable to craft rules to reflect these distinctions. The original International Trade Organization allowed for specialized arrangements for raw materials, but this approach disappeared with the rejection of the ITO. After the late 1940s, trade arrangements recognized sectoral distinctions only by formally or tacitly keeping certain sectors off the table.

Exceptions notwithstanding, the framers of the trade order wanted universal codes of conduct because their goal was to provide a few simple tools for trade in goods that could be used to dismantle what remained of the old imperial trade systems. They included several core rules and principles:

- Tariffs at the border are preferable to nontariff barriers. Contracting parties should strive for the general elimination of quantitative restrictions (GATT, Article XI).

- Concessions made to one contracting party should be automatically extended to all other contracting parties (general most-favored-nation treatment, Article I).

- Although there "is no single, sharply defined dispute-settlement procedure in GATT,"[12] tariff concessions by contracting

parties create GATT legal obligations that are subject to concil-
iation, dispute resolution, and enforcement under a variety of
GATT articles.

- Foreign goods that have cleared customs and legally entered a
  country should be subject to the same taxes and regulations as
  domestic goods (national treatment on internal taxation and
  regulation, Article III).

The policymakers and their economic advisers who created the
free-trade regime favored universality for at least four reasons. First,
they concluded that almost all markets that were organized for
competition should be subject to commodity-style competition.
Second, they felt that the chance for a negotiated bargain was
maximized by uniform rules that put everything on the table, thus
making packages more flexible. Third, they were convinced that
uniform rules made it harder for special interests to win special
privileges for their markets. Protectionists thus faced a double hurdle: they were fighting the free-trade norm, and they needed to
justify special arrangements that were inappropriate under the
GATT framework. Fourth, the framers worried that anything less
than universal coverage might reinforce the remnants of imperial
and preferential trading that the United States in particular had
vowed to dismantle.

THE TWO PILLARS THAT DEFINE THE RULES
OF THE WORLD ECONOMY

The first four pillars of the postwar market place concerned the
structure of governance of the world economy. The final two pillars
set forth the fundamental operating rules of the free-trade regime.

Promote Free Movement of Goods and Investment

The fifth pillar held that to promote market openness, governments
should promote the free movement of goods and investment across
national borders, even though trade and investment were treated as
distinct areas of concern. Although tradeoffs between trade and
investment rights were possible for sensitive industries, liberalizing

trade flows was the primary instrument favored by officials to integrate the world economy efficiently.

The GATT formalized the rules guaranteeing the freedom of movement of goods across national borders. New trade barriers should not be erected, and existing barriers would be dismantled over time. GATT rules call for transparency, reciprocity, and the reduction of national barriers to the movement of goods across borders. During negotiations contracting parties were expected to make equivalent concessions because otherwise the final compromises would not be politically acceptable at home. These rules were designed to transform global trade in goods into a commodity market. (Goods that are essentially interchangeable are considered commodities. Commodity markets are composed of numerous buyers and sellers with adequate knowledge about prices and other market characteristics. Contracts are reliable and enforceable, and negotiating and delivery costs are minimal.)

Trade arrangements help reinforce favored coalitions and resolve common political dilemmas. GATT negotiations were conducted on a bid-ask basis with the GATT secretariat acting as fair brokers. Countries offered increased access to their home markets contingent on receiving equivalent benefits in other countries' markets. The goal was to work out a bargain under which every country gained and granted access of roughly equivalent value. In addition, because the agreements were binding, members were less likely to abandon these undertakings during times of economic distress; this was a common-sense benefit that appealed to political leaderships in all countries with significant export industries.[13] At the same time, all contracting parties retained elaborate safeguards for their politically potent domestic industries.[14] Thus, the GATT permitted political leaders to avoid a common bad (the inferior outcome of trade wars), permitted selective liberalization over time of manufactured goods (the engine of the postwar economy), and allowed for ample safeguards against painful, rapid adjustments. Perhaps most critically, it allowed political leaders to package gains from export expansion to offset complaints by those concerned by import expansion.

There is no counterpart for the GATT for international investment, but numerous bilateral investment treaties and a substantial body of international commercial law support the rights and free-dom of international investors.[15] The most important right for foreign investors was national treatment—a guarantee that foreign firms, once they had established themselves in a national market, would be treated just like local firms. Most efforts to enforce special protection for foreign firms met with mixed success.

A series of assumptions about the ideal world market for trade and investment underlies the formal rules, including the following: information needed to buy and sell in the market is free and avail-able to all interested parties; there are no significant barriers to market entry; contracts among the parties operating in the market cover all contingencies and are completely enforceable. In short, the laws of Adam Smith rule the market. Had true commodity markets emerged, TNCs would have been less important. The rise of TNCs reflects the failure of politics, technology, and market conditions to conform to the assumptions of the classic commodity market. Al-though governments slowly developed implicit international invest-ment rules to deal with TNCs, it is not yet clear whether these same rules can be applied to ICAs.[16]

Just as significantly, the TNC reflected a fundamental political economic compromise that shaped the postwar order. As the discus-sion of automobiles in Chapter 5 illustrates, the United States implicitly accepted a tradeoff in politically sensitive industries. As long as U.S. firms were allowed to invest in a country of prime interest to them, the U.S. government did not vigorously protest barriers that limited trade access. For example, the United States accepted the possible negative (trade diverting) effects of the cre-ation of the European Community in return for protection of the right of its firms to invest. This crucial bargain meant that as long as investment options remained open, devices such as voluntary export restraint agreements (VRAs seems to be gaining more general usage than VERs) were less disruptive to the logic of the post-1945 order than is often asserted. However, this compromise also left the rights of foreign investment as the most important unfinished item on the postwar agenda.

Governments and international bodies recognized that the bur-geoning operations of mostly U.S.-based TNCs during the 1960s might undercut the rule of national comparative advantage. The

United States followed the tradition of the United Kingdom in advocating freedom of foreign investment. But it was not prepared to break up the regime over the issue. Compromise was possible.

National Comparative Advantage

The sixth pillar of the postwar free-trade system was drawn from classical economics. Advantages in the global marketplace were defined by revealed national comparative advantages.[17] The fundamental assumption held that international trade was commerce between two or more countries and that the basic characteristics of the world trade system were driven by differences among countries in such factor endowments as land, labor, and capital that were slow to change and hard for policy to manipulate. The explosion in intraindustry trade in recent decades reflected the specialized advantages that could flow from mixes in factors: a highly skilled workforce married capital investment with human resources. This seemed a logical extension of the model but also suggested to policymakers that competitive niches could be created through determined government action. Thus it ultimately opened the way to a more dynamic view of comparative advantage.

The comparative advantage model also implicitly presupposed that firms were national in character. The responsibility for regulating firms rested with national governments. Firms were incorporated in individual countries, and their home countries retained significant legal jurisdiction over them even when they operated abroad. Not even the rise of the TNC broke this assumption for many years because TNCs still largely reflected national advantages.

TNCs first emerged in the late nineteenth century.[18] But before 1945 foreign portfolio investment dwarfed foreign direct investment by TNCs as the dominant form of international investment. In fact, portfolio investment—-the buying of stocks and bonds in foreign enterprises—characterized the British empire. Such investments financed the expansion of the railroad systems of Europe, the United States, and South America. But these investments could be risky: defaults on foreign bonds by U.S. railroads in the 1890s were on the same scale as current developing country debt problems. Economic theorists view the rise of the modern TNCs as a political necessity and as a response to imperfect commodity markets. In theory, local producers should dominate national markets because they know the language, the customs, and the customers. In a true commodity market, foreign firms would have no special technological or brand-name advantages but would pay more than their domestic competitors to establish overseas operations. (The logic of national comparative advantages leads to exporting.)

Raymond Vernon developed the best-known explanation of the postwar rise of TNCs.[19] His product cycle theory suggests that individual industries have their own life cycles and that differences among countries also affect the behavior of individual industries. The product cycle theory hypothesizes that for any sector unique advantages based on technological ability, financial resources, marketing skills, managerial ability, or consumer reputation influence the development of new technologies and products. Technology, knowledge, and financial capacity are not spread evenly. Brand names matter. As a result, during the early phases of the development of an industry, several large domestic firms often emerge as effective oligopolists and quickly dominate global trade in their products. But in time, foreign firms, often bolstered by trade barriers, enter the industry. The creation of multinational production networks located in the territories of key national markets is one corporate response to greater equality among competitors and the erection of trade barriers. Eventually, the advantages of the dominant TNCs diminish, giving way to an industry where competitive strength is widely distributed among countries and companies.

The product cycle theory implicitly rests as much on the comparative capabilities of countries as on the characteristics of particular industries. The early domination of U.S.-based TNCs was, in part, explained by unique features of the U.S. economy, particularly its heavy investment in advanced technology, its skilled and educated work force, and its prosperous consumer society. The large, affluent U.S. market and its advanced technological base launched U.S. firms as early leaders in most new technologies. Foreign firms sometimes matched U.S. R&D spending initially, but no other country could match America's gigantic domestic market. The special advantages of U.S.-based TNCs remained until other countries rivaled U.S. affluence, education, skill, and R&D commitment. Policymakers deemed this unlikely to happen quickly because most of them doubted the efficacy of industrial policies to alter comparative national advantages.

Moreover, during the 1950s and 1960s most TNCs involved in manufacturing were less global than is commonly perceived. Although they had widespread international operations, most of their core competitive strengths came from the home market, and their home and global operations were not highly integrated. Analysts characterize such firms as *multicountry domestic firms* that try to exploit their special competitive assets on the world market through direct foreign production and marketing. Procter and Gamble exemplifies this approach: many of its international operations were virtually independent local operators that formed a global portfolio of assets for the parent firm.[20] For decades, ITT's manufacturing strategy for telecommunications equipment followed this model. Even some firms usually considered global in their strategy, such as General Motors, actually ran a set of loosely integrated national or regional companies. Moreover, the U.S. government and its firms never assumed that there should be a global plan for organizing the division of labor among firms. Comparative national advantages were revealed by experimentation and changed slowly over time.

For many years, firms, especially those involved in manufacturing, operated with fairly low levels of globalization and weak international partnerships. In its weakest form complementary relationships among firms of different countries arose to manage areas such as limited, long-distance trading, international interfirm licensing and consulting arrangements. U.S. international firms relied mainly on these methods when dealing with relatively closed markets, such as Japan in the 1960s.

Even if governments were inclined to let firms oversee national or international public policy arenas, domestic political pressures would prevent them from relinquishing control. Instead, officials are searching for new ways to combine innovative forms of market oversight with increased doses of competition. Paradoxically, the U.S. government is trying to use ICAs to help solve important trade disputes with Japan and to help negotiate standards in some areas, even though no government is ever comfortable that the motivations of private firms (especially those partnered with foreign firms) are congruent with its own. They continue to seek formal guidelines to structure the "private diplomacy" of corporate alliances and manage the world economy.

New issues such as R&D, government procurement, local regulations, and administrative regulatory procedures have begun to appear high on the trade agenda. As the United States reorients its global competitive approach, it also is demanding that Japan open its markets in new ways. The challenge is to find a balance: the United States needs to continue to oppose inefficient and discriminatory foreign practices that disadvantage U.S. interests, but at the same time, it must draw lessons appropriate to its history from the Japanese model and develop its own equivalent to an industrial policy to remain competitive. A major innovation sought by Uruguay Round negotiators was to establish a new principle— market access. This principle grants governments continued control over the rules and structures of their national economies but asks that governments also provide market access to foreign competitors on reasonable terms. ICAs and new commercial guidelines are first attempts by the private and public sectors to delineate a new model of industrial organization and global competition. Government policy and international rules need to define the context within which open, global competition takes place.

CHAPTER THREE

The Politics and Economics
of Market-Access Regimes

Politics and economics are moving the world economy toward a market-access regime. As GATT Director General Arthur Dunkel has argued, "Market access negotiations involve not just the reduction and elimination of tariffs and non-tariff measures at the border, but also corresponding commitments at the level of domestic policies that distort trade and competition."[1] Free-trade rules suffice for part of world commerce, but the world economic regime will become irrelevant unless it also incorporates the dynamic growth sectors in manufactured goods and services.

The new structure of international trade and investment has demanded that firms respond to these changes. This flow of international investment, particularly among industrial countries, has important implications for government efforts to manage the world economy and for firms that wish to remain competitive in the face of these changes.

THE CHANGING STRUCTURE OF GLOBAL COMMERCE

Interdependence: The United States as the Global Pivot

At the heart of the transformation of world commerce is the increased interdependence created by burgeoning foreign direct investment. Large amounts of investment can be tied entirely to a country's own region, or, particularly in France and Germany before World War I, loans and investment could be directed mainly to colonies or countries with close political ties.[2] In fact, the data suggest that the United States remains the linchpin of the world investment system. It is the major common denominator for most countries' outward investments. It also remains the largest investor in Europe and, although at much lower levels, the second-largest investor in Asia. For example, between 1984 and 1987 the bulk of British (81 percent), French (69 percent), and German (65 percent) foreign investment still ended up outside the European Community. By contrast 53 percent of Dutch foreign investments and 47 percent of Danish foreign investments were within the European Community. During this same period about 55 percent of U.S. investments were in the European Community but only 17 percent of Japanese investments.[3] Indeed, the European Community is by far the leading foreign investor in the United States. As Table 3.1 indicates, most of these investments involve acquisitions that are purchased largely with funds generated by existing U.S. subsidiaries.

Thus, when analysts talk about the emergence of regional blocks, they fail to recognize that this is likely to happen only if the United States adopts a defensive, regional strategy. European business is deeply embedded in the U.S. economy, and Japanese firms are rapidly expanding their investments. U.S. penetration of Europe is strong. American investment in Asia is thinner but still significant. The major gaps in interdependence arise because inward foreign investment to Japan is still relatively sparse and because Europe is weak in Asia as a whole. In the late 1980s the United States and Japan continued to dominate foreign investment in Asia. The United States was the leading investor in Hong Kong, China, and Singapore while Japan held the top position in Korea, Thailand, and Indonesia. Asia as a whole (including Australia) provided the only serious investment rivalry for the United States and Japan. In Singapore and Indonesia the combined investments from the rest of Asia presented a serious challenge. Although the Japanese solidified their lead after the late 1980s, American investment continued to be significant. It is the low European profile that is surprising.[4]

Table 3.1
U.S. Direct Investment Inflows in 1989 and 1990

	1989 ($ billions)	1990 ($ billions)
Type of investment:		
Acquisition	$59.71	$56.78
Establishments	11.46	7.65
Total	$71.17[a]	$64.43[a]
Source of funds:		
Foreign direct investment	$22.54	$12.50
U.S. affiliates	48.63	51.93
By national source:		
EC nations	$33.87	$30.91
Japan	17.41	20.50
OPEC nations	0.43	0.31

Sources: Mahnaz Fahim-Nader, *Survey of Current Business* (May 1991); *CTC Reporter*, no. 26 (Autumn 1988), p. 14.

[a] In 1989 the total assets of businesses that were acquired or established was $127.51 billion. In 1990, as the United States and other countries experienced a recession, the total of new investments fell to $95.01 billion.

Another way to consider the structural power of the United States is in terms of its role as a market for goods and services. Although the United States vies with Germany for leadership in world exports, at the core of its influence is its importance as the largest and most accessible market in the world. The comparative importance of the U.S. market has eroded: Asia is now the largest semiconductor market in the world (see Chapter 6), and the European Community is a much larger market for automobiles (13.4 million vehicles versus 8.7 million in the United States) (see Chapter 5). But the European Community usually makes no attempt to preempt significant national discretion in critical world markets. Thus, the United States is the largest market under a single political authority able to set uniform policies for the entire market (federalism muddles the picture somewhat). Although restrictions are increasing in the U.S. market, it almost always is still more open than other industrial centers. Firms from around the world still want to compete in the United States because no other market offers comparable access or returns on investment.

The Political Structure of the Future Economic Order

In short, U.S. dominance of the world economy has declined, but its strategic economic power remains considerable. The United States still is more than an equal partner. It possesses structural power because of its central role in trade and investment flows in the Pacific Rim and Atlantic systems. The functioning of the world economic system still depends on U.S. leadership,[5] and other countries continue to delegate power to Washington on a conditional basis. As long as their interests are safeguarded, Japan (because of its domestic politics) and to a lesser extent Europe (because of the difficulty of reaching common positions) do not want to bear the costs of being leaders or agents of change. The United States therefore has been able to push for reforms that fit the needs of the U.S. corporate sector. Only belatedly have Japan and the European Community argued that the U.S. interpretation of the global economic agenda may not be in congruence with their special concerns. The real challenge facing policymakers is to find ways to use minilateral and sectoral efforts to reinforce global economic integration, multilateral economic rules, and special priorities of each power center.

Japanese and European preferences matter more today than they did two decades ago, and their role in global economic management needs to be expanded to maintain global economic order and sustain an open regime. The implications of this diffusion of global power are not as dire as pessimists fear, but it results in higher transaction costs related to oligopolistic cooperation. The leading world powers gain much from cooperation, but new specialized arrangements are needed to minimize transaction costs while decision-making responsibility within the U.S.-Japan-Europe triad is rebalanced.[6] New institutional formats are needed that improve monitoring, transparency, and the ability to retaliate selectively against breaches of international rules. To the extent that governments trust their companies to act as their eyes and ears, governments can use ICAs to alleviate the problems of transparency and monitoring. Governments do rely on their firms for these purposes, but the private incentives of all domestic firms are not congruent. Therefore, ICAs contribute to the resolution of trade problems only if they operate in the context of general rules for government oversight of the markets. Moreover, oligopolistic collusion in support of the regime will force changes in the regime.

Strategic Preferences of Global Customers

When shifts in global economic power raised transaction costs among governments, the political preferences of leading countries and their firms about openness began to shift as well. The evolving preferences of large firms, and now medium-size firms, changed the global regime, and models of industrial organization that do not favor traditional openness began receiving more attention in the United States.

The preferences of firms about trade policy matter in all societies because firms often organize for political action. Moreover, in democracies, private firms employ large numbers of voters. As firms globalize to protect their domestic positions and earn overseas revenues, the firms and their workers are more likely to support international openness.[7] They are more likely to integrate their worldwide operations and enter into international partnerships to obtain selected competitive assets (technology and other assets needed to remain competitive) even as they cope with new problems. Even firms that worry that their foreign competitors are being unfairly helped by their governments generally favor protection only after they are unable to gain access to other countries' markets.[8]

Large customers also are becoming more assertive in using their bargaining leverage. Strategic users are organizing their interests on a global basis and are acting to maximize their interests as consumers, not just as suppliers. They are being forced to consider the bigger picture of world trade rules.[9] One result is that organizations such as the International Chamber of Commerce are acting more aggressively to encourage coordination of individual national positions. This is not unprecedented in tariff history: farmers fought protection for heavy industry in the nineteenth century to keep their costs down. This time, however, large corporate users, attuned to global, not national markets, are uniting to influence policy and outcomes.

Large global users are intent on organizing inputs to global production on favorable terms. As they become more sensitive to terms of supply and pricing of goods and services, they have emerged as potent supporters of global competition. This works in two ways: some markets, such as electronics, have concentrated, large industrial users; other markets are dominated by unorganized consumers. Politicians in many countries organize surrogate representatives of consumers.[10] The vigorous campaign of large banks and other transnational firms also is forcing reform of national communications markets and the pricing of international communications. In fact, the International Chamber of Commerce in late 1991 called for competition in basic telecommunications services and infrastructure as a way to guarantee better services and prices to large corporate customers.[11] Similarly, the new activism of large users of high-technology services such as banks and travel agents has helped eliminate anticompetitive practices restricting global trade in services. Large strategic customers also worry more about the health of their suppliers, especially those that provide strategic inputs that could be dominated by firms linked to their own competitors. Thus, the U.S. computer industry favors government support for U.S. chip producers and simultaneously opposes protection of domestic semiconductor makers because barriers would increase the cost of chips.

Pressure for more openness at home and abroad is coupled with the suspicion that classic free trade alone may be insufficient to overcome the weak ties between suppliers and customers that impede product innovation and cost improvements. Firms are experimenting with ICAs and DCAs to improve these links. The blurring of divisions between buyers and sellers means firms need access to their market counterparts in new and demanding ways. Automobile parts firms, for example, need access to foreign markets and flexible computer networks to tie them to their customers.

Global Strategies of Suppliers

The globalization and alliance strategies of firms are important because they increase the mobility of capital, information, technology, and personnel. Firm assets are mobile and can move geographically, can convert to other uses with reasonable rewards, and can sell at reasonable prices. This is true even for many industries where assets traditionally are fixed and hard to convert to other uses. (Not all industries have been transformed this way; most petrochemical complexes still are fine-tuned to serve specific markets.) The increasing mobility of assets encourages openness because pressure for protectionism increases in direct proportion to the immobility of assets.[12] Owners of immobile assets cannot easily switch to more rewarding uses if competition becomes intense. Conversely, immobility means that trade protection is likely to be more effective.

The knowledge and organization components constitute a growing share of the value of sophisticated manufactured goods. Substantially more than half the value of jet aircraft, computers, and telephone switches comes from these components. These assets always are mobile. Firms can use ICAs to leverage these assets when they underperform internationally, but their sale value on the open market is hard to evaluate. When McDonnell Douglas sought to sell 40 percent of its commercial aircraft operations for $2 billion to Taiwan Aerospace Corporation (29 percent of which is owned by the government), it wanted to compensate for its weak competitive position, sell aircraft in Asia more easily, and generate a needed infusion of cash. McDonnell Douglas recognized that it could not survive on U.S. sales alone and was uncertain whether it would be able to sell its competitive assets for an attractive price in a fire sale, particularly because no buyer could predict with certainty how the U.S. government would react to the sale. Instead of seeking U.S. government subsidies and protection, McDonnell Douglas sought to leverage its core assets in the areas of manufacturing, systems integration, and design by joining with a firm that needed a U.S. partner to enter and survive in the business.[13]

Firms still differ in preferences about openness because investment and trade flows are only imperfectly substitutable. At a minimum, there are one-time adjustment costs. Although several steel firms have entered into ICAs, most large U.S. firms with huge fixed-cost plants also want additional protection or direct assistance from industrial policy. Smaller steel firms in specialized markets where plants are depreciated rapidly are more willing to compete against international rivals head-on.

Generally, TNCs in industries with characteristics of strategic trading (such as declining marginal costs) prefer conditional openness. They believe the United States should keep its market open if and only if other key countries keep their markets open. This strategy requires more than "keeping your powder dry." To thrive the U.S. firms also must develop management structures and ties to other competitive assets around the world. Firms that already have paid a high price to globalize favor openness because they do not want to retreat. They support more global economic integration, seek new ways to take advantage of competitive assets abroad, and favor new investment safeguards that free-trade regimes, particularly those without true hegemony, cannot easily provide.[14]

The globalization of firms and the new models of industrial organization for government-firm relations also have changed the incentives for companies regarding two dangers of bilateralism—the risk that any given pair of countries will not create liberal packages because they have few interests in common and the risk that the two parties will create exclusive, bilateral cartels. These risks may be declining. First, new models of industrial organization mean that any specific negotiation—over aircraft or automobiles—also raises numerous adjunct issues, such as those related to antitrust law, subsidies, or R&D consortia. Implicit in single-issue talks are the linkages that negotiators might bargain for. Second, as firms globalize, their incentives to enter exclusive bilateral cartels also diminish. When ICAs provide links to third parties, those third parties may influence the outcomes of bilateral negotiations. U.S. electronics firms pushed for tough action to open the Japanese market but did not want to set precedents that might backfire for their European operations. Even in markets characterized by strategic trade conditions, TNCs seem to prefer opening the closed foreign markets of rivals over protectionism. (Of course, if firms can have both, they might welcome it.)

Despite the forces that are working for openness, genuine free trade is rare. Lawrence Krause estimates that only about 15 percent of all trade is truly free.[15] Agriculture, petroleum, chemicals, automobiles, airplanes, and semiconductors are just a few of the key commodities that are not traded freely because of various types of government controls or extreme forms of strategic trading.

Global Firms and Foreign Investment

Foreign direct investment rose from $47 billion to $139 billion annually from 1985 to 1988, about three times faster than the expansion in the value of trade. Nonetheless foreign direct investment is only about 10 percent of the size of trade flows in most years.[16] In this sense trade remains far more significant than investment for the world economy. But the aggregate data do not reveal how foreign investment shapes patterns of trade and international commerce.

Economic theory suggests that, in general, foreign owners should not possess enough competitive assets to dominate local firms across the board in industrial economies. But economic theory lacks a persuasive explanation of what constitutes a normal level of foreign investment activity. Analysts usually use the experience of leading European economies as a guide: their domestic economies are sophisticated and reasonably open to foreign investment, and unlike the United States they are small enough relative to global gross national product not to cloud the significance of foreign commerce.

Table 3.2 suggests that foreign corporations typically account for 15 to 17 percent of national sales, manufacturing employment, and corporate assets in Europe. But remarkably, foreign firms account for a quarter to a third of national imports and exports in most of these countries.[17] The United States was a laggard until the acceleration of inward investment in the 1980s but now seems headed toward European levels. Japan still trails the others for reasons discussed shortly.[18] It appears that U.S. and European levels of inward investment will continue to increase, but there is no reason to predict a stable equilibrium.

TNCs strongly influence international commerce in ways unrecognized by traditional trade accounts, although there are ambiguities about what constitutes foreign direct investment. Many official data series consider anything over a 10 percent share of equity in a firm to be foreign direct investment. By this standard Dupont is a Canadian foreign direct investment. Thus, the data

Table 3.2

Foreign Direct Investment as a Percentage of Total National Economy, 1977 and 1986

	U.S.		Japan		Germany		U.K.	
	1977	1986	1977	1986	1977	1986	1977	1986
Sales	5%	10%	2%	1%	17%	18%	22%	20%
Manufacturing jobs	3	7	2	1	14	13	15	14
Assets	5	9	2	1	17	17	14	
Exports[a]	23		2		24		30	
Imports[b]	34		15					

Sources: Graham and Krugman, *Foreign Direct Investment in the United States;* Julius, *Global Companies and Public Policy,* p. 45.

[a] Foreign-owned firms' exports as share of national exports.
[b] Foreign-owned firms' imports as share of national imports.

probably exaggerate the appearance of outright control. But they are a reasonable indicator of the level of national economic activity and of the growing link between foreign trade and foreign holdings. Minority equity shares in alliances and joint ventures do facilitate commerce between companies by reducing problems related to transaction costs. A significant part of national firms' foreign sales do not show up on national accounts because products are made and distributed from an overseas base. Local sales of U.S. firms in the United Kingdom, Germany, and France are on average five times greater than the level of U.S. national exports. However, they are only 30 percent higher than exports to Japan. In many industrializing countries, by contrast, U.S. exports dominate local affiliate sales of U.S. firms.[19] Moreover, intrafirm trade among units of TNCs now represents a major part of global commerce.

Table 3.3 provides a reconceptualization of global commerce based on the work of DeAnne Julius. Julius classifies commerce on the basis of the nationality of purchasers and sellers of products, not according to where they are shipped. For example, she deducts all U.S. parent-firm exports to their foreign subsidiaries from the U.S. export column (because these are transfers between two U.S. firms)

Table 3.3
**Relationships between Sales of Subsidiaries of TNCs and the U.S.
Balance of Trade Accounts**

Sales ($ billions)

Foreign sales:

Exports of goods and services	$304.0
less: Exports to U.S. subsidiaries overseas	71.3
Exports by FOF[a] in U.S. to home nation	50.7
plus: Local sales to FOF in U.S.	400.4
Local sales to U.S. subsidiaries abroad	865.2
Total foreign sales	$1,447.6

Foreign purchases:

Imports of goods and services	$439.4
less: Imports from U.S. subsidiaries abroad	65.6
Imports by FOF in U.S. from home nation	124.5
plus: Local purchases from FOFs in U.S.	616.5
Local purchases by U.S. subsidiaries abroad	558.5
Net foreign purchases	$1,424.3
Net U.S. trade balance	−$135.4
Net foreign purchases	$25.3

Source: Julius, *Global Companies;* Group of 20, p. 24.
[a] FOF = foreign-owned firm.

---

but adds sales by local U.S. firms in the United States to foreign firms operating in the United States. Following the same logic, she subtracts sales by American foreign subsidiaries to U.S. domestic firms from the U.S. import total and adds purchases by foreign operations of U.S. firms from suppliers in those countries to the American "import" total.

According to Table 3.3, foreign subsidiaries of U.S. firms purchase almost a quarter of U.S. exports and provide just less than a seventh of U.S. imports. When the impact of exports and imports of foreign TNCs operating in the United States is added, the share of total trade accounted for by intra-TNC trade reaches about 40 percent. In addition, adjusting for local purchases by TNCs greatly boosts the absolute levels of international commerce and transforms U.S. firms into net exporters to firms from other countries. These figures suggest that the globalization of firms is restructuring world commerce even more than traditional balance-of-payments data suggest. Nonetheless, this statistical wizardry cannot erase one central economic reality: the U.S. balance-of-payments deficit is the result of a large annual outpouring of dollars and of growing claims on the United States by the rest of the world. Ultimately, this deficit will have to be serviced.

Transnational investment already is a major force shaping world commerce and is prevalent in all major economic centers. At present, Japan is the outlier.[20] Table 3.2 shows that foreign subsidiaries in Japan do contribute a substantial share of its imports, but that otherwise inward investment has had little impact on the Japanese economy. (The figures indicate that foreign subsidiaries add little local value relative to their sales.) The full degree of Japan's difference is evident when it is compared to the rest of the world during the acceleration of foreign investment during the 1980s. Table 3.4 shows Japan was the fastest-expanding outward investor, but inward flows were negligible.

Japanese exceptionalism as an outward foreign investor is less acute but still significant. Japan started investing in OECD countries relatively late in the game, partly because of its late economic blossoming and partly because the Japanese pattern of industrial organization favored exporting.[21] Table 3.5 shows Japanese foreign

Table 3.4
Foreign Direct Investment by the G-5

	1989 Stock ($ billions)	Real Growth 1983–1989 (average annual percentage change)	Total Flow Outward	Total Flow Inward
U.S.	$385	33%	$218	$324
U.K.	226	17	175	99
Japan	158	37	140	2
Germany	91	18	66	15
France	69	26	55	32
Total	$929		$654	$472

Source: Julius, *Global Companies*, p. 5

Table 3.5
Japanese Foreign Direct Investment by Region

Annual Investment ($ billions)

	1987	1988	1989	1990	Cum. 1991[a]
To North America	$15.4	$22.3	$33.9	$27.2	$136.2
% of total	46.0%	47.5%	50.2%	47.8%	43.8%
To Europe	$6.6	$9.1	$14.8	$14.3	$59.3
% of total	19.7%	19.4%	21.9%	25.1%	19.1%
To East Asia	$4.9	$5.6	$8.2	$7.1	$47.5
% of total	14.6%	11.8%	12.2%	12.4%	15.3%
Total	$33.4	$47.0	$67.5	$56.9	$310.8

Source: Ministry of Finance and Japan's Economic Institute, cited in "A Trade Bloc in East Asia?," New Perspectives Quarterly 9:1 (Winter 1992), p. 10.

[a] Cumulative as of 1991.

direct investment by region from 1987 through 1991. Japanese investment in North America was more than double its investments in Europe and almost three times its investment in East Asia. However, it is notable that the Japan External Trade Organization estimates that "only 4 percent of Japanese companies' production is made outside of Japan compared with 20 percent for the Federal Republic of Germany firms and 17 percent for U.S. firms." The U.N. Center on Transnational Corporations attempted a similar comparison. It concluded that the U.S. share of world manufactured exports was 9 percent, and the exports from its foreign affiliates constituted another 9 percent. In comparison, in 1983, the figures for Japan were 9 percent and 1 percent.[22]

Although it was slow to start, Japanese foreign manufacturing investment is accelerating. (The capital squeeze on Japanese firms induced by the sharp decline of the Nikkei stock index and of real estate prices in Japan in 1991 and 1992 undoubtedly will influence the long-term picture of outward investments.) In the United States, where Japan has the most investment, Japanese plants fit the performance profile of European manufacturing plants in the United States in all respects but one—import propensity. Table 3.6 shows

Table 3.6
Characteristics of Manufacturing Foreign-Owned Firms Operating in the United States in 1986

	All Foreign-Owned Firms		Japanese Foreign-Owned Firms	
	Totals ($ millions)	Per Worker ($ thousands)	Totals ($ millions)	Per Worker ($ thousands)
Value added[a]	$65,282	$46.64	$3,199	$47.39
Compensation	46,029	32.89	2,362	34.99
Exports	12,573	8.98	906	13.42
Imports	20,791	14.85	2,936	43.48
Research[b]	n.a.	3.96	n.a.	4.81

Source: Graham and Krugman, Foreign Direct Investment, p. 61.

[a] Per worker figures in terms of gross product per worker.
[b] Total private R&D per worker.

that Japanese subsidiaries are somewhat more export prone but about three times more import prone than foreign-owned firms as a group. Dennis Encarnation argues that the imbalance in direct investment between the United States and Japan largely explains the trade gap between the two countries. About two-thirds of U.S. imports from Japan are done through trade between Japanese parents and their U.S. subsidiaries. The much weaker U.S. investment position in Japan puts the comparable U.S. figure at 50 percent, of which the majority is from U.S. subsidiaries of Japanese firms back to Japan.

Whether or not the numbers are precisely right, Encarnation is clearly correct that investment is shaping trade. The real question is whether Japanese firms are inherently more prone to rely on their home base of supply than U.S. or European TNCs and whether Japanese practices will change as the firms have longer experience with global production, as did both U.S. and European practices. Trade politics may expedite change for Japanese firms.[23] In the meantime, a United States interested in retaining an integrated global economy probably gains more leverage by encouraging European and Japanese inflows than it would by discouraging them.

The real question is what other policy actions should complement a policy of continued openness to flows of foreign investment.

The timeliness of data makes it difficult to judge whether Japan has displaced the rest of the world in organizing the Pacific Rim economy. But one important study suggests that in countries like Korea and Taiwan TNCs typically accounted for around 16 or 17 percent of national manufacturing output, 18 to 25 percent of all exports, and 26 to 32 percent of manufacturing exports. The shares of TNCs for the United States and Europe were similar. Japan was the most important foreign investor. The appreciation of the yen after 1985 triggered a move (endorsed by MITI) by Japanese firms to redeploy parts of their manufacturing structure to other parts of Asia. This reduced labor and resource costs while tapping the new technological infrastructure of these countries. In short, in the mid-1980s investment in the Asian region reflected the macropicture of the world: investment significantly shaped trade flows, the United States continued to be the linchpin of the world economy, while Japan was the dominant regional force.[24]

WHY DID FIRMS GLOBALIZE?

The changing patterns of world commerce that have just been described are important because investment flows shape trade flows. The transformation of this relationship underscores qualitative changes in the strategic dilemmas facing TNCs that the quantitative data does not tap and creates policy problems for the old and new regimes.

Postwar planners did not anticipate that TNCs would alter the international landscape in such complex ways, but as TNCs and ultimately ICAs integrated globally, they faced more complicated strategic choices and rising transaction costs. Firms made investments and entered into alliances to bolster their competitive position by bringing external resources under their control. (One way for companies to develop firm-specific assets is to develop unique assets internally: firms may improve their compensation systems or increase their research spending. This source of advantage does not depend directly on national advantages.) This interrelationship between international economic policies, corporate responses, and the management of the world economy is closely tied to the proliferation of globalized firms.

Why Firms Globalize

One reason that firms globalize is to cash in on success. Sometimes, strategic trade theory suggests, closing a market can help exporters build domestic scale economies and master learning-curve cost advantages that bolster exports. But global activities that go beyond exporting also are becoming vital to firms' long-term competitiveness. The need for economies of scale possible only on a worldwide basis may result in increased sensitivity to expand globally. Or firms may realize that unless they challenge oligopolistic foreign competitors in their own home markets, the rents they earn at home will be used to finance foreign entry. This was one reason that Motorola chose to fight to enter the Japanese market.[25] Theory suggests that companies that possess firm-specific assets need to globalize their operations to take full advantage of these assets.

Similarly, domestic firms often need resources and know-how that are available only globally. To acquire these resources firms may buy or contract for them or enter into partnerships with other firms. If there were no market imperfections or if firms wanted to sell their know-how in closed markets, firms should favor contracting for resources, perhaps by licensing a technology or hiring a foreign sales agent. But an asset's true value may be difficult to determine if markets are too thin (activity is too low) to work efficiently or information is unevenly distributed among a limited pool of buyers and sellers. Unless assets have intrinsic value or can be sold, transactions either will not be done or the market may be inefficient. Similarly, writing or enforcing contracts that govern arm's-length transactions may be complicated, especially for firms like specialized chemical plants that invest in assets that have value only as part of wider relationships. (Chemical plants may yield a feed stock that can be used only in plastic factories.) In short, small numbers of market participants, uncertainty, poorly distributed information, assets closely tied to one particular task, and hazy property rights boost transaction costs and undermine traditional contracts and licenses. This causes risks and losses to firms.

The traditional corporate response to such problems was to "go transnational," thereby internalizing transactions within firms. For example, instead of licensing a technology overseas a U.S. firm might choose to manufacture and sell it on its own in Europe. It was sensible for experienced U.S. firms to become TNCs so they could leverage their U.S. market base into a dominant competitive advantage. But as firms from other countries acquired important technological, processing, and distributional assets, U.S. firms no longer could compete just by buying them or making a competing direct investment. For example, Japanese firms' distribution networks depend on long-standing business relationships that would be weakened by foreign ownership. And the total is worth more than the sum of the parts: the value of specific engineering skills possessed by Siemens is enhanced because the skills in each division can be shared with other divisions of a diversified electronics firm or be made available to Siemens' allies through partnerships.

Global Attributes and Complementary Resources

To understand markets it is necessary to focus at least as much on attributes associated with the globalization of firms as on national comparative advantages. Globalization increases when firms develop strategies that depend on other nations' assets and firms for key inputs or complementary products.[26]

Globalization involves push and pull factors. The push factors are regulatory and competitive. Governments want more sophisticated local production because their competitors are becoming more sophisticated. The pull factor is that global operations improve competitiveness. Firms that learn more about their customers and tap specialized production assets on a·global basis are likely to do better than those that do not. This may include using advantages made possible by mastering national and local industrial and administrative policies in other countries. Taking local partners is the quickest way to learn these policies, but these partners need to possess genuine economic skills to be local assets. Partners can no longer act just as political fixers.

At one time the typical U.S. TNC tried to create linkage mainly by exporting technical resources and standards from the United States. Local partners provided marketing and helped with product adaptation from the "U.S. platform." Today U.S. firms want overseas operations to contribute significantly to their global business. As part of an integrated transnational strategy, firms are seeking complementary foreign assets. Ford and General Motors integrated their European operations into meaningful units in the early 1970s and approached global integration in the 1980s. Now their European divisions lead global production design for certain classes of vehicles, and General Motors is restructuring many U.S. operations according to practices developed in Europe. IBM achieved this sophistication much earlier. Japanese firms are striving to reach these levels of globalization. In many cases firms have identified access to national or regional efforts and to sectoral policies as critical to their strategy.

Knowing your customer was always good business, but sophisticated global customers make this approach doubly important for simple economic reasons. Unless suppliers pursue their national customers abroad and exploit the bonds formed in the home market, they will lose their customers to suppliers that they discover in overseas markets. U.S. firms began to refine and sell their products on a global basis after their control over many of their key users began to slip. Indeed, as the examination of the semiconductor industry in Chapter 6 shows, to maintain technological leadership companies must meet the needs of their most sophisticated customers and learn about new applications of their technology from those customers. If technology is innovative, not highly standardized, and requires extensive customization of products and constant innovation through the experience gained from servicing the products (the interaction of product and customer), then companies will prefer direct investment or corporate partners.[27] Distribution, customization, and other support services no longer can be parceled out to marginal, local partners. To find new ways to upgrade their local production and sales, firms form significant partnerships with firms that offer competing products.

As information and communication costs decline and global transportation and manufacturing infrastructure improve, global firms are freer to locate their operations wherever they can best use complementary assets to maximize their corporate positioning. Firms with complex alliances and extensive global strategies can find ways to internalize resources that used to be available only through public-sector programs in its home country. Blind faith in the market is shortsighted, but every deviation from the classic market does not demand a new government program. Firms are realizing that critical complementary resources—key value-added resources such as sourcing technology, competitive manufacturing capabilities, and marketing and after-sales support—are available only through global sourcing.[28] Complementary resources also take the form of pools of skilled labor (such as software programmers) and networking resources (such as global computer networks). Meanwhile, rapid innovation built on new technologies and regulatory changes is making old arm's-length ties anachronistic. Where interfirm deals once focused on technology or licensing agreements, today complicated efforts to develop uniform, interoperable architectures for products are the norm.

Firms with integrated strategies try to take advantage of local and regional policies in industrial countries. David Friedman's work on the Japanese machine tool industry and Michael Piore and Charles Sabel's analysis of numerous specialized manufacturers in Italy and West Germany strongly suggest that the success of firms often was tied to the way they used local and regional policies. These policies took various forms. Some tried to produce an educated, skilled pool of labor for regional firms, particularly specialized manufacturers. Other policies tried to induce local companies with specialized, complementary assets to work together.[29]

Dense concentrations of specialized firms in high-technology or skilled production often boost innovation rates. Silicon Valley is just one example. Various U.S. regions have adopted policies to attract and encourage specialized firms. The North Carolina Research Triangle and the state technology centers of Nebraska are two examples. Ports from Rotterdam to New York are moving into the information and communications businesses for similar reasons. TNCs are trying to affiliate with these specialized regional complexes to bolster their global efforts. Hyundai has moved its global headquarters for personal computers from Korea to Silicon Valley after concluding that the density of innovative resources it needed to meet its goals was available only in California.

Globalization and Alliances

Firms choose to enter ICAs because for large and expensive projects, it may be prudent for firms to share costs and spread risks among themselves. Alliances also permit firms to share resources in innovative ways to refocus their individual competitive capabilities. Thus, alliances lead to some of the same benefits that intraindustry trade provided for competition in traditional free-trade markets. (Intraindustry trade occurs when a country imports automobiles but exports automobile radiators and brakes. It blurs the line between winners and losers among countries in any industry and thus reduces the problems of free trade.) Some specific factors explain why firms enter into ICAs.

Transaction Costs   Transaction costs are critical. Partnerships are an intermediate strategy between contracting and ownership in a foreign country that lowers costs, boosts revenues, spreads risks, and provides access to needed specialized assets. Partnerships, however, have high coordination costs, and partners must share profits. Moreover, partners may turn out to be untrustworthy, applying inappropriate transfer prices, stealing technology, or offering competitive products independent of the partnership.[30] Nonetheless, by the mid-1980s joint ventures involving equity relationships may have accounted for 20 percent of foreign direct investment and 30 percent of manufacturing joint investment.[31]

Complementary, Specialized Assets   The need for complementary assets provides another piece of the answer to why firms enter into ICAs. As key competitive assets in research, manufacturing, and marketing develop in various countries, companies will rely on international operations to secure complementary assets. Moreover, companies may enter alliances because customers demand integrated product lines covering diverse technologies that no single company can provide. Indeed, it is likely that in the future alliances will incorporate key customers as members. Many current alliances are domestic because corporate customs and government support are easier to manage when all parties share a nationality. A distrust of strangers also makes DCAs appealing. But firms are learning that they need large numbers of ICAs and much more sophisticated foreign operations. Siemens, for example, supports European consortia *and* partners with IBM.

Important specialized assets, such as technology or technical standards, need to be established jointly because to be compelling any single product needs complementary technologies. Japanese firms embraced this philosophy long ago and relied on DCAs to achieve their goals. But even Japanese firms now recognize that ICAs offer advantages for this purpose. Thus, Toshiba now shares its most sensitive technology for liquid crystal displays with IBM in order to secure IBM as a customer and a partner in design challenges. U.S. and European firms are extensively linking their operations by developing international product networks on a global basis to take advantage of specialized assets. Pisano, Russo, and Teece show that a combination of joint technological development with work to obtain other significant complementary assets, such as distribution, will lead to corporate partnering. If the technologies are process oriented, rather than product oriented, companies will be more receptive to partnering because conflicts of interest are less acute.

These considerations have brought intellectual property issues onto the front burner of trade negotiations. One of the important interim results of the Uruguay Round trade negotiations was the acceptance of intellectual property issues as a key trade issue. Intellectual property, patents, and trade secrets are now high on the U.S. trade agenda. Indeed, in April 1992 the U.S. Trade Representative cited India, Thailand, and Taiwan under the so-called Super 301 legislation for their inadequate intellectual property enforcement.[32] These trade disputes, negotiations, and agreements about intellectual property encourage licensing and partnering agreements by protecting intellectual property. This is especially necessary because alliances and licensing help accommodate complex trading of patent portfolios where it is hard to evaluate the full worth of the property. For many industries patents are no longer the heart of intellectual property. The action is moving to copyright (as in the 1985 U.S.-Japan trade dispute about software masks) and also to trade secrets (proprietary knowledge that is not patented). Access to trade secrets (such as tooling for complex manufacturing) will require numerous difficult commercial and policy decisions. But the United States, whose approach to trade secrets differs from those followed by Japan and Germany, believes that its approach is economically more efficient. This suggests that more international negotiations on this topic can be expected during the 1990s.[33]

Alliances also are more likely if demand is concentrated in companies with global operations. The Digital Equipment Company (DEC) is linking with foreign companies to interconnect their product lines. DEC will share technology and enter joint engineering projects to help create products that work smoothly with DEC systems. The same pattern is evident in software and hardware. Sun Microsystems artfully built its leadership in work stations by encouraging others, even some direct foreign competitors, to use its key technologies, including its RISC chip technology, on favorable terms. Its object is to build a complementary range of products to Sun's work stations. Sun believes that it can handle direct competitors; it wants to avoid having its approach to computing frozen out by alternative approaches.

Two other cases illustrate important points. LSI, a leading maker of customized semiconductors, refers to its international strategy as "glocal." It combines a global customer base (which provides economies of scale and allows it to work with new technological innovation from Europe or Asia) with intensive design and prototype services to support local manufacturing. LSI also recognizes the political benefits associated with local manufacturing. Because "glocal" strategies strain corporate resources, LSI tries to share certain functions with other firms. It supports the formation of U.S. consortia because it believes they share compatible interest. Hence LSI sees DCAs as the key to globalization. Nonetheless, LSI withdrew from Sematech in 1991 because it wanted an organization that created more product rather than process technologies. More foreign firms now wish to join national research consortia that link together major suppliers and customers and define the next generation of technical standards. This function, once considered beyond the jurisdiction of GATT rules, is being internationalized.

Corning uses ICAs to build foreign business and provide the technical, marketing, and financial resources to generate successful application of its product lines globally. Corning will even consider withdrawing from successful ICAs that are committed to Corning products to release resources for a new ICA. In short, Corning believes in both "glocal" and in "global functional" specialization and uses ICAs to solve the problems.

Common Technical Infrastructures Another major reason for globalized alliances is that firms are investing in common technical infrastructures with partners. These investments take many forms. A large firm may build alliances with specialized suppliers around the globe for ongoing projects. For example, the Lincoln Town Car was long a mainstay in the Ford product line. But Ford chose a British firm to reengineer it, which in turn opened a U.S. office to coordinate its activities. The exterior body is produced by a U.S. plant created for this purpose by a Japanese metal-stamping firm. Ford created a new global communications network to tie together the firms.[34] Another example is that national stock markets are being tied together into a single whole by electronic trading.[35]

Several firms may discover that to operate globally they need to cooperate with foreign firms on minimum common technical standards and service support. They may worry that relying solely on governments to set standard processes may delay progress and contribute to discrimination against them in foreign markets. They may set up new product and service standards in conjunction with foreign firms and participate in common R&D for generic, precommercial technologies. The Corporation for Open Systems is both an ICA and a DCA (because it is organized with national branches) that sets standards and tests products for interconnecting computing systems. In its first phase the EC's European Strategic Programme for Research in Information Technology (Esprit) promoted precommercial research and tried to orient firms to common standards. A turning point in this trend was Japan's invitation to other countries' firms to join its national research effort on intelligent manufacturing systems. (The United States and the European Community insisted that there be joint government oversight of the commercial R&D to balance public and private investments.) Similarly, as flexible manufacturing systems proliferate, tighter relationships between component suppliers, manufacturers, and final systems assemblers are becoming common. These arrangements often lead to DCAs, but ICAs also are becoming more common.

Global Networking Advantages When firms join together to create a common international network, they all may gain global networking advantages. More critically, firms are recognizing that partners are needed to expand globally to ensure that the networks are not designed simply to advance the interests of one member. Moreover, common technical infrastructures may evolve into the joint development of strategic processes or products. A firm is likely to seek partners if economies of scope are important for the product and it cannot easily assemble the full range of products, distribution support, or technologies alone.[36]

Interconnection also is the new norm within sectors. Joint development arrangements are especially popular in services such as value-added networks. For example, many firms are turning to global electronic data interchange (EDI) to link manufacturers, their suppliers, and their customers. The goal is to make them more efficient managers. A textiles or apparel firm might benefit enough from the efficient management of their inventory and production runs to offset differences in labor costs between the United States and Asia. Thus, the Society for Worldwide Interbank Financial Telecommunication (SWIFT) provides interbank clearing functions globally for the banks that are its members. Each week the value of interbank transactions is equal to the total annual value of global trade; it is crucial that these transactions are cleared quickly and efficiently.[37] Similarly, SITA, the Société Internationale de Télécommunications Aéronautiques, allows international airlines to track luggage and passengers around the world, and airline reservation systems such as Sabre and Apollo in the United States, Galileo and Amadeus in Europe, and Abacus in Asia provide a similar service for the airlines. Moreover, these regional airline reservation systems are being linked to create global advantages. Indeed, Apollo and Galileo actively explored merging their operations.[38] Along the same lines, Reuters has created a new global ordering system that for the first time allows long-distance competition in many automobile parts markets. A final example is the ICA that ties DHL and its German and Japanese air freight partners to create a more effective global delivery system. DHL's expertise in logistics and cost controls could not be exploited without complementary capabilities in local logistics and airport landing facilities. These examples reflect a dual trend. Greater communications capabilities allow firms to globalize and also to work efficiently with others to build cooperative networks geared to global markets.

Joint Development of Common Products In many industries fixed costs are rising and product cycles are shortening. Firms respond by entering ICAs to share the cost of research and product development, especially in Europe. In the absence of a unified market, European firms faced a unique challenge. Although European TNCs now are as large as their American counterparts, their small home markets and the increasingly competitive European regional market have forced them to diversify more than U.S. firms, especially in electronics and chemicals. Although R&D as a percentage of sales is as high as in the United States, European TNCs must spread their efforts more thinly over a wider range of products. This causes problems as product cycles shorten and manufacturing process work becomes more vital. It is no longer enough to be a close second in key markets or to be smart on products but not services. This set of problems reinforces the pleas of major high-technology firms in the European Community to continue as the disproportionate recipients of government R&D funds.[39]

Firms are emphasizing rapid, global product positioning to earn the margins needed to cover research costs. They are enhancing economies of scale and scope in manufacturing by combining global and regional production platforms to keep core production skills in each parent. At the same time they are combining resources to quickly customize products and meet additional regional capacity needs. Similarly, consortia for joint development of specialized input technologies are emerging to support the product offerings of member firms.[40] However, although the pressures for joint development projects are growing, most firms worry about the integrity of their production capacity.

Examples of joint-development ICAs abound. Ford and Mazda have an alliance that has gone beyond a common technical infrastructure to joint development of common products. Motorola and Toshiba each have independent production capacity, but they contemplated a common position for memory chips in Europe until they concluded that it was cheaper to export to the European

Community.[41] Joint-development ICAs may stabilize, especially if market closure by governments makes local allies critical just when fixed costs make global positioning essential. The commercial aircraft, aircraft engine, and satellite sectors are moving in this direction. In commercial aircraft, for example, the "timing and choice of partners for multinational development and production programs are key strategic choices that can plug holes in product lines, block other alliances from forming, and spell the difference between commercial success and failure. Such programs also inevitably accelerate the international flows of technology and program management skills." For example, Airbus has over 30 percent U.S. content in its airplanes.[42] Similarly, the Rank-Xerox and Fuji-Xerox alliances are designed to place Xerox at the heart of a crucial specialized global market. The McDonnell Douglas deal with Taiwan on commercial aircraft was a quest for capital and an effort to build a partner to anchor the Asian market.

At their strongest, joint-development ICAs may result in firms with strong independent identities as commercial suppliers. Airbus and Intelsat are examples. Firms also may try to form product families in which each family member contributes specialized inputs to a common product line. An explicit division of labor among firms is maintained and specialized assets are shared by the firms to assist each part of the ICA. AT&T, to enter Europe, tried such a strategy with Philips for network telecommunications equipment and with Olivetti for office automation and communications. It formed substantial ICAs with each firm and then tried to orchestrate both ICAs collectively. Both ICAs failed: AT&T's ICA with Olivetti dissolved, and Philips is liquidating its position in the joint-venture firm. Nevertheless, AT&T has brought Italy's STET and Spain's Telefonica into the ICA it once shared with Philips. And Olivetti tried once more in 1992 to refocus its competitive strategy by letting DEC buy almost 10 percent of its stock and agreeing to build its future product line around new DEC technology.

Dominant market leaders like Boeing and Toyota usually resist corporate alliances of such daunting ambition, but when market power is relatively evenly distributed or demand is growing rapidly and unpredictably, alliances should increase in number. Alliances also should be more common among followers than leaders. In general, for example, joint-development projects are more common among second-tier automobile firms than in the first tier.

Will ICAs Last?

In general, it is difficult to sustain ICAs because their transaction costs are high. They may offer fewer incentives to defect from cooperative R&D ventures, but usually when partnerships start jointly producing a critical product for world markets, tough safeguards against defection are needed. One way to provide such safeguards is to forge broad-ranging relationships that extend beyond the immediate project.[43] With this kind of arrangement a partner that failed to meet its obligations in one partnership could be punished in other partnerships. Banks developed another safeguard against defection by making syndicated loans to developing countries. If a single participant in any syndicated loan declared the borrower to be in default, cross-default clauses kicked in that threw all syndicated loans to the country into default. This method allowed every bank to have an equal chance to attach assets owned by the borrower. To the extent that global networking provides economies of scale, scope, and learning traditionally associated with such networks as telephone systems, they may prove highly viable. But transaction costs may be so high that more nimble solo ventures may triumph through quicker innovation.[44] Joint development also may be easier if there are significant political constraints on market entry and high economies of scale that make it difficult to offer a reasonably priced product through national production alone. In the case of aircraft engines, for example, scale problems and political barriers prevent any firm from defecting from a global consortia to go it alone.[45] Similarly, the return of the chemical industry to its historical origins, stressing heavy commitment to R&D and technological innovation, strongly suggest that major chemical companies will need to continue to build strong technological and business links spanning many countries.[46]

Another way alliances break down is when one partner forges ahead independently on production or technology while its partners rely solely on the ICA. Over time, the partnership becomes a mismatch. Tension also occurs when partners that once boasted complementary skills and technologies find their expertise converging.

For example, Fuji-Xerox, a successful alliance for over a quarter of a century, faces new tensions because Fuji's photographic expertise and Xerox's copying technologies are converging. In the past, their technologies generally complemented each other rather than overlapped.[47]

The Globalization of Commerce

Firms frequently believe they need partners to succeed and see quasi-integration through ICAs as a way to center their strategies productively. They do not want to commit to joint development but realize that traditional licensing, original equipment manufacturing, and sales agent agreements are not sufficient to meet their needs. As firms forge links through common investment and commitments to codify and share tacit technical knowledge involving particular technologies or sets of systems architectures, they can widen the range of available suppliers and buyers for any single firm by making specific technologies interoperable. Still other ventures selectively share proprietary knowledge.

These developments are producing fundamental systemic changes that go well beyond individual firms. The globalization of assets through integrated transnational strategies and ICAs are making global firms more vulnerable to opportunistic behavior in global markets. TNCs now presume that if they share risks on major projects with foreign corporations, they will gain important know-how, products, and financial leverage. Even firms that make strong pleas for limited protection would be negatively affected if the world economy suddenly limited flows of products, technologies, and investments. At the same time that protectionist temptations are offset by strategic interdependence, token access to foreign markets is no longer enough. For example, LSI wants each major international partner to be represented in a "collegial" management structure. This is costly and makes sense only if the firm believes that it must be local in each regional market and must rapidly disseminate technologies and products to quasi-independent regional groups. Thus globalized firms are more sensitive to all forms of barriers that prevent them from operating in specific national markets. They do not want simply to "get in" and then be protected against new competitors. As globalization proceeds, they are likely to push strongly for openness.

These new forms of cooperation go beyond traditional licensing agreements, even if they fall short of creating unified global firms. They depend on complementary resources acquired from other countries or their firms and are provoking new corporate and regulatory strategies within the international economic order.

Globalization is not a homogeneous process. The enormous variations in globalization, and the risks and opportunities it creates, demand detailed rules to guide world commerce for particular industries. The traditional six pillars of the world economic order are buckling because they can no longer support the plethora of specialized arrangements for each industry made necessary by globalization. A new architecture is needed.

CHAPTER FOUR

The Six Emerging Pillars
of a Market-Access Regime

Academics and policymakers clung tightly to the old, comforting rhetoric of free trade and to the pillars on which it was built because, despite occasional dips, global commerce continued to grow. Noting that the United States is more, not less, international than it was two decades ago and that trade and investment are up, not down, analysts and officials concluded that adjusting and adapting the old regime was sufficient to prepare it for the 1990s and beyond. They failed to appreciate that a market-access regime was emerging—not because it was planned but as a result of market developments and corporate strategies.

New principles are taking shape to help governments guide, but not micromanage, international commerce: as power diffuses, bargaining problems change; as firms globalize, their preferences change; and as different models of industrial organization become dominant, international regimes must be modified to preserve openness.

Market-access regimes are most likely to occur when firms are highly globalized and governments use open industrial policies to promote their industries while still accepting foreign penetration of their markets. Open industrial policies permit foreign and domestic competition but assume that governments will play a role in shaping competitive advantages. Industrial policies have different goals.

Many such policies support public infrastructure, assist industries that are being resized in response to foreign competition, and promote R&D projects involving generic technologies (rather than specific products).[1] East Asian governments often orient their public policies to promote the growth of selected sectors. But when national policies deprive foreign firms of access to the domestic market, the country is not conforming to the market-access regime.

Firms and governments have turned their attention to market access. U.S. bilateral trade negotiations with the European Community and Japan showed that major firms now evaluate market openness in terms of rights and tradeoffs related to trade, foreign investment rights, and industrial policies. In the late 1980s U.S. trade officials began to assert that market access was more important than any other individual principle of free trade and developed the concept of market access in drafts of interagency working papers. The U.S. position on trade in telecommunications and information services during the Uruguay Round negotiations, for example, focused specifically on market access. The United States argued that countries should permit effective market access because the conduct of trade and investment increasingly requires it. Although countries will retain substantial latitude in choosing domestic industrial policies, these policies should not discriminate too harshly against foreign firms. Therefore, domestic regulations should be subject to review with regard to transparency, national treatment, and strategic trade implications. (Chapters 5 and 6 explore how the world automobile trade and the semiconductor regime are emerging market-access regimes.)

In short, the six original pillars of free-trade regimes have eroded and are being replaced by the six emerging pillars of a market-access regime (see Table 4.1).

THE FOUR PILLARS THAT PROVIDE STRUCTURE FOR THE MARKET-ACCESS REGIME

Pillar 1: From the U.S. Model to the Hybrid Model of Industrial Organization

After 1945 the global economic regime coincided with U.S. preferences and was constructed on the basis of the U.S. model of indus-

Table 4.1
The Old and the New Pillars of World Trade

Old Pillars *of the Free-Trade Regime*	*New Pillars* *of the Market-Access Regime*
Structure	
1 U.S. model of industrial organization	Hybrid model of industrial organization
2 Separate systems of governance	Internationalization of domestic policies
3 Goods traded and services produced and consumed domestically	Globalization of services; eroding boundaries between goods and services
4 Universal rules are the norm	Sector-specific codes are common
Rules	
5 Free movement of goods; investment conditional	Investment as integrated coequal with trade
6 National comparative advantage	Regional and global advantage

trial organization. A model of industrial organization is both political and economic: it assumes a role for government and a structure for firms.

The U.S. model assumed that domestic markets allowed free competition and that foreign firms could enter national markets without overcoming undue barriers. In the late 1960s, Europe worried that their indigenous high-technology firms would be routed by IBM and other U.S.-based TNCs.[2] Twenty years later many Americans fear that U.S. firms cannot compete effectively with the Japanese and that Japan will dominate U.S. financial markets and own a majority of assets in the United States.[3]

As economic power and capabilities diffused, the Euro-Japanese models of industrial organization gained prominence, and the openness of the global economic regime receded.[4] DCAs and ICAs are one consequence of changes that have swept the global economy, and they are central to the search for a new formula for corporate structure and for government oversight. Significantly, these alliances are geared to more global competition, not to more protectionism. If Japan, South Korea, and others desire export-led expansion and protection at home, then overseas expansion is critical because it eventually forces new forms of globalization. Countries with open strategies have firms facing greater pressure in their home markets. At least for sophisticated firms in imperfect markets, a rational response is to prefer international expansion rather than simple protectionism.[5]

Even if every country accepted the U.S. model of industrial organization, with its emphasis on transparency and relatively open, "leaky" relationships among firms, these developments would pose vexing problems. The diffusion of economic power means that many critical market decisions now are made far from U.S. shores. The origins of corporate alliances and their implications for the international economic regime reflect not whether Japan is a predatory economic power but that Japan and to a lesser extent Europe have different models of industrial organization that are less committed to transparency and arm's-length relations between firms and governments—key features of the U.S. model that once defined the parameters of global competition.

In addition, antitrust enforcement under the Japanese and European models traditionally was permissive. These models accepted tight links among industry, finance, and government. Local, national, and regional industrial promotion and coordination policies were commonplace. By contrast, trade protection for strategic industries and controls on foreign investment were not prevalent in the United States.

The Japanese Model   The Liberal Democratic Party (LDP) and the Japanese electoral system play crucial roles in Japanese economics.[6] Japanese elections, because of the structure of the Japanese electoral system, are based on patronage benefits, not on contests over public policy, and patronage works best when the economy is highly regulated and politicians have ample funds with which to court voters. Politicians regularly collect benefits for being the court of last appeal in a regulated economy. The LDP's electoral success, which has allowed it to rule continuously since 1956, has produced a circle of politics and economic policy: the bureaucracy knows what is expected politically and in return has considerable discretion in guiding the economy; the major Japanese firms obtain what they need to grow internationally in return for their support of the LDP.[7]

MITI's industrial policies promoted competition among Japanese firms or groups of firms, encouraged Japanese firms to export, and simultaneously protected the internal Japanese market from foreign penetration, thus providing Japanese firms with sufficient economies of scale to make them efficient producers. The Japanese keiretsu is the most celebrated offspring of the production policies of the new industrial models. The classic keiretsu includes a central group bank, a trading company that imports raw materials and exports group products, and an assortment of independent companies with extensive cross-stock holdings. There is no central holding company, and coordination is loose and voluntary. But the financial system provides stable funding for aggressive investment plans, protection against takeovers, at a financial premium that is equivalent to a charge for an insurance policy.[8]

Japanese firms also created contractual and equity relationships that promoted quasi-integration. Quasi-integration occurred when a major firm like Toyota, NEC, or NTT shared its production and design skills with its suppliers. Product components were designed with a particular system in mind. To maximize overall performance, the system maker transferred some of its technology to the component producer.[9] Indeed, in many cases the component maker was simply provided with specifications and told to design the item; the maker was free to draw on technology and capital of the system supplier as necessary. This linked production system made it difficult for outsiders to become core suppliers to major Japanese companies.[10] It also encouraged Japanese firms to supply all major pieces of a system and thus discouraged the pattern of intraindustry global trade that characterized the U.S. model of industrial organization.[11]

The Japanese approach to production worked most easily when firms produced at home and exported. Long after formal import barriers began to decline, Japanese firms deviated from the typical transnational pattern of extensive production abroad coupled with significant imports. Only when pressure by foreign trading partners began to mount did Japanese firms belatedly start to become more global. Even then, Japan's keiretsu system encouraged Japanese firms to invest abroad in ways that reinforced domestic patterns. Thus, medium-sized Japanese firms in sectors such as automobile parts invested overseas to follow their large group members abroad. Sophisticated local content is much lower for Japanese operations than for their U.S. counterparts. This made Japanese foreign investment disruptive to recipient countries. It was inconsistent with typical patterns of postwar intraindustry specialization that allowed countries to define new niches in response to new foreign competitors.

The collision of permissive industrial policies with different patterns of collaboration among firms created serious consequences for research and development. Lifetime employment and the near total ban on mergers and acquisitions in Japan helped persuade Japanese firms to invest in each other and develop cooperative R&D projects to fuse technological capabilities.[12] Government ministries advanced part of the money and served as brokers for the projects. Many non-Japanese companies complain that although Japanese technology is critical to their operations, it is poorly reported in professional journals and it is difficult to license Japanese technology. To tap Japanese skills, leading foreign firms are entering elaborate partnerships in Japan, and their ability to do so on equitable terms is becoming critical for global economic integration. Having belatedly recognized this reality, MITI now is making all consortia under its sponsorship open to foreign firms. Significantly, MITI is not taking steps to reduce consortia or government oversight; instead, it is simply making foreign firms into junior partners in its regulatory net. Our case studies demonstrate that Japanese officials would like to open Japan by incorporating foreign firms into a global version of Japanese industrial organization.

The European Model Across the Atlantic, the EC 1992 program is part of an attempt to adapt European industrial policy by applying lessons learned from the Japanese model. The 1992 program will create an internal market large enough to provide major economies of scale. The European Community, the member governments, and ICAs all are trying to create European counterparts to Japanese practices.[13] European firms are expanding by buying out one another and increasing their position in the United States. Meanwhile, new DCAs and ICAs in high-technology sectors in Europe are diverting a large share of R&D funding away from national governments to the European Community. EC initiatives such as Esprit, Research in Advanced Communication Systems for Europe (RACE), and Basic Research in Industrial Technologies for Europe (BRITE) were devised in part to encourage the formation of inter-European alliances large enough to compete successfully against U.S. and Japanese firms in key high-technology sectors.[14]

Esprit, an EC program for cross-national research for the information industry, had a budget from 1984 through 1988 of 1.5 billion European currency units (ECU) (half from the Commission, half from participating firms). To put this figure in perspective, Esprit and other programs administered by DG-XIII, which is in charge of efforts related to the telecommunications and information sectors, account for approximately 45 percent of EC R&D expenditures. Firms in collaboration with academic researchers undertook in-depth work on microelectronics, software, computing, and computer-integrated manufacturing.

Esprit and RACE were meant to emulate the Japanese R&D model. They were designed to spawn generic manufacturing processes that would serve the major European producers. (In its second phase RACE is supposed to focus on applications and bringing products to market.)[15] U.S. firms that produce specialized components and manufactured products worried that if they were shut out of the research programs, they would be at a competitive disadvantage in Europe. Almost certainly the European Community would gear its VRA and other programs to ensure substantial regional production by companies headquartered in Europe.

But these efforts ran into difficulty.[16] By early 1992 key DG-XIII officials privately conceded that Esprit was a failure and that RACE was largely a failure—mostly because of the intransigence of monopolistic European telecommunications operators that failed to open up to greater competition, which in turn meant that European equipment companies kept misreading opportunities. (Europe appears to have failed to move fast enough to follow the United States on local- and wide-area networks and on inter-wide-area-network networking.) Officials are determined that if there is another round of RACE R&D projects, over 40 percent of the funds will go toward telematics applications (such as information and communication systems for hospitals). The European Community will not give up collective R&D, but its latest conclusions fit our thesis: competition and more market-focused policies to promote industries are not mutually exclusive. Still, it is significant that the European Community by the early 1990s was spending about 6 percent of its R&D funds in consortia; by contrast, only 4 percent of Japanese R&D funds flow through them, and only 1 percent of U.S. R&D funds. (Motorola, however, because of the global nature of its business, reportedly spends 10 percent of its R&D on consortia.)[17]

In short, the international economic order implicitly rested on the idea that the United States was its key economy and that the U.S. model of industrial organization was relatively transparent and open. The global dispersion of economic power forced firms, especially U.S. firms, to adopt complicated strategies to obtain technology and other assets needed to remain competitive. This alone would have challenged existing corporate structures and rules governing international competition, but the dispersion of power also made other models of industrial organization more influential. Dealing with government support for industry and national efforts to foster their own firms' advantage is increasingly more difficult while simultaneously ensuring the transparency and enforceability of the rules of international commerce.

The Emerging Hybrid Model The Euro-Japanese models add to the managerial complexity that arises from globalization, raise new organizational challenges, and make it harder for firms to compete. It also is more difficult for governments to create the rules that provide fair and efficient international competition. In short, we expect the world economy to undergo a process of "reverse restructuring" as more elements of the Japanese and pan-European models for competition are incorporated into the global regime for managing the world economy. The implications of these changes help explain the erosion of the other pillars.

Countries are not moving to a single model of economic organization, any more than a single model existed when the U.S. example predominated. But trade policy cannot succeed if it has to carry the load of industrial adjustment and promotion policies. Put bluntly, other countries are telling the United States that it cannot rely on trade policies to fix the adjustment problems of the automobile and other industries. Other policies must complement trade policies if the world economy is to remain open and foreign firms are free to contest local markets.

All three power centers are restructuring their models of industrial organization to balance international obligations with national aspirations. If they do not, managing the global economy will become more difficult because the diffusion of international power and the emergence of a hybrid model of industrial organization raises complexity and increases the chances of misunderstanding, cheating, unjustified reprisals against trivial errors, or other transaction costs. This is what pessimists fear for the future.

Another reason that oligopolistic cooperation spurs changes is that the emergence of new great powers reopens a recurring problem that besets global regimes. Great power promises about the regime must be credible because great powers are in the best position to cheat. Therefore, all countries benefit from features of a regime that solidify domestic support for the regime in the great powers.[18] For example, when the United States became a world power, the International Telecommunication Union (ITU) sanctioned private ownership of U.S. international communications carriers, making it easier for American firms to operate abroad.

By the same logic, the emerging international regime will have to take into account the idiosyncrasies of the domestic Japanese and European political economies. Japan and the European Community inevitably will promote different degrees and kinds of government oversight and collaboration among firms. The revision of international patent conventions at the World Intellectual Property Organization, for example, appears likely to lead to strengthened global property rights, which would reinforce openness. To accomplish this, the United States will have to accommodate the Euro-Japanese models of patent claims that emphasize first applicants for patents, not first inventors of the technology. This reflects how the Europeans and Japanese balance protection against competition in their economies. In short, the definition of what constitutes an open market changes because the underlying model of industrial organization has changed.

The corollary to a shifting definition of openness is a transformation in the industrial organization model of the major powers.

Convergence is an overblown notion, but all three power centers are undergoing significant changes. As the case studies show, Japan is creating foreign access under the auspices of government oversight. The European Community is trying to restructure its firms to increase their scale while creating a unified market and a coordinated system of industrial policy assistance. The United States is reluctantly experimenting with relaxation of its antitrust policies, new forms of R&D collaboration with industry, and radical tactics to pry access into foreign markets that require closer collaborations between the government and various DCAs and ICAs.

In short, a hybrid model of industrial organization is likely to prevail. It will be taken for granted that important markets feature active adjustment and promotion policies by governments and various measures to increase local value added. But foreign firms must still be able to contest the market effectively except in clearly delineated and announced segments of the market reserved for local firms. More bilateral and regional arrangements are likely to arise within a multilateral framework because it is simply too complicated to negotiate these arrangements globally. (The likely compromises needed to create this new model and the politics of implementing it are explored in Chapter 9.)

Pillar 2: Moving to Internationalized Domestic Policies

Under the second pillar of the free-trade regime, bureaucracies were viewed as discrete and independent entities. Today, the lines demarcating global rules for trade, investment, and money are blurring, as are the lines between these and domestic regulatory and industrial policy systems. Bureaucracies must cooperate if they hope to craft reasonable, complementary, far-sighted policies.

The Convergence of Trade, Investment, and Monetary Policies The relationships among trade, investment, and monetary policy are growing more interdependent. During the Uruguay Round negotiations officials from finance ministries negotiated beside trade officials. The United States campaigned to open Japanese financial markets, in part to win business opportunities for U.S. banks, and to liberalize outflows from Japanese capital markets so that capital costs would equalize globally. In noting that Japanese banks had displaced U.S. banks at the top of the financial rankings, Washington believed that Japanese business enjoyed unfair advantages as long as it was the sole borrower with easy access to the vast pool of Japanese savings.[19]

In essence, the blurring of boundaries separating trade, investment, and finance means that a single economy has replaced a dual economy. The new problems that now face firms and governments cannot be solved by old policy prescriptions. To sell more U.S. telecommunications equipment in the semiclosed markets of Europe and Japan, the United States must encourage competition in telecommunications and computer services, since service providers will help manufacturers enter their markets only if they believe they need their equipment to compete. By the same token, if governments exercised less control over their airlines, the world aircraft industry would be transformed, since commercial aircraft procurement in Europe and the United States was never guided solely by market considerations.[20]

Overlapping Domestic Regulations and International Industrial Policies Under the free-trade system national economic and regulatory policies and international economic policies were separate and assumed to be independent of each other. Although major countries were acknowledged to steer the world economy, policymakers went to great lengths to protect their national economic choices against outside influences. The sovereign control over the national economy was a right that all countries guarded. The increasing globalization of firms and sectors has made it impossible to isolate national economies from international influences, however, and the relationship between domestic and international economies now clearly runs both ways.

On the one hand, international developments undermine efforts to set national economic policies. The members of the European Community were the most forthright in recognizing this new reality. The twelve member countries passed control for external trade policies to Brussels years ago. With the announcement in December 1991 of their intention to proceed to a single European currency and a single European central bank, European leaders conceded that although economic union would be difficult to achieve, their affairs are intermingled. They have acknowledged that attempts to set national and regulatory powers that are not coordinated with their neighbors will be ineffective and perhaps counterproductive. In contrast, U.S. officials were reluctant to be fully candid with other utility regulators about how a GATT services code might raise questions about their practices.

On the other hand, focused industrial policies also distort the operations of global markets. Countries that devise clever strategies to maximize the advantages of their national firms may prosper at the expense of others. In addition, domestic industrial and regulatory policies may create trade and international economic distortions of major proportions. Strategic action by governments and companies may turn losers into winners and make winners into losers.[21] For example, subsidies may create export advantages and build learning curve economies at home by discouraging the competitive entry of rivals. Strategic trade policies might produce enduring market advantages in high-technology markets. New technologies with features like high fixed costs, significant learning curves, or specialized but competing technical standards put pressure on firms to globalize. Firms need more markets with a wider range over which to spread costs and hedge risks against and to build support for the standard—the same features that increase the risk that oligopolistic strategies might undermine some advantages associated with free trade and openness. Profits in these markets may be abnormally high and are likely to be captured disproportionately by market leaders.

The chances of distortions due to domestic industrial policies rose significantly as the dominant U.S. model of industrial organization declined. Indeed, some Japanese economists now argue that such industrial policies actually improve global welfare by bolstering competition internationally. But they concede that there are high adjustment costs for long-established winners. As a result, they argue, innovations in international trade and investment policies, along with adjustments in domestic economic policies, may be necessary to reconcile massive global adjustment and improved efficiency.[22]

The same boundary issues that plague national decision making haunts negotiators trying to reach agreements in international and especially multilateral negotiations. Thus the Uruguay Round negotiators disagreed about whether investment issues fell under GATT auspices and could be addressed at all during trade negotiations. Ultimately the principle of market access, a shorthand that covered both trade and investment, emerged as the core of the negotiations. Issues related to the movement of labor, which before the Uruguay Round had always been treated as an immigration question, suddenly found their way onto the agenda for trade negotiations.

The Consequences of a Global Economy The blurring of boundaries between trade and investment and between domestic and international policy realms has complicated national policymaking and international negotiations. Officials once felt free to concentrate on the domestic consequences of their policy choices, as long as they abided by a few fundamental global principles. This was a reasonable assumption when the United States, the fulcrum of world commerce, abstained from extensive micromanagement of dynamic world markets. (When the United States deviated in a key world market, like oil, the world market diverged sharply from the GATT ideal.) But as U.S. centrality declines and the U.S. policy mix shifts, regulators must consider whether they and their business constituents care enough about the fate of the global market to take measures that secure the welfare of foreign business. ICAs are devices that major businesses can use to establish private covenants that govern how foreign firms will be treated in national markets.

The struggle by governments to cope with globalization and new models of industrial organization has had two consequences for domestic policies: substantive domestic policies are being revised as a result of international negotiations, and irrespective of the substance of the policies, countries are beginning to acknowledge that they have an obligation to make their domestic policies and policymaking subject to international review. This does not mean that every policy is going to be subject to a trade dispute, in part because foreign firms do not want to annoy local governments and customers. But a precedent concerning the political oversight of domestic administrative laws is evolving. Slowly, governments are acknowledging that outsiders are entitled to appeal domestic decisions and to have access to information that they need to ensure that the global system responds to trade agreements and other political actions. Therefore, governments are accepting a greater obligation to make their policy-setting process transparent to foreign firms (including the workings of industry advisory groups). In addition, there is a greater expectation that governments will expedite appeals on trade-related complaints. (See Chapter 10 for a variety of devices for creating self-binding behavior by states through declarations of intent and interpretation of the rules.)

Pillar 3: Global Services Resemble Global Goods

The third old pillar, closely related to the second, distinguished between internationally produced goods and nationally produced services. This conception of a dual system is outdated for at least five reasons. First, the distinction between goods and services is eroding. Most manufactured goods contain a large and growing amount of service inputs. Most of the cost and value added that go into the development and production of everything from steel to computers to commercial aircraft are services. Most customers understand that "solutions" are the joint product of services and manufactured goods. Pieces of hardware cannot solve problems alone. Management consultants cite the example of the consultant who is credited with helping Black & Decker realize that it was in the business of producing holes not drills.

Second, most markets are becoming more global in high-technology manufacturing sectors and in the key segments of more sophisticated services sectors such as telecommunications, finance, and advertising. Major producers all target the same relatively small group of about 1,000 critical customers, and success depends on winning and holding the business of a significant portion of that list. Customers, particularly in the services industries, are demanding global service at competitive prices and are organizing to improve their bargaining position. Producers are complying. In the 1960s U.S. banks followed U.S. manufacturers abroad; twenty years later U.S. law firms are repeating the process. Telephone companies are rushing in the same direction as they enter into a stream of new ICAs, as is discussed in Chapter 7.

The mingling of goods and services and the growing competitiveness of services are not just extensions of free trade to the services arena. A third factor is that services are becoming more competitive at the same time that restrictions on services are affecting competition involving goods. The union of goods and services in new packages and the flux in restrictions on the sales of goods and services pushed companies to form ICAs. In a complicated world, niches are less secure, so firms combine their political know-how and technical expertise within ICAs to compete globally. Many firms are ready to jump from multicountry domestic strategies directly to transnational strategies. Motorola is forming joint ventures in Japan and Argentina for the supply of cellular telephone networks. Each network buys Motorola's equipment technology— a multicountry domestic strategy. Motorola also wants to enhance its individual national advantages by soliciting support for Iridium, a global satellite service that will use satellites in low orbits to link its national networks on low-cost terms. (The United States secured the spectrum allocations required by Motorola to operate Iridium at the ITU's World Administrative Conference, which concluded on March 3, 1992.) Moreover, Motorola has embraced strategic alliances on semiconductors on a global scale to meet the next generation of challenges in miniaturization.

Fourth, the status of services changed when the United States decided to actively join in the continuing transformation of the world economy. It is no longer accurate to portray goods as being traded while services are produced and consumed nationally. Firms recognized this new reality in the 1960s; the U.S. government began adapting its policies in the mid-1970s. Starting with the Trade Act of 1974, Washington began to focus on services and embraced competition in services and free trade in services. As U.S. firms adapted their competitive strategies to changes in the domestic environment and the opening of the U.S. market to foreign competitors, the U.S. government made the international liberalization of services a priority. Other governments are today struggling to do the same.

Fifth, foreign direct investment trends also demonstrate the growing role of services. As services become subject to international competition, it is often impractical to deliver them without direct foreign investment. As a result, as Table 4.2 indicates, from 1981 to 1985 services accounted for more than half of the investment out-

Table 4.2
Service and Foreign Investment Flows (in $ billions and as a percentage of average annual foreign direct investment)

	Japan	United States	Germany	United Kingdom
Outward flows				
1975–1980	$4.0 (41.8%)	$15.6 (34.3%)	$8.9 (49.1%)	$2.3 (43.6%)
1981–1985	$9.4 (62.2%)	$9.1 (53.2%)	$12.7 (58.4%)	$5.0 (38.2%)
1986–1989[a]	$28.1 (73.0%)	$17.5 (57.0%)	$11.0 (64.0%)	$29.5 (38.0%)

Source: Calculations based on *CTC Reporter* (Autumn 1988), p. 14; United Nations Centre on Transnational Corporations, *World Investment Report, 1991* (United Nations, ST/CTC/118, 1991), pp. 10, 16.

[a] Percentages cover period of 1985–1989. Japanese data not adjusted for reinvested profits on foreign investments.

flows of Japan, Germany, and the United States, up sharply from the 1975 to 1980 period, and the percentage continued to climb thereafter.

The globalization of services and their increasing importance, in tandem with goods, for global commerce has at least three important consequences. First, even if the Uruguay Round fails or produces only paltry results on trade in services, the promotion of services onto the global trade agenda signals an enormous shift in approach. At a minimum, countries are acknowledging that it is possible and probably desirable to negotiate trade rules for services. Foreign service providers are likely to be guaranteed some general rights of establishment in the economies of signatory countries. In addition, it is likely that national treatment will be extended to service providers, making it more difficult for countries to prohibit foreign entry, even where services are provided by monopolies at home. Countries probably will open up slowly and reciprocally. The firms of countries that allow access to their markets are likely to be granted wider latitude in their partners' economies. Ultimately, sector codes covering telecommunications, tourism, financial, and other services are likely to be established to evolve over time.

Second, the rising importance of globalized service sectors is redefining the relationship between the GATT and traditional international organizations concerned with services, such as the ITU, the International Maritime Organization, the International Civil Aviation Organization, and even the World Bank and Bank for International Settlements. As the GATT intrudes on their turf, they resist. However, the external threat posed by trade officials has forced these sleepy organizations to begin to reevaluate their roles. They are becoming more proactive and potentially more important even as they are forced to share their turf with the GATT and trade officials.

Third, despite initial efforts by developing countries to segregate goods and services during the Uruguay Round negotiations, the GATT is likely to sanction cross-retaliation between goods and services. This approach makes sense. Firms and countries now recognize and accept that there are linkages between sectors like telecommunications and semiconductors or finance and steel. Natural pairings are beginning to emerge so that countries found to be providing GATT-illegal support for their firms in one sector can be retaliated against in a different but linked sector.

In short, the boundaries between goods and services as well as between domestic and international are collapsing. The behavior of firms helped blur these boundaries, and firms continue to advance the process as they globalize their operations. Governments are pulled along and are beginning to act on a cooperative, global basis.

Pillar 4: Industry Codes Are Necessary Supplements to Universal Principles

The GATT usually presumed that one set of rules fits all, but this is no longer possible. Many industries have special political or economic conditions that force a departure from classic GATT principles. Improved universal rules and dispute settlement procedures may help to resolve this issue, but the Civilian Aircraft code and the new services codes probably are closer to future approaches. More than ever before, many industries are subject to ad hoc understandings governing the fundamentals of market access. But these ad hoc solutions are dangerous: they could lead to conflicting rules and the diversion of trade, which happened in the U.S.-Japan-EC maneuvering over the semiconductor market and again in the U.S.-Japan automobile "understandings."

The writing and negotiation of these rules may ultimately not be GATT's strong suit. GATT negotiations cannot easily displace the efficiencies of keeping the negotiating numbers small when dealing with some issues of coordination of industrial policies. But GATT does have a vital role to play in reconciling minilateral initiatives with global obligations. Properly handled, the distinctions between bilateral, minilateral (more than two, but not everybody), and multilateral negotiations can be artfully blurred. Unfortunately, at present much of the needed problem solving can be undertaken only at the fringes of the GATT. (Chapter 9 expands on this idea.)

THE TWO PILLARS THAT PROVIDE THE RULES FOR THE MARKET-ACCESS REGIME

Despite the reasonably evident changes in the structure of the postwar free-trade system, most economists continue to cling stubbornly to the stylized models that formed the basis of their training and on which they base their research and writing. The underlying theories remain powerful, but their application is only now receiving a needed review.

Pillar 5: Investment Becomes an Integrated Coequal with Trade

Free trade and the parallel but distinct freedom to invest across national borders were presumptions that were at the heart of the old regime. Today, trade and investment are treated by firms and governments more as coequals. Nevertheless, the agriculture and energy sectors always were riddled with protectionism.[23] The Seven Sisters were not a cartel after 1945, but they did try to manage the oil market and had no use for the GATT. OPEC members have even less interest in putting oil on the trade table. Indeed, for years a single staffer at USTR was responsible for the global trade in oil, chemicals, and fertilizer; everybody else worried about the other half of world trade. In the area of textiles and footwear the United States never accepted free-trade discipline despite calls for openness by developing countries.[24] Automobiles and steel have a spotty history of free trade, and services were not even considered to be tradable. As protectionist sentiment rose in the United States during the 1980s, the new strategic trade theorists raised the prospect that under some circumstances trade protectionism might be economically efficient.[25] Indeed, about 30 percent of the huge trade in electronics (about 7 percent of world trade) already is subject to managed trade arrangements.

Despite these exceptions, openness increased dramatically after 1945 and did not in fact decline during the 1980s, even though TNCs compromised the postwar free-trade system. In effect, the unspoken understanding was that major countries would continue to open their home markets in sensitive sectors by allowing freer trade and more foreign investment, but only at the urging of a major trading partner like the United States. When U.S. interests were at stake, the game was different. Managed market arrangements for textiles were perfectly acceptable, and U.S. firms supported import substituting industrialization in developing countries for most capital goods.[26] Large firms also supported such policies for intermediate and consumer goods. There was an element of "hear no evil, see no evil" to the system. Over time, however, the distinctiveness of trade and investment flows broke down. Governments still were expected to allow considerable competition from foreign firms, but the emergence of three new issues began to change the ground rules, ultimately suggesting a set of new rules.

The spread of TNCs and the emergence of ICAs and DCAs shifted the delicate balance between trade and investment flows. These new global firm architectures raised at least three new concerns in board rooms and national capitals: (1) demands for market access increased, causing governments to begin to rethink international investment rules; (2) the globalization of firms, particularly those based in Japan, led Washington and Brussels to focus on local-content issues and rules of origin capable of assessing where value was added; and (3) the globalization of firms and the blurring of boundaries between trade and investments highlighted issues of what constituted unfair competition and spurred greater interest in antitrust rules.

Increased Demands for Market Access Enduring political legacies of TNCs were the elaborate new policies that countries instituted to supervise competition from inward investors. Many countries limit the amount of foreign ownership that they permit in various industries. Foreign firms involved in local manufacturing activities often are required to export some portion of their production. In addition, governments frequently demand that TNCs produce some minimum percentage of the total value of their products locally. The United States has fewer rules of this type than most countries, but foreigners are not permitted to own U.S. broadcasting companies, and in late 1986 the U.S. government objected to and blocked the purchase of Fairchild, a major semiconductor producer, by Fujitsu, a Japanese company. At the time, Fairchild was controlled by Schlumberger, which is technically not a U.S. firm. Similarly, in the early 1970s the Canadian government blocked Citicorp from acquiring the Canadian-based, but European-owned Mercantile Bank.[27]

Barriers to foreign investment range from outright prohibitions to complicated local content rules or value-added provisions imposed on foreign investors. Japan and other countries directly or indirectly restrict foreign buyouts and takeovers of local firms, particularly hostile ones. The absence of the takeover option may encourage alliances but weakens the position of foreign competitors. In addition, foreign firms wishing to invest in Japan often are so delayed by bureaucratic rules that when they finally set up business in Japan, they find that domestic firms already have developed and marketed competing products or services and won consumer loyalty. Some countries require firms investing in their economies to take domestic partners; other countries require foreign companies to enter entirely on their own. (In Uruguay Round negotiations on trade in services the United States wanted investors to be guaranteed the right to choose to invest on their own or to take partners.)

Increasing Local Content Concerns The introduction of export target rules sped up the move toward global manufacturing. Key factors in the production process began to change. TNCs started moving people, management skills, money, communications networks, and data around the globe. These actions accelerated the progress of the services revolution and muted protectionism (because factor mobility undermines protective tariffs).

Today, concerns about local content are proliferating. Now that banking, telecommunications, reservations, and other infrastructure services are as internationalized as goods, new ways of determining where value was added to goods and services are needed for market-access regimes to function. Governments worry that firms might join ICAs to circumvent antidumping rules or voluntary export restraints. For example, a Japanese firm subject to antidumping actions might enter an alliance with a local firm or a third-country firm so its products will be less Japanese and therefore exempt from antidumping penalties. Such alliances might even add considerable value.

However confused governments may be, they are not helpless. Their weapons include countervailing duties and antidumping laws, which are legal under the GATT. In addition, the GATT articles and codes recognize that governments reserve for themselves absolute control over the rules of origin for goods. For customs and antidumping purposes, governments alone determine where goods were produced. To ensure that products and services sold in their markets contain sufficient local content, governments are refining rules of origin. (See Chapter 10 for a discussion of rules of origin.)

In short, local-content concerns are generating immense interest in rules of origin. Governments may raise local-content issues to force the review of whether sensitive products of an alliance should be granted access or tariff preferences. At present, producers of such products have minimal internationally accepted rights and duties. These rules may erode the markets for third-country firms involved in alliances with firms from countries subject to various trade complaints. To mitigate these potential problems, Hong Kong and Japan led the push for coverage of these issues in the Uruguay Round.

Concerns about Fair Competition Raised by Alliances Governments also possess a formidable arsenal of weapons for responding to perceived instances of unfair competition. The spread of ICAs and the extraterritorial impact of DCAs also raise significant antitrust issues. How can officials determine whether a specific set of relationships among firms has anticompetitive effects? This question is at the core of the trade dispute between Japan and the rest of the world about keiretsu structure. Similarly, the European Commission, particularly through DG-IV, the Competition Directorate, is seeking new ways to prevent unfair competition within Europe as an integrated internal market is created, and trade complaints related to the conduct of Japanese subsidiaries in the United States also focus on unfair collusion among Japanese firms that undercut fair competition. Still, it often is unclear whose rules and what basis decisions should be based on. These kinds of concerns are likely to lead to increased efforts to extend or create new national, regional, and global antitrust rules.

To illustrate the challenge, a particularly prickly problem high on the current agenda is when DCAs or ICAs should raise antitrust issues. The United States passed the National Cooperative Research Act in 1984 to provide new research and development consortia with an antitrust waiver. Creating Sematech and MCC would have been much more difficult without this waiver. Still, these consortia are not totally exempt from legal risks.[28] Incoming investment, takeovers, and joint ventures in the United States have always been subject to antitrust review, but as a rule, only horizontal combinations (for example, between two stainless steel producers) were subject to challenge. During the 1980s even ventures that fell into this category usually did not have to worry about the Department of Justice unless the total market share involved approached 20 percent.[29] However, in an attempt to understand whether a foreign firm, because of the competitive nature of its home market, represented an anticompetitive threat, the Exon-Florio amendment, part of the Omnibus Trade Act of 1988, authorized special review of any takeover or joint venture in industries important for U.S. national security. Similarly, ICAs will be subject to antitrust review in Europe, but the European Commission does not have clear standards governing their acceptability.

To meet the conditions raised by increasing demands for market access, growing concern about local content, and worries that ICAs and DCAs have unfair competitive advantages, governments are beginning to institute new foreign investment rules, revise and expand rules of origin, and update antitrust laws. These three types of measures are needed to allow governments to treat investment as a coequal with trade in the world economy. (Strategies for creating and implementing such measures are discussed in Chapters 9 and 10.)

Pillar 6: From National to Regional and Global Advantages

The sixth traditional pillar held that most trade takes place between firms located in different countries on the basis of national comparative advantages. This kind of trading was believed to be the best way to integrate the world economy because national comparative advantages were slow to change and largely revealed by market dynamics, not by global planning. This also meant that accountability and control of the world economy was effectively in the hands of national governments.

The growth of TNCs with manufacturing operations and distribution channels encircling the globe altered this picture long ago. The rise of alternative models of industrial organization, the blurring of boundaries, and the globalization of the firm had at least three complicated, unexpected effects on comparative national advantage: (1) alternative models of industrial organization transformed assumptions about how national comparative advantages develop; (2) with the partial exception of firms based in Japan, firms no longer define their competitive advantages on the basis of their home nation's position; and (3) the link between trade policy and competitive advantages on world markets is weakening. As a result of these three changes governments will need to recast their policies in terms of fairness.

The Impact of Alternative Models of Industrial Organization As was noted earlier, the changing meaning of comparative advantage under the Japanese and European models of industrial organization erodes the pillar of national comparative advantage. Although the efficacy of various forms of export-oriented industrial targeting is debated, an emerging consensus is that it is legitimate for countries to foster industrial transformation by investing aggressively in specialized infrastructure. There is ample evidence that some forms of traditional national comparative advantage still prevail. Japanese customers shopping for household electronics place a premium on innovative products that save space, and Japanese firms gained a global advantage by serving this local demand. Making capital investments in Japan was less risky than elsewhere because the Japanese inflation rate was low. Likewise, heavy Asian investment in educating engineers paid off for local enterprise. In mature industrial economies these types of national comparative advantages shift slowly and are less distinctive than they once were, but the situation is more dynamic in industrializing countries.

It is significant that Japan and other Asian countries are openly discussing the creation of global blueprints for the international division of labor—an idea that is anathema to the traditional notion of national comparative advantage. Japanese policymakers suggest that it is foolhardy for countries to randomly seek new industrial niches. Instead, they argue, governments should coordinate the development of public infrastructure. If countries agree to allocate segments of an industry among themselves according to a consensual blueprint, they can encourage complementary investments.[30] If this kind of hierarchical structuring of world competition becomes commonplace, even if it rests on benign intentions, it poses a profound challenge to the existing global order.

Implementing this plan may prove difficult. Asian countries, for instance, were reasonably successful in resisting the plans of Japanese automobile producers. Moreover, Japanese firms are recognizing that they will need to provide substantial local value added in their operations in other industrial countries. Although they may, in the manner of U.S. firms, wish to engage in global product mandating that gives specific regional subsidiaries jurisdiction for particular global products, they cannot simply make components in a major region.

The Globalization of Firms Nonetheless, Japanese policymakers have understood something that others have misinterpreted: rising regional integration is part of globalization. Both Europe and North America already are sufficiently integrated that firms may think in terms of regional advantages and strategies. Huge regions enjoy scale economies and supply consumers sophisticated enough to support competitive global efforts. U.S. firms once could do this on their own but found it more difficult as the U.S. share of world output dropped. For example, to protect their positions, European banks have created at least eight major networks of cross-shareholding agreements within the European Community. Each group consists of three to fifteen banks. Unlike the earlier consortia, which member banks ran as a separate organization, the member banks generally buy stakes of a few percentage points in some of the other banks in the network.[31] A similar phenomenon arose in the United States in the early 1980s. Large regional banks, fearful of national expansion by the big money center banks in the wake of deregulation, began to buy small shares in each other and to cooperate on specific systems and services.

Regional agreements are a logical complement to the redefinition of the national supply base of specialized production equipment, components, and design capabilities. Firms recognize that they have to decentralize ever more complex functions globally, including advanced production and design. But they also are trying to avoid disastrous splits between their top management and research teams and their distant production sites and suppliers. They are refining and strengthening a core competence in production at home while also producing more elsewhere. In Europe, the Americas, and Asia, this effort requires a redefinition of the home supply base to encompass complementary resources of their broader geographic regions. This regionalization of the home base then produces incentives to deepen specialized regional agreements to govern commerce. As long as the agreements are not exclusionary, the same pacts can assist the operations of foreign firms.

This leads to an extraordinary paradox: the growth of highly integrated regional economies makes it easier to reconcile local value added with efficient global production strategies. Integrated European and North American markets make it possible for foreign firms to produce large shares of even sophisticated systems such as telecommunications switches on a regional basis. Individual countries in a region can be assigned specialized product mandates because the countries in the area are highly integrated. Moreover, specific regions can be assigned worldwide mandates to develop specialized design and component technologies. The most acute crisis concerning equity and efficiency occurs when smaller markets are not integrated on a regional basis. Countries then may be trapped trying to produce globally because of the economics of a single firm or can resist and try to compete with inefficient local production operations. Thus, major TNCs may have a strategic interest in regional economic integration as a complement to global integration. Indeed, TNCs of all countries are being tugged to globalize their operations.

The Weakening Link to Trade Policy A third reason for the decline of the pillar of national comparative advantage is that, besides the effects of ICAs, links between trade policy and the competitive advantages of countries have weakened. Trade still may mean that a manufacturing firm in one country sells goods to an importer in another country. But it is just as likely that a manufacturer from one country will produce a good in a second country for shipment to its own subsidiary in a third country where further value will be added to the product before it is sold to an importer in a fourth country. For example, the Ford Capri subcompact convertible that was introduced in 1990 was designed by Ford in Michigan, engineered by Mazda in Japan, and built by Ford of Australia.[32] This kind of trade complicates international commercial affairs by weakening the link between cause and effect in trade policy and raising firms' transaction costs.

At one time only tariffs and quotas were needed to reward or punish a country's exporters, and these simple tools usually allowed trade policymakers to achieve their goals. But as major national firms began to produce and distribute their products overseas in complicated ways, the political congruence between trade policy and national interests diverged. Today future advantages may depend more on the attributes of firms than on the national factor endowments of countries.[33] If so, old remedies for national trade problems may no longer work as expected. For example, economists and policymakers know that a large dollar devaluation will eventually improve the competitiveness of U.S. goods and services. However, the value of the dollar matters less than it once did.[34] In fast-growing, lucrative markets characterized by oligopoly and imperfect competition, advantages possessed by individual firms may be a better predictor of success than the national exchange rate. For ICAs that depend on inputs from several countries, exchange-rate changes may cancel out.

The emergence of ICAs raises other important, hard-to-resolve new issues about nationality. To illustrate, during photocopier anti-dumping proceedings within the European Community, the European Commission had to determine whether firms qualified as being European. Rank Xerox, Olivetti, Oce, Tetras, and Develop had brought the complaint, but all were closely tied to non-European producers. Rank Xerox owned a significant share of Fuji Xerox, a major Japanese producer, but wanted to protect its European output from other Japanese firms. Canon owned part of Tetras, while Oce and Olivetti imported their copiers from Japan. Ultimately, the Commission excluded only Develop (because it was taken over by Minolta) when assigning a 20 percent duty in 1986. Subsequently, Olivetti built a joint factory with Canon in Italy. It then joined Rank Xerox in petitioning for renewed protection in 1992 on the grounds that its joint venture with a Japanese firm would be endangered by Japanese competitors.[35]

Should Amdahl and Honeywell, once major U.S. computer manufacturers, be eligible to join U.S. consortia for joint research and development involving microelectronic technologies and manufacturing processes now that they have significant foreign ownership? Amdahl and Honeywell now are involved in strategic alliances with Fujitsu and NEC under which they share many key products and considerable know-how with their Japanese partners. Bull of France now owns a majority of Honeywell Computers, and NEC and Honeywell retained minority shares. Although Europe's semiconductor research project JESSI allowed IBM to participate in projects starting in late 1990, it removed British International Computers Ltd from three of five projects it was pursuing in JESSI after Fujitsu acquired it.[36] At some level they are no longer truly American firms, and government efforts aimed to bolster U.S. technological innovation may be undercut before they begin. Similarly, Nippon Telegraph and Telephone (NTT), the dominant Japanese telephone company, is central to Japanese research and high technology and in 1986 formed an alliance with IBM in the field of data communications. To the extent that this is a meaningful alliance, one of the principal supporters of Japanese efforts in computers and communications technology is now sharing its secrets and know-how with one of Japan's leading competitors. This kind of arrangement is not always well received: some Canadians criticize Northern Telecom, in which Bell Canada Enterprises maintains a 52 percent interest, because it hired a U.S. citizen as chair and more than half of its production comes from the United States so that it can qualify as a U.S. firm.

ICAs raise new questions about government oversight, and globalization raises even more subtle issues. In 1987 the United States was outraged when it learned that Toshiba had transferred to the Soviet Union sensitive technology obtained from U.S. firms, which made it easier for Soviet submarines to escape detection. The protest took a traditional form—one government protesting the behavior of a firm of the second government. It would have been more complex if the culprit had been Airbus, a major manufacturer of commercial aircraft that is jointly owned by several European countries. No single country bears responsibility for Airbus. The EC can be held accountable; in a showdown Airbus could not escape major confrontations with its national parents. In the area of international finance, partnerships in specific business areas linking Citibank and Dai-Ichi Kangyo Bank, Goldman Sachs and Sumitomo Bank, American Express and Nippon Life, and Credit Suisse and First Boston make it difficult to determine which countries have regulatory responsibility.[37]

Moreover, traditional trade and industrial support policies, such as R&D or protectionism, take on strange twists when alliances enter the picture. U.S. congressional representatives were initially enthusiastic about supporting a policy to subsidize high-definition television (HDTV) and prohibit foreign firms from joining the research group. Their intent was to revive U.S. electronics production and protect the last remaining U.S. maker of televisions, Zenith. However, it soon turned out that the largest U.S. producers of televisions were Thomson and Philips, and both were union shops. This example could be multiplied many times over with a variety of twists.

The Need for Fair Trade Rules for Procurement, R&D, and Standards Instead of national comparative advantages, the sixth pillar of new market-access regimes obligates governments not to unfairly use their government advantages to manipulate markets. The goal is not to end government agreements on rules for government procurement, government ownership of industries, government-sponsored research, and development and standard-setting practices. Instead, the intent is to apply trade and international competition rules to the basic tools for modern industrial policies while avoiding massively protectionist policies. A particularly vexing problem facing trade negotiators is to modify principles, rules, and means for resolving disputes.

Government Procurement The Government Procurement code, one of the major successes of the Tokyo Round of GATT trade negotiations, clarified the circumstances under which signatories could discriminate in favor of local suppliers and narrowed the amount of price differential permitted for governments to favor their own firms. A goal of the Uruguay Round was to strengthen and extend the Procurement code to new areas and to expand the number of signatories. The forms of preferences are coming under sharp international scrutiny for two reasons: (1) government procurement is so large that it represents an unacceptable portion of total trade in an age of more competitive global markets; and (2) governments too often use procurement policies to provide local suppliers with an unfair advantage, particularly in high-technology sectors. This is significant because government procurement may be more critical for research and development success than straight research funding.[38]

Firms often use corporate alliances to hurdle barriers to sales imposed by procurement codes. Indeed, this effort is the glue that links many ICAs in the high-technology realm. ICAs may qualify for government contracts from which foreign firms are excluded. If procurement became progressively more open, the number of ICAs might diminish. But there is little evidence that greater liberalization in procurement would result in real arm's-length exporting and contracting for major items.

Research and Development R&D has always proven a sensitive issue for TNCs because all countries prefer to receive larger transfers of technology. Important questions will arise about how to attribute R&D spending for the purpose of meeting local content agreements for government procurement. More speculatively, it is possible that "informal" requirements for significant regional design facilities may become another local content demand.

By the late 1980s, R&D had become a central feature of many domestic corporate alliances. DCAs organized around R&D usually emphasize precommercial technologies or process technologies. (Japanese issuers of credit cards, however, have long worked together to rate the creditworthiness of their customers. American Express and other foreign firms that issued charge cards were excluded from the club, and they complained that their exclusion made it difficult for them to conduct business in Japan and thus constituted a trade barrier.) These types of DCAs are common in Europe, North America, and Japan and allow domestic firms to increase their competitiveness in critical sectors. The central issue that continually provokes debate is deciding which firms should be allowed to join these consortia. For instance, the Center for Advanced Television Studies and the MCC in the United States both exclude foreign firms. In the U.S. debate surrounding high-definition television, for example, Philips would like to participate in U.S. R&D consortia but would prefer Sony to be barred from membership.[39] Japanese and European high-tech consortia have been just as reluctant to invite participation from firms based beyond their borders. They liberalized membership rules only under massive pressure from the United States. On this matter, the GATT has said nothing, but guidelines covering the trade-related impact of R&D probably are inevitable. (Chapter 10 offers some detailed suggestions about the generalizable rules lurking behind numerous ad hoc actions.)

Technical Standards R&D within DCAs also is of growing importance for standard-setting exercises. In Europe, participants in the EC-sponsored ICAs such as RACE are designing key standards for the European network. Should RACE and other R&D groupings that have significant influence on trade-related policies such as standards be exempt from GATT supervision?

Standards also matter when DCAs and ICAs begin to produce products closer to final end users, promote systems architecture, or invest in selective sharing of proprietary technical data. For example, the Open Systems Foundation, an alliance that ties together many international computer firms, focuses on alternative solutions beyond those afforded by the conventional personal computer. Competitive promotion of new software standards on a global basis is one way that ICAs might shape trade advantages outside the traditional mechanism of industrywide committees.

Part one has shown why the world trade order is changing and where it is going. Part two illustrates how this general transformation varies according to industry. The mismatch between the general framework for trade and special arrangements for specific sectors increases problems with protectionism.

Sectoral Studies

CHAPTER FIVE

The Automobile Sector

The automobile sector was the largest manufacturing industry for decades. By 1977 foreign subsidiaries of automobile companies produced 20 percent of global output. In 1980 automobiles accounted for about 5 percent of world trade, and about 30 percent of world automobile output was exported.[1] The patterns for trade and investment in automobiles mirror the strains in world markets caused by shifts in the center of power and industrial organization and changing patterns of globalization in the industry.

The political economy of the automobile industry never fit the classic model of free trade, but the six pillars of the old regime served as a basis for the global automobile regime. Moreover, over time liberalization did occur through foreign direct investment led by U.S. firms. As was typical under the U.S. model of industrial organization, these firms considered exports and overseas production to be interchangeable. A crisis occurred in the world regime for automobiles when Japan's new model of industrial organization fundamentally altered the industry. Japanese firms introduced new production practices and emphasized export-led growth while benefiting from a protected home market. When foreign firms belatedly took the Japanese expansion seriously, they had no reason to avoid trade clashes with Japan.[2]

Japanese competitive pressure and U.S. and European government efforts to respond to that pressure have prompted a massive reorganization of the global strategies of both Japanese and non-Japanese firms. Ford and General Motors are integrating their global operations more thoroughly, while European and Japanese firms belatedly are becoming genuine TNCs with significant production and distribution networks outside their home countries. In this sense globalization is deepening the traditional direction of TNCs, pulling European and Japanese firms steadily into these patterns. More profoundly, with the partial exception of a few of Japan's leading producers, all automobile makers now need to share financial risks, key technologies, and products through DCAs and ICAs for vehicles and their components. Even sophisticated Japanese components makers are being driven to join new alliances. Thus, even as high adjustment costs push U.S. and European producers to promote new commercial restrictions, they are becoming embedded in alliances that scramble techno-nationalist strategies. Governments must adapt their trade policies covering items such as rules of origin to coordinate regional positions on domestic regulation. These forms of government intervention have produced market distortions, harming marginal efficiency, but they have not blocked the fundamental reorganization of the industry that is the main source of efficiency gains.[3] Indeed, the new organization of the industry conforms reasonably well to the pillars necessary to support a market-access regime.

THE POLITICS OF THE POSTWAR AUTOMOBILE REGIME

The political economy of the automobile industry reflects its size. Automobile firms are major employers and purchase huge quantities of other firms' products. They are particularly important for regional economies within countries and for union work forces. Indeed, their role is so massive in many economies that shifts in foreign purchasing patterns can significantly alter balance-of-payments performances. An extreme example was the $31 billion 1990 U.S. automobile trade deficit with Japan, which constituted about three-quarters of the total U.S. trade deficit with Japan.[4] The automobile sector is always politically sensitive because it affects the economic well-being of grass-root constituents and the voting public knows it.

The free-trade ideal was never approached in the automobile industry. Classic liberalization was postponed because after 1945 all key countries made the protection of their long-standing local producers a high priority. Countries accepted an implicit compromise: countries where major firms were based were expected to liberalize access to their markets only if other countries explicitly demanded it; if countries chose to restrict imports, they were expected to allow foreign firms to invest in their economies. (Trade was preferable, but foreign investment was better than closure and might even stimulate new, related trade flows.) In short, government action to protect the market share of domestic producers was tolerated. Japan and other countries could delay liberalization until they became important markets.[5]

In practice, these rules produced a highly regionalized world market. In the European Community imperfect internal liberalization was the norm. Foreign investment by U.S. firms usually was permitted, but domestic firms in Britain, France, West Germany, and Italy dominated their own markets. The United States welcomed foreign imports, but the huge bilateral trade flows with Canada were managed by a special free-trade pact: the United States was promised flexible sourcing and manufacturing throughout North America, and in return Canada was guaranteed local content. As Japanese imports surged, the U.S.-Canada Free Trade Agreement prevented Japan from circumventing voluntary export restraint agreements (VRAs) by importing to the United States through Canadian ports. (The U.S.-Canada Free Trade Agreement authorized free trade in used automobile parts and slightly stiffened the requirements for local content. But significantly, free-trade guarantees were not extended to new assemblers setting up in Canada.)[6]

The global automobile regime focused on the producers of automobiles. This made sense under the old model of industrial organization. The assembly business—the manufacturing of the vehicle—was the political heart of the industry because it shapes the components business, which accounts for 80 percent of the total value added. But the reorganization and globalization of the industry slowly forced greater policy attention to the trade in components. Firms relied more on independent suppliers of components, and even the parts makers' alliances with assemblers became the subject of trade controversies. This occurred while the U.S. market remained preeminent, despite some slippage. The growing weight of Europe and Japan as centers of production and consumption reinforced the salience of components issues because those regions always had relied more on independent suppliers. (Of expected world vehicle sales of 34.6 million units, the U.S. market accounted for about 8.7 million units, Japan for 4.7 million units, and Western Europe for 13.6 million units—almost 80 percent of the world market, a somewhat lower figure than for most other advanced technologies.)[7]

The United States

By the 1920s the U.S. automobile industry—led by Henry Ford and Alfred Sloan—was dominant. Although in its early days the automobile market was dominated by low-volume, luxury cars built by small crafts specialists in Europe, Ford and Sloan's strategy was based on large economies of scale, highly specialized work tasks, vertical integration of assembly and components, and strong industrial concentration at the "assembler level."[8] General Motors, Ford, and Chrysler dominated assembly, and to take advantages of economies of scale, all manufacturers relied on the same narrow range of mechanical technologies. The result was a homogenous U.S. market. The U.S. government supported the industry by keeping gasoline taxes low and by following proconsumer economic policies.[9] Simultaneously, strong antitrust enforcement discouraged links among automobile makers.

Until the 1970s the global regime for automobiles mirrored the organization of the U.S. industry. General Motors and Ford sought majority ownership and sole control over their foreign operations. They ran regionally self-contained operations in North America and Europe. They were reluctant to take on local partners. The Big Three often located assembly operations in developing countries that relied heavily on imported components. For the most part they operated as multidomestic firms overseas, conforming to local product traditions in major markets. Their reach was global, but their strategy and products were local.

Europe

After 1945, Europe's economic and political divisions reduced U.S. dominance. Every European country had different income levels, tastes, technical standards, and vehicle taxes.[10] After the creation of the European Economic Community in 1958, governments spent heavily to promote and protect their national automobile champions. European market leaders enjoyed secure home bases from which they selectively expanded to take on Detroit's European operations. Although until the 1970s European firms usually could not produce as cost-effectively as their American counterparts, they tried to differentiate product lines while producing enough vehicles to take advantage of scale economies. After adjusting for exchange rates and labor costs, European costs were higher and productivity and costs for European firms stills lag well behind U.S. and Japanese automobile makers.

European firms achieved only moderate concentration in the assembly stage, but Europe boasted a strong, independent components industry. The major automobile firms in Europe were Volkswagen, Renault, Peugeot, Fiat, Volvo, Ford, and General Motors. Second-echelon producers ranged from producers of luxury vehicles such as BMW and Daimler Benz to low-end national producers such as Leyland. European firms often collaborated to produce components such as engines that their partners could use in their product lines. The efficiencies derived from these joint production agreements and the existence of strong part suppliers helped European firms enter the U.S. market for small and specialty vehicles in the 1960s even as competition within Europe increased.[11]

Europe's success in the 1960s posed the first test to the automobile regime. Although Ford and Chrysler (but not General Motors) quickly joined the United Auto Workers (UAW) in endorsing import limits, the success of Volkswagen and other European imports in the late 1960s was not a major threat to Detroit's core business.[12]

Japan

As long as a label reading "Made in Japan" was a sign of inferior quality, Japanese firms played little role on the international scene.

Their home market was small; their exports were minimal. Japanese protectionism extended even to foreign investment, but it was over-looked until 1971. Foreign firms had some successes in entering the Japanese component market: Borg Warner fared well in the trans-mission business. In the late 1960s the United States pressed Japan to allow U.S. automobile makers to buy minority positions in Japanese producers. Detroit wanted to build automobiles in Japan, but the Big Three were willing to settle for equity positions that created bases from which they could source smaller automobiles to fill in niches in their product lines that they deemed unimportant. (They mistakenly assumed that there would be abundant gasoline available at low prices during the 1970s and beyond.)

The Old Pillars and the Automobile Sector

How did the automobile regime conform to the six pillars of the postwar free-trade system? Until the Japanese onslaught the U.S. model of industrial organization dominated (pillar 1). National bureaucracies, usually ministries concerned with commerce and industry, worked diligently to strengthen and promote their own national automobile sectors. There were few challenges by foreign firms to domestic regulations as long as access through investment was available (pillar 2). Automobiles were considered to be critical manufactured products. The service inputs that went into their design, production, and maintenance were ignored by trade policy-makers (pillar 3). Even before the 1980s the giant automobile firms were considered to be too important to be lumped with other manufacturing companies for trade agreements. Special deals were common (pillar 4). Thus the automobile sector was consistent with the first three pillars that defined the governance of the postwar free-trade system but diverged somewhat from the fourth pillar.

By contrast the two pillars that defined the rules for a free-trade system were often ignored for automobiles. Instead of trade and investment the international operations of the automobile industry were characterized for a long time by the assumption that countries would grant free trade *or* investment (pillar 5). Finally, many countries, particularly in Europe and later Japan, viewed the automobile sector as so critical to their national development and prosperity that they insisted on championing the industries even when they possessed no revealed comparative advantage (pillar 6). In short the structure for free trade existed in the postwar automobile industry, but national priorities never allowed free-trade rules to take hold.

THE TRANSFORMATION OF THE OLD REGIME FOR AUTOMOBILES

The Japanese Breakthrough

Ironically, Japanese firms ultimately gained ascendancy because the Japanese market was so crowded that it was impossible for a few giant firms to capture scale economies. When, despite MITI's opposition, all the major keiretsu decided to enter the automobile sector, competition and overcrowding became inevitable even in the absence of foreign competitors.

Eventually Toyota developed an organizational model for production that reorganized workers into multiskilled teams and established long-term alliances with quasi-independent component suppliers. Toyota produced only 20 percent of its components itself, but its "family" of suppliers provided an additional 50 percent of its components under the "just-in-time" system that minimized inventory costs. Japan achieved the lowest cost in the world at intermediate production scales with slightly lower levels of concentration at the assembly level than in Europe. Today the three Japanese global firms are Honda (an independent), Toyota (an independent with close ties to the Mitsui group), and Nissan (an independent with close ties to the Fuji keiretsu and a major stake in Fuji's automobile division). Mazda (part of the Sumitomo group, which rescued it from near collapse in the mid-1970s) and Mitsubishi Motors are in the next tier. Mitsubishi recently climbed to third in Japan. Suzuki, Fuji, and Isuzu are in the third rank. Hino and Daihatsu are niche suppliers affiliated with Toyota.

Japanese firms also led the way in building their domestic production around exports. Japanese production techniques worked best with tight coordination with traditional industrial partners. Japanese firms feared that they would lose the competitive edge if they produced overseas. Honda, Toyota, and other Japanese firms thrived because they offered a wider range of distinctive automobiles, kept their costs down, and consistently had the shortest innovation cycles in the industry to target specialized niches. Their superior management practices moved products from the idea stage to the customer faster than their competitors: the Japanese development cycle is about three years or even a little bit less, whereas U.S. and European automobile makers take up to five years to develop a new automobile. Japanese producers also offer about double the number of models of U.S. firms.[13] In addition, their huge production base, made possible because foreign buyers liked their exports, further reinforced their position in high-quality compact vehicles. Once they dominated the small-automobile niche, they upgraded and targeted midsize and luxury markets (in part because VRAs forced them to upgrade to keep revenues growing). Japan's competitors were compelled to reorganize to emulate Japanese practices.[14]

Japan's success in the 1970s and 1980s threatened automobile trade arrangements because exports caused local unemployment and national producers suffered heavy losses that were not balanced by gains for their workers or suppliers. The Japanese expansion also created massive surplus production capacity, which became a major economic burden during even small global economic slowdowns.

By the time negotiations began to open the Japanese market to foreign firms, the Japanese firms were so entrenched in all but the luxury niche that reciprocal access to Japan was slim compensation for foreign firms. More direct action was required. Table 5.1 tells the story.

The U.S. Response

The Japanese challenge highlighted the disarray in Detroit and Europe and prompted significant restructuring during the 1980s. The first step was to try to restrain the Japanese behemoth. General Motors finally joined Ford and Chrysler in supporting restrictions on Japanese automobile imports. A formal voluntary restraint agreement was negotiated by 1981 that was replaced after 1985 by voluntary unilateral restraints set by Japan. In 1984 Japanese automobile imports were limited to 1.68 million units; the limit increased to 2.3 million units per year in stages.[15] Japanese "trucks" are not covered by the agreement, and by the mid-1990s "trans-

Table 5.1
Shares of Japanese Automobile Imports in 1990[a]

	Percentage
VW and Audi	24.1%
Mercedes Benz	17.5
BMW	16.5
Rover	6.2
General Motors	3.8
Honda	3.4[b]
Ford	2.7
Jaguar	1.6
Rolls-Royce	1.5

Source: *Economist*, June 22, 1991, p. 68.

[a] Total units = 221, 706 (5% of the Japanese domestic market). Although sales of U.S. models in Japan climbed in 1991, total foreign sales dipped in 1991.
[b] Exports from overseas plants.

plant" factories in North America will produce another 2.5 million vehicles per year (double the 1989 output).

The VRAs increased Japanese profits per vehicle by creating an artificial scarcity of Japanese vehicles. U.S. manufacturers also profited because they exercised pricing leadership in light trucks (where the threat of VRAs may have slowed Japanese entry).[16] Both the United States and Japan considered voluntary limits politically superior to a steep, temporary tariff: Washington did not want consumers to notice the overt price effects of tariffs; Japan did not want to pad the U.S. public purse at the expense of its producers.

The crisis in Detroit was not simply of Japanese origin. Only rarely did U.S. firms offer competitive compact and subcompact vehicles of their own design and manufacture. In 1989, for the first time, the largest-selling model in the United States was foreign—the Honda Accord. When the new Saturn division of General Motors belatedly reentered this market, consumers were so disillusioned with Detroit that Saturn had to be marketed as a new company, not as part of General Motors. Detroit's market share fell to less than 70 percent before bouncing back to 72 percent in 1992. In 1990 Japan hovered around 27 percent of the U.S. market, of which 3 percent was sold by the Big Three under their own names, and Chrysler's long-term future was still in doubt despite marked improvement.

One significant change has been the growing fleet business. The Big Three have bought automobile rental companies and loaded their sales there, so that, excluding these sales, by the early 1990s the Japanese and U.S. firms were about even in their retail sales in the U.S. market.[17] Despite significant progress by Ford and Chrysler, the top Japanese companies still have some cost advantages, especially if the costs of idle capacity and employee benefit packages are considered. In contrast, by no measure is General Motors competitive in its average vehicle costs.[18]

Detroit's supplier base faces a more subtle threat. The Big Three are trying to imitate their Japanese competitors by outsourcing more of their product. They are even cooperating with each other under the U.S. Council for Automotive Research in eight DCAs to develop certain key components such as batteries for electric automobiles. But the Japanese transplants to the United States bring their keiretsu-based supplier network with them. As a result, the U.S. component industry is eroding, to repeated charges that Japanese firms are not fulfilling their claims that they provide 65 to 80 percent local U.S. content.[19]

In 1991 pressure grew in the United States to cap Japanese sales by creating a quota on combined imports and local production. The UAW supports an absolute limit on combined imports and local Japanese production in the United States, mainly because most Japanese plants resisted organizing. The UAW also demands strict local content tests. Chrysler chairman Lee Iacocca endorsed a cap on Japanese sales in 1991.[20] President Bush's dramatic decision to invite the chairmen of the Big Three to accompany him to Tokyo in January 1992 reflected the intensity of the pressure for quotas. Such an initiative illustrates how the world market could become less open but still highly globalized and competitive.

There are some bright spots for the United States. U.S. consumers gain because competition is tougher than in the past even though VRAs retard price competition. Detroit is achieving much higher quality at lower cost, has markedly reduced the total number of vehicles that it must sell to break even, and is raising the manufacturing productivity of its U.S. supplier base.

In addition, the industry is going through another round of further globalization. The Big Three are diversifying their partnerships. New alliances are being formed with European firms, second-tier Japanese automobile makers, and even with South Korean producers. Moreover, Japanese-owned and -operated plants in the United States are entering the export market themselves and promise to cut the U.S. trade deficit somewhat. And Japanese firms are beginning to modify their market strategies in response to pressure from MITI and, more vitally, to rising capital costs. By 1992 Japanese firms were finally paying rates for capital equal to the rest of the world (in part due to financial deregulation in Japan opening its savings pool up to foreign borrowers). Maximizing market share by proliferating product lines, huge capital spending, and low profit margins is giving way to pruning product lines, reduced spending, and higher margins. This may provide Detroit with enough financial room to finish its refurbishing while leading to new U.S.-Japanese alliances.

The European Response

For decades Spain and Italy allowed only token imports of Japanese vehicles. France negotiated a VRA limiting Japanese firms to 3 percent of its market. By contrast, since 1977 the United Kingdom has allowed Japan up to 11 percent of its market, and West Germany imports are at about the same level. By 1991, Japan held about 11 percent of the European market.

One goal of the EC's 1992 program was to improve European competitiveness as the Japanese increased their efforts in Europe. Market integration will improve economies of scale by removing hidden trade barriers and forcing producers to control costs. Price competition will benefit consumers and rationalize resources used by the automobile industry to the benefit of national economies. A new program to limit long-standing state aid to automobile makers will accompany internal harmonization. EC cases against state aid to Renault and Rover extended Commission oversight over these subsidies, but the European Community is unlikely to cut off adjustment funds entirely.

These changes should help Ford and General Motors, which have a highly diversified European base of operations and are less subsidized than their European counterparts. But they too are weak in markets such as France and Italy. Collectively, they are trying to regroup their global operations to strengthen their home base. They therefore are seeking new alliances with European producers to fine-tune their product efforts.

Japan's potential strength in Europe is clear. It already has a 26 percent market share in countries without quotas or VRAs.[21] The fear of the Japanese entry into the rest of Europe through these countries slowed progress on harmonization of internal technical standards, taxes, and other items. For example, automobile dealers won a ten-year block exemption from EC competition rules, which will inhibit the growth of new Japanese dealer networks.

VRAs were the strongest response to Japan's global breakthrough that threatened the regime for automobiles. European companies worried that Japan's VRAs with the United States would divert additional Japanese exports to Europe. European automobile makers united to demand an adjustment program to govern Japanese expansion. Fiat, Renault, and Peugeot were joined by Volkswagen and BMW in seeking tight limits. General Motors and Ford (major players in the United Kingdom and Germany) also favored limits. Daimler Benz was silent. Countries with weak domestic companies, like the United Kingdom and the Netherlands, were more receptive to Japanese expansion. Germany favored less sweeping restraints. EC voting rules made it possible that a British-German coalition could water down strict dirigiste rules. In July 1991 the European Community finally reached a VRA agreement with Japan that set important international precedents, even if the language was deliberately ambiguous.[22]

Restraints under the VRA are intended to be in force through 1999. Its major innovation is that it formally covers exports and implicitly covers direct production subsidiaries in Europe. Exports are restrained at current levels of 1.23 million automobiles and light trucks. The EC claims that there is an "understanding" that Japanese production in Europe is not to exceed 1.2 million vehicles (compared to 760,000 in 1990). But the annexes to the official "elements of consensus" show that Japan never accepted this interpretation.

It seems likely that MITI recognized the calculus of the European Community. MITI was not inclined to accept local production caps because it would be difficult for the European Community to legislate the rule. As the United Kingdom noted, such legislation might violate the Treaty of Rome. Nonetheless, Japan's real objections likely are to how the cap might force a cut in Japanese output if market growth is slow during the 1990s. MITI argues that it is entitled to sell 2.43 million vehicles in 1999; the European Community says that Japan is bound to hold its share to 16 percent of the total European market. This arcane distinction is important if European sales do not reach the 15.1 million units projected for 1999. Japanese officials tried to mute Europe's unhappiness by predicting that Japanese production in Europe would reach just one million units by 1999.

The total EC figure is political dynamite in several sensitive national markets. Hardliners like France and Italy remain determined to nurture their national champions. They acquiesced to a Europe-wide figure because they need the jobs Japanese plants will provide and because they do not want to be blamed for paralyzing integration by sealing their markets from neighboring Japanese plants. But they insisted on an EC monitoring program that is designed to slow the growth of Japanese imports into the most protected markets.[23] What counts as a Japanese vehicle remains a matter of dispute. Is a Honda station wagon that is intended for sale in Germany but that is produced in the United States Japanese? It is easy to predict that the European Community will insist on rigorous EC scrutiny of the rules of origin for Japanese production plants in Europe.[24] In addition, the European Community will press Japan to open its markets to more European exports beyond what has been achieved by BMW and Mercedes. In short, this agreement extends the scope of protectionism to foreign investment for the first time and at the same time grants a major increase in the Japanese share of the total market.

By the spring of 1992, the European Commission, led by the Commissioner for Industry Martin Bangemann, forced Japan to accept even more restrictive terms. Japan agreed to export 6 percent fewer vehicles to Europe in 1992 than in 1991. If the EC figures— 1.2 million imports and 300,000 automobiles made by Japanese transplants—are accurate, Japan's share of the market should decline slightly to 11 percent in 1992. (The EC and Japan disagree over whether the Japanese allocation should increase or decline in 1993.) At the same time the European Commission unveiled a much more interventionist industrial plan to boost European productivity and help the European automobile industry compete against Japan. It is estimated that it takes thirty-five work hours to put together a car in Europe versus seventeen in Japan. To close this gap Bangemann proposed in January of 1992 to spend $4.3 billion over five years to help European industries become more competitive. The European Community expects to spend close to $900 million on training in the automobile sector in the next few years and may cut 200,000 jobs (but retain displaced workers) in the component industry to cut costs and raise productivity. Although European R&D spending is at world levels, the program is designed to provide more product-oriented R&D funding. Bangemann also favors slowing competition across borders by slowing the abolition of exclusive automobile dealerships.[25] If the European Community agrees to fund the Bangemann program, it will be reflecting a belief that protectionism does not block increased foreign access to the European market but simply caps the rate of change and introduces an expensive system for rationalizing and upgrading European competitors.

GLOBALIZATION AND ALLIANCES

The dramatic changes in the world automobile industry and its trading rules unloosed radical moves toward globalization by most firms, last and most dramatically by the Japanese. A web of ICAs linking Japanese, European, American, and even Korean firms is emerging to share the risks of developing, building, and bringing expensive new products to market and to cope with adjustment stresses that government policy cannot resolve.[26]

U.S. (and European) firms want to focus on acquiring Japanese know-how and on learning how to lower their costs. These alliances may retard new independent entry by foreign firms. To bolster their competitive positions, U.S. and European automobile makers also are forging deals with third-tier producers that make specialized niche vehicles.

U.S. Alliance Strategies

General Motors General Motors is involved in a vast array of alliances that are not clearly part of a centrally articulated, integrated strategy. Joint production plants with other companies often have run into problems on managing costs or implementing flexible switching products to meet new demands of consumers.[27] General Motors' Chevrolet division hopes to reinvigorate its small automobile sales by creating a new family of Geo vehicles. A different manufacturer makes each vehicle: the Metro is produced by a plant in Canada that is jointly owned with Suzuki; the Prism is a repackaged Corolla produced by GM's NUMMI venture with Toyota in Fremont, California; the Storm is built by Isuzu in Japan; and the Tracer is built in Japan by Suzuki. The Geo division in 1990 increased General Motors' share in the U.S. market.[28] In theory, General Motors adds value by blending the Geo vehicles into a coherent product group. General Motors has large holdings in Isuzu, operates a joint plant with Isuzu in Canada, and is linked with Suzuki to build specialized vehicles.[29] Suzuki also is in a joint venture with Fuji. General Motors is working with Isuzu to build vans in the United Kingdom and has bolstered its luxury specialty automobile line by buying 50 percent of Saab. General Motors built its Pontiac LeMans automobiles from its 50-50 partnership with Daewoo (formed in 1984) on a comprehensive components and assembly venture. But poor quality, strikes, and escalating labor costs along with fundamental differences in the companies' managerial outlooks doomed this venture. The divorce became final when General Motors sold its share of the venture to Daewoo.[30] This reduced its Asian presence to Japan and an assembly venture for light trucks in China, but General Motors was looking at India and Indonesia for new ventures. It is mounting significant ventures in component and vehicle assembly operations with local producers in Eastern Europe and the Soviet Union. General Motors announced an ICA with a Czech firm for transmission production and vehicle assembly, and it kept pace with Volkswagen's ambitious strategy for old East Germany by picking up a venture with Wartburg. It also made deals in Hungary and the Soviet Union. Fiat also moved vigorously into these markets.[31]

But so far General Motors does not run the total network of its alliances with anything like the degree of coordination and oversight that characterize a Japanese keiretsu.[32] Although it has made a notable effort to diversify its business and add unique technological strengths by bolstering its aerospace (Hughes Aerospace), electronics (Delco partnered with Hughes), and information systems (Electronic Data Services) groups, its costs remain higher than Ford's. Nissan and Toyota also are experimenting with diversification and technological specialties tied to automobiles, such as investment in cellular telephone networks. Just as significant as the attempt to ally with other firms was the internal reorganization of General Motors. Its old pattern emphasized quasi-autonomous regional firms. A boardroom revolt in 1992 brought a new management team drawn heavily from its profitable European operations. These executives promptly indicated that General Motors would now operate as a more integrated global firm. This would include using European suppliers for U.S. production, and vice versa, on a scale and on a basis for selection heretofore unknown to the insular giant. In short, the renovation plan emphasized globalization, even at the level of components suppliers.

Ford Ford epitomizes the strategy of adopting Japanese industrial techniques to lower costs and bolster quality. Its most efficient plants now are fully cost competitive. Ford blends global product mandates for regional divisions and international corporate allies to allow specialization in the deployment of its resources. The strategy relies heavily on a solid alliance with Mazda, which Ford has owned 25 percent of since 1979.[33]

Ford has declared that it needs to boost spending on new products, but it is wary of simply building a new plant for each new offering because it foresees a 20 percent surplus of global capacity for automobile and truck production. Instead, it seeks more flexibility in its existing factories, partners to share the output for specialized new vehicles, and partners to reduce its design and engineering costs. It gets its Probe vehicles from Mazda's Michigan plant and produces vehicles for Mazda and Nissan.[34] This formula should allow it to focus on maintaining the core production competence in which it has some comparative advantages—U.S. production of midlevel vehicles.

Ford Europe thrived mainly because of its expertise in midsized models. (However, Ford has been a leading advocate of European limits on Japanese automobiles because it has been less successful in upgrading its German manufacturing facilities than General Motors or other European firms.)[35] Ford Europe is now in charge of all Ford R&D for midsize automobiles and Detroit engineers and builds large vehicles. Ford ceded control of its new small automobile development around the globe to Mazda. For example, it uses a Mazda-designed compact in Germany and the new Escort is a Mazda 323 that is built by Ford. This strategy allowed Ford to build an entry-level vehicle in the United States for $2 billion, a considerable cost saving. Ford and Mazda also are sourcing automobiles (the Festiva) that were designed by Ford and engineered by Kia in South Korea. (Ford owns 10 percent and Mazda holds 8 percent of Kia, which introduced utility vehicles in the United States in 1992.) Ford cut its purchases from Kia (which also has a large domestic market) in protest against South Korean government discrimination against Ford imports.[36]

With small trucks and minivans, which have captured a growing share of the automobile market, Ford has used a mixed strategy. It produces a four-wheel-drive, sports utility vehicle that Mazda also markets and is developing and manufacturing a compact pickup truck for Mazda. (Mazda estimates that the 25 percent U.S. tariff on imported pickup trucks will lower its exports from Japan by $400 to $500 million per year.)[37] Ford formed a joint venture with Nissan for minivans in the United States, a product where neither has excelled. Ford will manufacture the minivan in the United States; Nissan will design it.[38] Ford and Volkswagen also will produce a minivan in Europe. This follows their merging of many Latin American ventures in the 1980s. Ford also looked for European opportunities to develop the luxury automobile niche. Ford bought Jaguar and took a 75 percent share of Aston Martin; deals that did not materialize included a major alliance between Ford and Fiat for European operations and, on the rebound, a flirtation between General Motors and Fiat. Neither Ford nor Fiat would consent to giving up control over the partnership that both agreed could be a major boon.[39]

Chrysler The history of Chrysler's alliance with Mitsubishi Motors parallels the fluctuating fortunes of Chrysler and the rise of Mitsubishi Motors. Indeed, Mitsubishi Motors' global expansion took place against a backdrop of alliances. The U.S. government pressed Japan to allow Chrysler to buy a share of a second-tier Japanese automobile producer, and Mitsubishi Heavy Industries spun off Mitsubishi Motors to rationalize this relationship. Over the years Mitsubishi Motors used its link with Chrysler to gain more independence from Mitsubishi Heavy Industries, but Mitsubishi was never entirely happy with its relationship with Chrysler. Although Mitsubishi received important technology and assistance in the United States market, Chrysler had negotiated well.

Initially, Chrysler had the sole right to sell Mitsubishi Motors automobiles in the United States. By 1981, Chrysler's market position was eroding at precisely the time Mitsubishi Motors desperately needed U.S. sales to win a share of the new VRA quotas set by MITI. Therefore, Mitsubishi Motors pressured Chrysler into renegotiating their bargain, promising to help Chrysler modernize in return for the right to market its own automobiles as well as supply Chrysler. This worked for a time, but the VRAs limited what Mitsubishi Motors could sell on its own. Faced with Chrysler's renewed weakness, Mitsubishi Motors again pushed to renegotiate the relationship. It consented to enter a joint venture with Chrysler (Diamond Star) for a new plant. Chrysler gained access to new production facilities. Mitsubishi Motors faced less risk as it began production in the United States. It also added a new product to sell in the United States that was not counted against its VRA limits.

As Chrysler continued to wane, Mitsubishi made a dramatic move. Mitsubishi Motors used its 15 percent stake and long-standing (since 1973) technical cooperation agreement with Korea's Hyundai to limit its future links to Chrysler. Mitsubishi Motors will no longer supply Chrysler with Excels to market in the United States. Hyundai will supply Chrysler instead, thereby freeing Mitsubishi Motors to market its own product itself. Mitsubishi's alliance with

Daimler Benz and Mitsubishi Motors' decision to stop marketing Chrysler products indicate that Mitsubishi no longer feels it can rely on Chrysler. As a sweetener for Chrysler, however, Mitsubishi Motors calmly agreed to let Chrysler realize a $310 million profit by cutting its equity share in Mitsubishi Motors from 21.8 to 12.1 percent.[40] Then, to ensure that Chrysler's troubles did not endanger its important capacity at Diamond Star, it agreed to buy out Chrysler's stake in the plant while still supplying it with automobiles from the output. This occurred even as Chrysler continued to complain that unfair Japanese tactics endangered its profitable minivan series. Mitsubishi reportedly feared a Chrysler bankruptcy and was supposedly also offering to help Chrysler design a new car line for a much lower fee for its design services.[41] By 1992 Chrysler had reduced its stake in Mitsubishi Motors to less than 6 percent.

This complicated renegotiation leaves Chrysler with no major sales base outside North America. It gambled everything on an innovative design and production system that fielded a new set of vehicles for North America. If it can reposition itself as a prosperous U.S. producer, it might once again try to develop its international business. Chrysler signed a separate deal in Japan for distribution and tried unsuccessfully to consummate major deals with Renault and Fiat, especially for the sale of Jeeps in Europe. But talks failed by 1990. The weakened Chrysler Corporation did buy Lamborghini and opted for an ICA in Austria with Steyr-Daimler-Puch, a noted supplier of components, to capitalize in Europe on its strong position in minivans. The EC promptly began to threaten higher tariffs on the minivan if Austria did not trim its aid to the venture. It is no accident that Chrysler is the most hard-nosed company on trade issues: it is the least global of the significant automobile firms. Although about 9 percent of its sales are foreign vehicles, none of the proposed protectionist packages would seriously threaten its access to these vehicles, and Chrysler hopes that foreign sales will decline as a share of its sales.[42]

European Alliance Strategies

The European producers are not yet as global as their American and Japanese counterparts, but they have regrouped. In the first wave of rationalization smaller, national firms consolidated. For example,

Fiat absorbed Alfa Romeo.[43] Next, foreign partnerships prolif-erated. The primary thrust was to rationalize pan-European pro-duction and product offerings. A second priority for the strongest firms was to improve their North American position. There also was pinpoint targeting of the Japanese luxury market and the emerging Chinese market.

France is awash in deals. Renault, the second French producer, was not satisfied with the regrouping of French producers. Renault was partially privatized, so it could enter a sweeping ICA with Volvo for major equity swaps to facilitate joint production of automobiles and trucks. In February 1990 Volvo agreed to take a 20 percent stake in Renault, and Renault took a 10 percent stake in Volvo's Swedish parent company, a venture that required approval by the EC competition authorities. But as soon as this approval was in hand Volvo entered an additional joint venture with Mitsubishi and the Dutch government to build small automobiles in the Nether-lands starting in 1995. Renault provided the transmissions for the automobiles. It now appears that far closer Renault-Volvo coopera-tion could emerge. In late April 1992 Volvo chairman Pehr Gyllenhammer strongly hinted that it would consider becoming a minority partner in a single automobile firm merging Renault and Volvo operations.[44]

Germany's Volkswagen, which again became the top company in Europe in 1990, has fewer alliances than its U.S. counterparts, but it needs help. It has shored up its European position by buying 90 percent of SEAT, the leading Spanish automobile firm, and wooing Skoda, the leader in Czechoslovakia. These plants open markets and lower labor costs, which are 50 percent lower in Czechoslovakia than in Spain. Despite rumors about a possible alliance between Peugeot and Volkswagen, in 1991 Volkswagen teamed with Suzuki to produce European sports vehicles.[45] Mean-while, Volkswagen's U.S. position has dwindled to 1.6 percent of the market, a level too small to sustain. Consequently, it is spending significant sums to revive its U.S. share, spending $1 billion on its major subsidiary in Mexico (sales of 200,000 per year), considering building a North American plant for its Audi subsidiary, and enter-ing joint ventures with Ford in Argentina and Brazil.[46] It also is the largest force in production in China and is improving its share in the

Japanese luxury market even as Japan is challenging its Audi line. Volkswagen will be hard pressed to maintain success in Europe without notable new successes outside of Europe. More generally, there are signs that German firms once again believe that they need production capacity in North America. Daimler Benz is investing $175 million in a heavy truck subsidiary in Oregon and is considering a Mercedes production facility in the United States. BMW plans to spend between $318 and $636 million to build a plant in South Carolina.[47]

Politics matter in these ventures. The expansion of foreign direct investment and alliances raise intricate issues for firm-to-firm and firm-to-government diplomacy. In 1989, for example, General Motors was interested when the British government sought a large private investor to buy and modernize Rover and its uncompetitive plant, but the Thatcher government worried that it would be criticized for selling another British firm to foreigners (Ford, after all, had just bought Jaguar) and that Honda, which was providing Rover with indispensable technical assistance after buying 20 percent of Rover in 1980, would be unhappy. Rover was sold to British Aerospace, perhaps at a depressed price. The deal was sweetened with under-the-table aid to British Aerospace that the European Community later ordered the company to return.

The Japanese Alliance Strategy

The motivations for Japanese firms were somewhat different. They wanted to exploit their competitive advantages in the 1980s but were stymied by export restrictions. Their solution was to invest in local production, which raised new problems for them. The general political rage directed against Japan forced Japanese companies to consider whether an expanded market share would be tolerated even if it was achieved through local production. Nissan, for example, discovered when moving into Britain that it was not easy to determine how much local content was necessary to be treated as a local producer. Local partners might prove an asset. Moreover, Japanese firms were not experienced as global players. They had much to learn about managing foreign work forces, local suppliers, and the myriads of other details that their finely tuned production systems depended on. Foreign partners might provide these management skills.

The Japanese firms were the last to start building alliance structures, and even so, the three largest Japanese firms are moving toward globalization while minimizing alliances. Toyota, Honda, and Nissan—the three Japanese giants—have the resources and political motivation to be integrated transnational firms by going it alone. At the urging of MITI, a small number of automobiles are being imported into Japan from their overseas factories.

Local content and ownership rules forced much of Japan's earliest overseas production into Asia. This was especially so for Mitsubishi Motors, which lagged at home. Partly because of their inexperience overseas, Japanese firms were more accepting of local partners than were U.S. firms. Like U.S. firms, Japanese investors deplored sophisticated local content rules, but they were responsive to production incentives and political pressure. One response was to nurture horizontal divisions of labor for specialized components among regional firms. Mitsubishi Motors and Toyota led the way in developing cross-regional sourcing of parts. Japanese interest in elaborate plans for regional divisions of labor made it possible that a general production plan for assembled vehicles might emerge. The Association of Southeast Asian Nations (ASEAN) has explicit rules permitting plans for intraregional distribution of labor by automobile firms. Approved plans receive special, reduced tariffs. However, so far, South Korea, Malaysia, and other Asian industrializing countries have opted for increasing local production of core vehicles, even while accepting efforts at regional specialization.[48]

The move into production in the industrial countries took longer. Japanese companies have reduced their risks on new models and foreign plants by bringing in foreign partners, which provide them with valuable design engineering and specialized R&D and even products to fill in their own product lines. At first, partners in these ventures exchanged Japanese production know-how for U.S. marketing channels and information about the U.S. production base. As U.S. firms upgraded their production facilities and lowered their costs, these ventures frequently began to share costs and technical know-how to produce the niche vehicles that the firms needed to fill out their product lines. U.S. firms also used ICAs as "exit vehicles" so that U.S. firms could continue to offer products in a market where they had ceased to compete. Honda and Nissan gambled on mastering the new terrain on their own and established independent operations in the United States. However, to increase the percentage of parts bought in the United States, Nissan decided to buy parts from the U.S. manufacturer Associated Fuel Pump Systems, a joint venture of Nippondenso, the largest automobile parts producers affiliated with rival Toyota.[49] Other Japanese firms used partnerships to explore the market. The most celebrated joint venture was the General Motors–Toyota NUMMI plant in Fremont, California, which was subject to strict antitrust guidelines, including a 1996 deadline for its termination (which the partners hope to have extended). Direct entry along the lines of the partnership between Mazda and Ford was more typical.

It is always difficult to move from an alliance based purely on cross-marketing to serious joint development. Thus, many of the early Japanese-European alliances, which have far less experience than the U.S.-Japanese ventures, will fail as the partners seek to upgrade them. Consider the alliance between Daimler Benz and Mitsubishi Corporation (the trading house), which was supposed to go well beyond their existing efforts at cooperation in the automobile sector. Mitsubishi already sells Mercedes in Japan and hopes to double sales to 70,000, versus sales of 250,000 in the United States. When the two firms discussed swapping small portions of their equity in their automobile groups to develop a new all-terrain vehicle, they found deep differences in methods and goals that thwarted progress. Daimler Benz is a $43 billion group, and the Mitsubishi Corporation is a $100 billion behemoth with total group sales of about $200 billion. Both are well suited to act as part of a global keiretsu, but an earlier venture to develop a common vehicle in Spain failed in 1988, as did a joint venture to create a global sales network. Although the partners have produced diesel engines in Europe, friction is reported in corporate operating styles. Nonetheless, the earlier failures prompted a significant effort to stabilize their joint projects by building a wider, deeper relationship. (See the discussion of the stability of alliances in Chapter 3).

The Mitsubishi Motors–Daimler Benz effort illustrates a key pattern of ICAs in the automobile assembly industry. The second-tier global producers (General Motors, Ford, Fiat, Volkswagen, Peugeot, Renault) produce in massive volume, but their costs are higher and their innovation cycles are slower than the first-tier Japanese firms. Mitsubishi and Mazda are slightly smaller but have the other advantages of Japanese producers. All of the second-tier firms are building ICAs that share engineering, design, and sometimes production. In general, economies of scale are greater for components than for assembly. Ideally, firms would like to source components on a global scale but face two obstacles: product designs vary regionally so components must often vary, and local content rules influence sourcing. As a result, ICAs share engineering, tooling, and R&D costs globally.[50] In addition, they all are signing long-term product contracts for key parts of their product lines.

Japanese firms predict that exports from Japan will decline while overseas production with extensive local content of 80 percent or more will expand rapidly. Nissan has committed itself to cutting exports by 50 percent from its peak level in 1986. It plans for a trilateral production structure with 100 percent local content in the triad regions and active cross-trading of specialized vehicles within its corporate channels. Other large producers vow to match the tripolar cross-trading structure. For example, Honda and Nissan want to source some of their demand in Europe and the Asian developing countries from the United States. In 1989 Honda pledged that half of its 150,000 automobile output from its new Ohio plant would be exported. Toyota has pledged to export 10 percent of its U.S. output. This arrangement also pleases countries, such as Taiwan, that want to relieve trade frictions with the United States because of their own huge trade surpluses with the United States.[51] One estimate is that Japanese plants in the United States will ship 300,000 vehicles per year to Japan by the mid-1990s. These efforts also will extend to assisting the exports to Japan of U.S. and European vehicle and component makers. In this spirit, Toyota is negotiating a deal to market Volkswagen products in Japan and was offering the same bargain to General Motors even before President Bush's trip in early 1992.[52] General Motors declined.

President Bush's January 1992 trip with an entourage that included the chairmen of General Motors, Ford, and Chrysler resulted in headlines announcing the dawn of a new era of managed trade in U.S.-Japanese relations. Most journalists missed the point. These key countries always managed key aspects of the trade in automobiles. Insistence on local production and on more local value added in that production is standard fare for every country except the United States. The sole true innovation, which mirrors exactly the 1986 U.S.-Japan semiconductor agreement, was a high-level Japanese pledge to increase Japanese use of foreign components from the United States and to provide a more hospitable climate for foreign vehicle sales in Japan. For example, in addition to opening Japanese dealerships to U.S. vehicles, U.S. firms may benefit from new financial assistance to foreign firms establishing Japanese facilities. Although estimates differ, it is plausible to project that Japanese imports from the United States could reach $6.4 billion by 1994.[53] Thus the agreement increased integration of the global industry by marginally prying open some Japanese industrial groups.

But there are three troubling aspects of the agreement. First, as Tables 5.2 and 5.3 indicate, there is no provision in the agreement for other third-party suppliers. This is a dangerous precedent within a purely bilateral agreement. (USTR officials defend the pact by noting it was only an understanding and that it pledged access to all foreign interests; few believe this.) Indeed, the European Business Committee immediately counterclaimed that European imports

---

Table 5.2
Japanese Automobile Makers' Goals for U.S. Vehicle Imports

Distributor/Source	Import	Annual Sales Target	Target Year
Toyota	General Motors	5,000	Not set
Nissan	Ford	3,000	Not set
Mazda	Ford	4,500	FY 1992
Mitsubishi	Chrysler[a]	6,000	FY 1995

Source: "Carmakers Set Goals for U.S.-Made Parts," Nikkei Weekly, January 18, 1992, p. 7.
[a] Production to be done at Mitsubishi plants in the United States.

Table 5.3
Japanese Automobile Makers' Goals for Local U.S. Vehicles*
(in $ billions)

Company	Purchase in FY 1990	November 1991 Target for FY 1994	Revised Target for 1994
Toyota	$2.600	$4.60	$5.28[a]
Nissan	1.300	3.30	3.70
Honda	2.770	4.50	4.94
Mitsubishi	0.675	1.40	1.60
Mazda	1.186	2.16	2.30
Total	$8.531	$15.96	$17.82

Source: "Carmakers Set Goals for U.S.-Made parts," Nikkei Weekly, January 18, 1992, p. 7.
* Includes purchases from Japanese subsidiaries in United States.
[a] Estimated imports of parts into Japan will be $1.46 billion.

should account for 10 percent of Japan's market in 1995 and 17.5 percent in 2000. (The figures did not include exports of vehicles produced by Japanese firms in Europe for reexport back to Japan.)[54] Second, although the agreement is likely to reduce the U.S. trade imbalance, it saddles the economy with the inefficiencies that arise from any set of arbitrary market supply targets, in part because local content rules in the NAFTA agreement were quickly distorted by demands for strict accounting on such items as seat belts. Nonetheless, Japanese firms may experience lower adjustment costs because they have pledged to export from their own U.S. production facilities. Third, all this activity may have little effect on the fundamental problems of Detroit. Much of the promised U.S. content is likely to be provided by Japanese transplants in the United States. Moreover, Japanese firms resisted all efforts to cut their export caps to the United States, partly because they could not agree among themselves. The only solution to these problems may be new U.S. measures to assist U.S. automobile makers, including new investment incentives and increased assistance for joint research products by the industry.

A more profound innovation would occur if the United States adopted a policy that capped the combined Japanese sales of exports and locally produced automobiles in the United States. As noted earlier, Europe took this position in its negotiations with Japan in 1991. The dramatic Bush initiative was partly designed to ensure that General Motors and Ford would not strongly back a Democratic bill to retaliate against Japanese automobiles by cutting imports of Japanese vehicles by 250,000 units per year in the event that Japan failed to cut its total trade surplus with the United States by 20 percent per year. The administration's goal was to forestall this possibility.

Other Lessons from Automobile ICAs

Despite the prodding of VRAs, ICAs are unlikely to be as important for Japan's Big Three as for the other giant firms in the industry. These second-tier firms are selectively working out marriages for design and product supply among themselves and developing a set of specialized alliances with smaller third-tier firms. The first two tiers are becoming more integrated transnational corporations. It is unlikely that a few ICAs will dominate the assembly business, but as competitive advantages equalize, firms are sharing technology, designs, and products on a selective basis. Another subtle change involves the rise of domestic corporate alliances, even in Japan: Mazda is sourcing engines, transmissions, and other key components for its new minicar in Japan; Isuzu and Fuji have a deal under which Fuji sells a four-wheel drive made by Isuzu and Isuzu will sell a small passenger vehicle of Fuji. The Detroit manufacturers are finally heading toward much more extensive collaboration on developing some components. In the future the leading global firms are likely to broker more deals similar to the Mitsubishi Motors-Hyundai-Chrysler arrangement. All the firms below Japan's Big Three may find that their identity and economic prosperity depend on their selection of alliances. (There are even some signs that Nissan may join the alliance movement.) They will share some technical infrastructure, long-run design and engineering cooperation, and cross-supply contracts for selected product lines (rather than jointly owned production ventures, which often prove difficult to manage). The biggest tensions over cross-supply contracts may arise from VRAs when a company like Chrysler cannot move the product and a Mitsubishi is not free to increase independent sales on its own.

If there is a fundamental split within the ranks of the second-tier firms, it is between European firms with global ambitions and those rooted to Europe. Volkswagen, Daimler Benz, and Volvo are more outward looking; Fiat, Renault, and Peugeot seem more inward looking. These differences were reflected in the attitudes of national governments toward the VRA with Japan.

The proliferation of ICAs for production also reflects two subtle changes sweeping the automobile sector. The Japanese model of long-term alliances with independent suppliers and just-in-time delivery has been augmented by American advances in running integrated global data networks. As U.S. and European firms move to match Japanese organizational efficiency in product development, the software side of global design (computer networks) should rise in importance. And as James Womack observes, open-minded alliances are ideally suited to supply components for technological reasons. For example, the refinement of electronic controls and the introduction of new materials has revolutionized the production on many automobile component parts. Marriages are needed to develop new technologies. Domestic corporate alliances arise among local firms, but ICAs that take advantage of new technologies and technological components not available in any one country are logical outgrowths of current demands for local added value. Toyota expects to buy electronic components from General Motor's Delco to help meet its goal to procure 10 percent of its semiconductors from foreign suppliers. In 1976 Nissan set up a joint venture with Bosch and one Japanese component manufacturer for electronic emission control and other parts. Mazda later joined this venture, although it also had a joint venture with NEC since 1987 for supplying high technology equipment. But many cutting-edge ventures remain basically Japanese: Fujitsu and Isuzu have formed a joint venture for high-technology car parts, while Hitachi teamed with Nissan in 1990 to pursue telephone and navigation systems for automobiles.[55] It is not surprising, but it is troubling, that new DCAs such as the Advanced Battery Consortium in the United States reject any notion of Japanese participation, even though the U.S. Department of Energy is a member.[56]

Alliances also may prove irresistible to firms like Japanese component makers that are charged with unfair trading practices.

Such complaints usually come in two forms. First, U.S. parts distributors argue that keiretsu-linked parts makers charge outrageous markups or withhold parts from independent distributors. (Presumably manufacturers promise keiretsu members favors such as guaranteed purchases and investment help in return for help in bolstering profits.) These actions could form the basis for antitrust action.

Second, U.S. parts makers complain that Japanese automobile firms are so closely tied to keiretsu members that they will not import foreign-made parts. To sell, foreign suppliers must provide much higher quality at much lower prices. Worse still, Japanese automobile firms in the United States mainly source from new U.S. plants of their traditional Japanese partners. A 1991 U.S. Department of Commerce study predicted that the U.S. automobile parts trade deficit with Japan will grow from $10.5 billion in 1989 to $22 billion in 1996. Japanese automobile assemblers claim they purchased $9.07 billion in U.S. parts in 1990, but most of these parts came from Japanese transplants in the United States.[57] Japanese producers argue that this is largely a transitory problem because Japanese parts and automobile firms are now coinvesting with U.S. and European firms in ways that will increase local shares of the Japanese components market.[58] Nonetheless, the Auto Parts Advisory Committee to the U.S. government recommended that Washington initiate a Section 301 action against Japan. This case once again raises the question of whether ownership is more significant than the location of production.

There still is room for new marriages. The intertwining of the Japanese model of supply with American data technology is at the heart of the boom in electronic data interchange (EDI). Global networks are linking suppliers, assemblers, and distributors in new ways, and firms that create and participate in new networks gain vital, global competitive advantage. Detroit wants its network standards to become global standards, particularly because of high U.S. production in Europe.[59]

More fundamentally, a new world market is emerging. For example, an ordering service introduced by Reuters has made it possible to develop a previously unimaginable open world market to trade automobile parts. By combining components and information systems it seems possible to produce an infrastructure support system for automobile vehicle companies with common technical infrastructures, product networks, and joint development efforts. The market will be far more open, allowing much more flexible location decisions on manufacturing and perhaps allowing tightly focused, specialty assembly firms to survive. This should be good news for many European and developing-country firms. At the same time, rules of origin and antitrust issues related to the global supply structure of assembly firms are likely to rise to the top of the policy agenda. Although in the past the assembly business was not particularly global, renewed competitive pressures and growing trade conflicts are forcing the top two tiers of major automobile firms to become transnational corporations with integrated and global design and production strategies.

AN EMERGING MARKET-ACCESS REGIME FOR AUTOMOBILES?

The automobile industry shows both the continuities and the innovations in the world political economy. Free-trade liberalization never dominated, but a regional trading economy emerged that was linked by overseas regional operations of U.S. transnational firms and global imports into the U.S. market. Export-led expansion by Japanese firms using new production methodologies disrupted the old regime. European and American response forced Japanese firms to globalize and other leading firms to reorganize. Corporate alliances are important, but they are only one facet of competition moving to regionally based local content and reliance on intra- and intercorporate trade channels.

The VRAs for exports and investment have focused mostly on slowing Japanese expansion. VRAs are an imperfect policy tool, but they are especially troublesome when combined with expansive interpretations of dumping and large government subsidies. If VRAs make sense, it is as a tool of adjustment. Market shares shift, but losers lose more slowly and have a chance to rationalize their operations. But dumping protection and subsidies can blunt the incentives to change and compound market distortions created by VRAs.

Any VRA program raises the issue of how to judge local content and rules of origin. The European Community has set precarious precedents for trade by declaring that Japanese plants in Europe, irrespective of local content, will be considered foreign and subject to output restrictions—an approach that diverges from its own policy in other sectors. In fact, the United States has protested some EC rulings in electronics that treat Japanese-owned factories in the United States as Japanese.

Even leaving aside questions of origin, determining the degree of local value added is leading governments into difficult terrain. For example, General Motors recently protested a U.S. Treasury decision disallowing the interest paid on a loan as North American content for factory tooling in its joint-venture plant with Suzuki in Canada. At the same time Honda was embroiled in controversy over whether its Civic plant in Canada met the 50 percent content test. There was some thought that Honda might escape because the engine installed in Canada is assembled in Ohio. The engine has at least half of its parts from the United States so it qualifies as U.S. content, and under the bilateral trade pact must be counted as 100 percent U.S. content.[60] The relationship between Japanese firms and their keiretsu suppliers which colocate in the United States and Europe is even more contentious. How will their content contributions be judged?

The content issue raises fundamental questions about Japanese business practices involving horizontal and vertical keiretsu. Japanese component suppliers often enjoy firm specific advantages unmatched in the United States and Europe. But if Japanese firms do not use ICAs to transfer technology, then the problems discussed earlier will prevail.

Japanese automobile firms must consider whether to start incorporating foreign-controlled firms into their vertical keiretsu. There are some obvious candidates technologically due to U.S. leadership on electronic data interchange (EDI) and certain types of pollution-control technologies for automobiles. MITI officials suggest that automobile keiretsu in Japan are becoming more likely to choose suppliers outside their "family" because the sophistication and costs of new component technologies do not lend themselves to a unique supplier for each major assembler. They also hint that foreign firms may soon join the ranks of component suppliers.[61]

The real import of alliances in the components trade is that the reintroduction of intraindustry trade fostered by ICAs reinforces international openness. The traditional free-trade order prospered partly because intraindustry trade made most countries winners and losers in the same industry because of extreme specialization. ICAs may blunt automobile trade imbalances by fostering a new form of intraindustry exchange. If such exchanges do not grow, the U.S. Justice Department may follow through on its threat to sue over antitrust violations by keiretsu involved with the sourcing of components. Such a suit would charge the Japanese parents and their U.S. subsidiaries with unfair practices using the logic that antitrust violations in Japan injure U.S. firms selling in both the U.S. and Japanese markets. As Robert Baldwin has noted, antitrust has been a major gap in trade laws since the ITO Charter failed to win acceptance.[62]

Controversies in the automobile sector also inevitably raise the twin issues of the integration of regional markets and the opening of Japan. If local content rules, VRAs, and the like are to keep local employment up and permit the fruits of new production techniques, the market for local production must be capable of sustaining the production of a core set of automobiles at world-class levels of scale economies. Thanks to Japanese techniques, this scale is smaller than in the past, but it still substantial.

The integration of regional trading blocks helps this new form of globalization. The regional blocks are interdependent enough to induce governments to accept content contributions from throughout their region as tantamount to national content. Obvious problems arise where there are no major regional economic groupings. One possibility is the Japanese strategy for centralized benign coordination of national contributions, as it has discussed in Asia. However, such planning is difficult to sustain in a decentralized world, and certainly it is politically explosive. Regional trading groups may become more attractive because they can permit flexible alternatives for foreign investment. ASEAN has been slowly promoting this type of regional strategy of complementary development for automobiles.[63]

Still, the movement of the factors of production through investment or transfers within corporate trading networks is insufficient unless the entire global industry has some stake in a global market. This means that Asia, and particularly Japan, has to open up to foreign firms. Formal targets may be less vital than steady growth of opportunities in Japan. It would be preferable if a significant share of these sales involved foreign firms, at least by sourcing their Japanese partners, but the bulk of the total almost certainly will be through internal trading with Japanese global subsidiaries.

The new political economy of the globalized automobile industry generally conforms to the six new pillars of market-access regimes in the international political economy. The U.S. model of industrial organization has been replaced by a hybrid model strongly reliant on Japanese organizational innovations. The automobile sector, perhaps more than any other industrial sector, conforms to the hybrid model of industrial organization—the first new pillar of a market-access regime. The proliferation of VRAs aimed at Japan illustrates that it is impossible for any domestic automobile maker to survive, much less thrive, without domestic policies attuned to international realities, thus the second pillar of the new regime also is evident in the automobile sector. Even Japanese officials and industrialists accepted this new reality and altered both their foreign investment and import policies. Similarly, the U.S. government awakened belatedly to the necessity of having an activist domestic policy if it wants to avoid truly managed trade. The third new pillar focuses on the erosion of boundaries between goods and services, and R&D costs for automobiles and the international financial and communications networks that now are fundamental to all automobile manufacturing ventures demonstrate that services are critical to the industry. At the same time, the automobile sector almost certainly will continue to conform with the new fourth pillar of a market-access regime, which predicts that there will be more regional and sectoral agreements.

Two new pillars establish the basic rules of a market-access regime. The fifth pillar predicts that access will be defined in terms of either relatively free trade or investment policies, and in North

America, Europe, and developing countries governments are slowing increased imports from Japan or the newly industrializing countries but remain open to new Asian investments, as long as significant value is added domestically. The sixth emerging pillar, the reliance by firms on regional and global advantages and not just national comparative advantage, is already the rule not the exception in the automobile sector, which is more and more dependent on globalized firms, often acting through ICAs in their conduct of business. These new relationships will minimize the need for an ornate global code for the automobile industry. Indeed, the process of reconciling U.S. and EC demands of Japan may force some trilateral understandings so that bilateral agreements do not stimulate domestic political demands. The operations of the global automobile sector in the early 1990s and governments' efforts to balance fairness and openness in managing it are clarifying the way that other sectors will be managed in the future.

CHAPTER SIX

The Semiconductor Industry

Semiconductors are the critical building blocks of electronics technology.[1] In 1989 the semiconductor business was a $50 billion global market,[2] and the market has been growing about 15 percent annually. Over 30 percent of all semiconductors are exported.[3] It is not surprising, therefore, that the semiconductor industry was viewed as strategically important from its earliest days.

The semiconductor industry is unlike the automobile sector[4] in that its key technologies are more proprietary and its products have a shorter product life cycle. Its rate of technological advance is much higher than for automobiles. In addition, unlike automobile owners, end users of semiconductors have little brand name loyalty as long as price and performance levels are comparable, and they derive no particular pride or status from using chips from specific suppliers. "Loyal" customers are likely to be locked into subtle technical standards or to have coinvested with the supplier to perfect component technologies. Although the cost of developing new products is high in both industries, semiconductor manufacturers use a much smaller network of suppliers than leading automobile makers. The unique characteristics of the semiconductor business raise special competitive challenges for manufacturers and increase the pressure on government officials to find new ways to manage this sector.

The traditional free-trade pillars could not address many of the fundamental issues of semiconductors even though trade grew rapidly. Small entrepreneurial U.S. high-technology firms, heavy government procurement of advanced technologies, and strong basic research in universities propelled U.S. firms to an early lead in all major markets except Japan, which was highly protected.[5] To help Japan catch up with American pacesetters, MITI sponsored numerous domestic consortia to advance basic technology and applied manufacturing skills and at the same time tightly restricted foreign firms' access to the Japanese internal market. The Very Large Scale Integrated (VLSI) Circuit Association—consisting of five large firms plus the Electro-Technical Laboratory of MITI—was organized with one common laboratory and two group labs (one representing NEC and Toshiba and the other incorporating Hitachi, Fujitsu, and Mitsubishi). From 1975 to 1979 its $308 million budget included $132 million in low-cost government loans. The Japanese government also invested $309 million in a parallel effort, NTT's three-firm VLSI project.[6]

As the dominance of U.S. firms waned and the industry grew more global, the United States government has moved, particularly through the United States–Japan semiconductor agreement of September 1986 (which was renewed in 1991), to help U.S. firms retrench, redraw the ground rules for semiconductor competition, and gain access to the Japanese market. Europe, where leading electronic firms were slow to recognize the importance of semiconductors, designated semiconductors as a priority when belatedly it began to modernize its high-technology industries. The European Community supported European firms as they struggled to regain market share at home but exerted less effort to forcibly enter the Japanese market. American and European firms responded to the Japanese challenge by forming domestic alliances, mainly to concentrate on R&D and production.

Overall the global market has closed marginally. Although the European Community imposed tougher restrictions on foreign access and the United States quietly introduced barriers, Japan relaxed its policy of closure and adopted a more open industrial policy. Global partnerships often share intellectual property and provide access to users that may make important contributions to the technology. Partnerships among component and systems producers often try to create new common technical infrastructures more rapidly than would be possible through formal standard setting processes. However, the leading chip producers are slower to establish advanced production facilities abroad than many other industries. The industry remains skeptical that it is possible to diversify production globally without sacrificing key competitive advantages. The close connection between product design and process innovation is one reason for this doubt, especially as U.S., Japanese, and European market leaders are establishing some joint production facilities. U.S. and European ties are less risky and less technologically significant for U.S. firms, in part because Europe lags on most fronts. But U.S. and European efforts to establish DCAs to bolster global competitiveness may ultimately promote their bilateral ties. At the same time, the United States and the European Community both are altering their industrial structures to mimic the Japanese emphasis on common development of product and process technologies. Efforts initially focused on issues such as reviving the "supply base" of regional producers of production equipment. In addition, these initiatives are resulting in complex ICAs among chip makers to swap fundamental production know-how, some of which will be fed back into the local supplier base. Along the way their companies may create loose divisions of labor in specialization to match some benefits enjoyed by Japanese keiretsus. The European Community and, to a lesser extent, the United States also are making foreign entry conditional on protecting a core base of domestic suppliers of products and process technologies. In essence, although not a perfect fit, the emerging structure of competition and cooperation in the semiconductor industry can be viewed as conforming to the six new pillars of the emerging market-access regime.

THE POLITICS AND ECONOMICS
OF THE SEMICONDUCTOR REGIME

Initially, when the United States held at least a 50 percent share of all major markets except Japan, the United States could afford to keep its markets open, with one exception: government procurement remained exempt from GATT rules and spurred innovation by U.S.

firms.[7] The European Community had open industrial policies. During the 1970s U.S. firms moved into Europe in response to high EC tariffs, British and French pressure to produce locally for military procurement, and a growing need to coordinate design with local customers. U.S. firms also established offshore supply plants to source all of their markets.

Japan, by contrast, was at best a semiopen market. Japan imposed high tariffs on all but Asian suppliers and blocked all U.S. investment except by Texas Instruments (TI), which agreed to license invaluable patents as the price to enter Japan. At first, U.S. firms sourced out of Asia to overcome the tariffs. But Japan soon declared that the United States was the true origin of all products (a position similar to one espoused today by the United States and the European Community).

As the industry matured, the sale and production of semiconductors grew more global. Most important, the Japanese broke through in world markets, greatly weakening the U.S. industry and further threatening an EC industry already dwarfed by U.S. entrants. When the U.S. industry for dynamic random-access memory (DRAM), the standard memory chip, collapsed in the 1980s under pressure from rapid innovation and steep price cuts by Japanese firms, semiconductors became a key trade issue. At the beginning of the 1990s DRAMs accounted for about a quarter of the market, and Japan dominated the production of DRAMs and many other specialized chips (such as those for video screens). U.S. firms still were preeminent in microprocessors (the "brains" of computers, like the IntelCAD 386 chip) and in application-specific integrated circuits (ASICs) that are custom-designed to perform particular tasks. Europe was behind on virtually all fronts.

Increasing concentration, not free trade, was the norm for semiconductors. As the capital intensity of the semiconductor industry increased, the global concentration of production grew. Eleven companies produce over 95 percent of the DRAMs sold on open markets. (Giant firms like IBM, however, are heavy producers of DRAMs for internal consumption.) By 1991 the total market for semiconductors reached $60 billion. As Table 6.1 shows, by 1991 six of the top ten semiconductor manufacturers were Japanese, three were American, and number ten was European. The second

Table 6.1
The Twenty Largest Semiconductor Vendors
in 1987, 1989, 1990, 1991 ($ billions)

		1987	1989	1990	1991
1. NEC	(Japan)	3.368	4.964	4.322	4.774
2. Toshiba	(Japan)	3.028	4.889	4.202	4.579
3. Intel	(US)	1.491	2.440	3.171	4.019
4. Motorola	(US)	2.431	3.322	3.539	3.801
5. Hitachi	(Japan)	2.618	3.930	3.516	3.765
6. TI	(US)	2.127	2.787	2.574	2.738
7. Fujitsu	(Japan)	1.801	2.941	2.599	2.705
8. Mitsubishi	(Japan)	1.492	2.629	2.108	2.303
9. Matsushita	(Japan)	1.457	1.871	1.826	2.037
10. Philips	(Neth.)	1.602	1.690	1.955	2.022
11. National	(US)	1.506	1.618	1.653	1.602
12. Samsung	(Korea)	0.327	1.284	1.315	1.473
13. SGS-Thomson	(Italy/France)	0.859	1.301	1.441	1.436
14. Sanyo	(Japan)	0.851	1.132	1.196	1.362
15. Sharp	(Japan)	0.590	1.230	1.194	1.318
16. Siemens	(Germany)	0.657	1.194	1.204	1.263
17. AMD	(US)	0.986	1.082	1.053	1.226
18. Sony	(Japan)	0.574	1.077	1.010	1.196
19. Oki	(Japan)	0.651	1.125	0.954	0.981
20. Rohm[a]	(Japan)	n.a.	n.a.	0.759	0.934

Sources: Kenneth Flamm, "Semiconductors," in Hufbauer, ed., *Europe 1992*, for 1987 and 1989 data, and *Financial Times*, September 2, 1992, p. 13, for 1990 and 1991 data.
[a] Rohm displaced AT&T at #20.

ten included five more Japanese companies, two from the United States, two from Europe, and Samsung from South Korea.

The Economics of Semiconductors

Seven rules of thumb highlight the economics of the semiconductor industry (the middle three apply especially to DRAMs):

- *High, fixed R&D costs are associated with semiconductor production.* The five leading Japanese firms invested $3.2 billion on R&D to develop the 4 megabyte DRAM chip. U.S. firms estimate that the cost for a firm to convert from a 1 micron to a $1/6$ micron chip technology will be about $250 million. These figures imply that minimum annual sales of $750 million are needed to keep costs competitive and carry the R&D expenses. (To be profitable the cost of R&D to develop a new chip should amount to no more than 10 percent of total sales revenues. But in a petition to the U.S. Trade Representative dated February 16, 1990, the Semiconductor Industry Association indicated that R&D costs accounted for 11.5 percent of sales revenues. IBM estimates the R&D bill for the 64 megabyte chip will be $1 billion and the cost of one plant will be $2 billion.)[8]

- In the semiconductor industry *product generations are short*, usually lasting less than five years, because technological innovation is so rapid. It follows that semiconductor plants and specialized equipment also have extremely short life cycles.

- *Learning curve economics for all semiconductors and economies of scale are critical* for DRAMs and other relatively standardized chips. The more units a plant produces, the less the cost per chip. Thus all firms have an incentive to rapidly build massive capacity, make deep price cuts to win market share, and leap ahead on the learning curve. To illustrate, although 1990 demand for 4 megabyte chips was projected at only 23 million units, Japanese plants may have the capacity to produce 70 million units annually.[9]

- *There is a high rate of innovation* in process technology. The simplest way to amortize these costs is to sell process technologies to DRAM manufacturers, which must themselves spend relentlessly to keep their plants at the state-of-the-art level. U.S. and European producers fear that the Japanese will control this supporting technical infrastructure because Japan already dominates DRAM production and holds a 75 percent share in some key process technologies.

- *Production process innovations improve product R&D effectiveness.* When production specialists and product innovators are separate, speedy innovation and product reliability are harder to achieve. The key Japanese breakthrough came when the Japanese rebundled design and manufacturing processes after U.S. firms split them haphazardly and consigned significant amounts of "lower-level" manufacturing abroad. But as pressures on Japan to globalize mount and U.S. firms scramble to better integrate design and process, alliances may help repackage these activities. Strategists hope to cooperate with specialized alliance partners on process and innovate on design. Many U.S. firms also are determined to emulate Ford's strategy of retaining core manufacturing competence for key product lines.

- In all phases of the semiconductor industry *there is a movement to consolidate more functions onto a smaller set of chips.* Thus, there are fewer types of chips on a circuit board, but each chip performs more functions.[10]

- *Computer-assisted design tools are revolutionizing the industry,* especially customized chips. This is the main saving grace for the United States because American firms may be widening their lead on computer-aided design and computer-aided manufacture.

Table 6.2 begins to show how companies position themselves according to these rules of thumb. In particular, it indicates that in their efforts to survive and excel U.S. firms are investing heavily in R&D and most are spending heavily to modernize their operations: they are, in effect, betting the company on each new offering. If their new products fail in the international market, or they are shut out of important markets by trade barriers, they are in danger of going under. U.S. firms are more vulnerable than their Japanese competitors because except for IBM, Motorola, Texas Instruments, and AT&T they derive a large proportion of their total revenues from the sale of semiconductors.

The Importance of DRAMS

Many believe that DRAM production is the key to the long-term health of the U.S. semiconductor industry. DRAMs are the only portion of the market that provide sufficient economies of scale and scope to finance manufacturing-process innovations necessary to keep the general semiconductor industry viable. This argument

Table 6.2
U.S. Semiconductor Firms in 1990

Firm	R&D as Percentage of Total Electronic Sales	Capital Expenditures as Percentage of Total Electronic Sales	Foreign Sales as Percentage of Total Electronic Sales
AMD	19.2%	28.7%	35.7%
C&T	15.5	4.6	0.0
Cypress	24.7	16.2	22.0
Intel	13.2	17.3	46.0
LSI Logic	9.2	9.5	43.8
Micron Tech	10.7	24.0	22.7
Motorola	9.3	11.5	54.2
Texas Instruments	8.2	13.8	33.2
VLSI Technology	16.5	10.9	44.5

Source: Electronic Business, July 22, 1991, p. 60.

assumes that components are vital to leadership in high-technology products and that DRAMs are crucial to success in higher-level semiconductor technologies.

Critics counter from two directions. The milder attack concedes the situation is sticky but argues that the United States and Europe need only revive a competitive fringe of DRAM producers to erode the rents being earned by Japanese producers. By 1992 Korean producers had seized almost 15 percent of the market, Taiwanese entry was coming, IBM announced plans to sell to the open market for the first time, and capital costs for Japanese firms had risen, which meant that Japanese firms might no longer be able to win special financial advantages from DRAMs. The even tougher line of attack argues that DRAMS are not the issue. Software matters, silicon does not. DRAMS are not the key to the information age in the same measure that gasoline was the key to the automotive age. In 1992 Siemens decided to cut back the scale of its future participation in DRAMs precisely because it argued (or rationalized) DRAMs were no longer so critical to mastering the industry.[11]

Critics always note that the U.S. industry has done well at the upper end. Capital requirements for state-of-the-art production are not as great as for DRAMS, and U.S. firms hold larger shares of the world market to meet these investment requirements. Moreover, the strongest challenge in microprocessors, NEC's major effort, has stumbled in comparison to the rapid innovations achieved by U.S. firms. If there are dangers on the horizon, they arise more from shifts in U.S. competition and technology than from the erosion of the financial base of U.S. leaders like Intel and Motorola. U.S. clones for the 386 and 486 chips have arrived, and RISCs (reduced instruction set chips) are threatening standard microprocessor architectures.

Pessimists note that at the same time, laptop and other compact computing systems are giving Japanese firms their first major challenge to the U.S. leadership in computing systems. Japanese system sales are not overwhelming, but Asian components provide up to 90 percent of the value added of system parts. In short, pessimists caution that current leadership may be a product of advantages from proprietary chips and computer systems that will soon disappear.

On balance, U.S. companies can lead on the next generation of advanced chips, such as RISC, but competition will stiffen as other Asian countries move up in the market. In addition, the relationship between components and systems remains complicated.

Systems and Components

The relationship between systems and components shows why hardware still matters. The information age is a long way from arriving as a seamless web of high-performance, low-cost technology delivering ever more imaginative products. Most delivery technologies are expensive compared to the marginal utility of individual applications (many of the best video games require a computer, not just a television), and the few remaining Betamax users will attest that technologies do not easily interconnect. Similarly, as producers of 3-D movies know, the design of applications is highly sensitive to assumptions about the hardware that will be available to deliver it. Moreover, many products can be produced economically only if both the basic chip and the detailed applications are built into a single chip. This is leading to downstream integration by DRAM makers, upstream integration by integrated circuit makers into DRAMs (like Texas Instruments), and downstream movement from processors to products (as in the Intel computer line). (Intel supplies other firms with personal computers. It attempts to avoid direct competition with major customers by investing in products like massive parallel processing computers, which few of the established giants compete with.) Many of these ventures are completed through alliances with firms in a complementary part of the industry. For example, Micron Technology, one of the last U.S. firms in DRAMs, bought a share of a U.S. firm with a promising flat-panel display screen for computers. Micron, a relatively small firm that had $425 million in revenues in 1991, gambled on this deal, hoping to source chips if the product took off.[12]

In short, the early innovators that successfully optimize hardware and content will likely emerge as the leaders in the information content industry. For example, Reuters successfully created modern foreign-exchange trading by figuring out how to combine inexpensive computer terminals with a reliable, customized communications network. Which operating system will be most appealing on what type of chip probably will be the crucial determinant of leadership for software operating systems and computer chips. Microsoft may emphasize operating systems for RISCs to ensure that UNIX cannot win market share via this chip's popularity.[13] More generally, successful, vertically integrated chip makers have incentives to withhold key components from competitors.[14] The United States cannot discard hardware for thoughtware.

Nonetheless, all major markets will not necessarily fall to firms with large DRAM outputs. Firms specializing in systems integration can win. U.S. firms hold a large share of the Japanese market for graphics chips (and visual technology is supposed to reflect the Japanese invincibility). U.S. success in this area is based on the systems integration capabilities of these chips, which U.S. firms achieved by working their systems integration expertise back into the chip. While Japanese firms concentrated on turning chips for conventional communications systems into commodities, U.S. firms refocused their efforts on higher-growth new specialties. For example, Motorola grabbed a leadership role in cellular phone system chips, a major growth market.

The Old Pillars and the Semiconductor Sector

The semiconductor industry illustrates the limits of the six pillars of the postwar free-trade system. The semiconductor industry was created in the United States, and, not surprisingly, a U.S. model of industrial organization defined the industry and its relationship to the government in its heyday. But even the U.S. market had a tighter government support structure than most other sectors (pillar 1). In the United States, Department of Defense procurement initially boosted the market. In Japan, by contrast, MITI made semiconductors one of their highest priorities and worked diligently with NTT and Japanese firms to overtake their U.S. counterparts via joint R&D and NTT procurement programs. Both the U.S. and Japanese efforts were outside the domain of traditional trade policy and negotiations (pillar 2). Semiconductors were quickly recognized as strategically important goods. AT&T, NTT, and European state telephone companies were key customers and providers of R&D for the industry. They could afford these expenditures because they were national monopolies whose R&D and procurement practices fell outside the GATT. Service monopolies were incubators of manufacturing markets shielded from competition (pillar 3). No one contemplated a special set of trade codes for semiconductors (pillar 4). In practice, the semiconductor industry was consistent with the four pillars that defined the governance of the postwar free-trade system even though the pillars missed some aspects of the logic of high-technology industries.

As a newer industry than automobiles, the two pillars that defined the rules for free trade were more often followed for semiconductors than for automobiles. A large share of semiconductor output was traded, although investment in foreign manufacturing operations became quite common as well. The demand for semiconductors grew so rapidly that countries unable to get into the business themselves imported freely. Japan, which discouraged imports and investment while building its own industry, was the major exception. Multinational output climbed rapidly in Europe, but for the most part firms used production in other venues to serve their home (i.e., U.S.) market (pillar 5). Japan deemed semiconductors so important that MITI was determined to create comparative advantage in Japan from the start. Europe, by contrast, largely was content at the start to allow revealed comparative advantage to unfold as it would (pillar 6). In essence, in its formative years the semiconductor industry conformed reasonably well to both the structure and the rules of the free-trade regime.

THE ROOTS OF JAPANESE ADVANTAGE IN SEMICONDUCTORS

More than any other market, semiconductors raise the question of why Japan surpassed U.S. and European firms. Unlike U.S. automobile firms, U.S. semiconductor makers were excellent and subject to strong market discipline. Japan did dump chips overseas while protecting its home market, but Japanese industrial organization— the ways in which firms are organized individually and collectively—mattered too. Early analysts emphasized Japanese culture or government leadership; more recent critics stress that Japanese firms found new organizational solutions to problems facing all firms. Much of the policy debate in Washington and Brussels concerns (1) whether U.S. and EC firms need to emulate the size and scope of the Japanese keiretsu[15] and (2) whether small, innovative firms are the key to the future.[16]

The basic argument for the former position is that Japanese success in microelectronics is mainly the result of a marriage of the keiretsu system with vigorous industrial policy. Because the importance of industrial policies has declined, today the key challenge is to match the economic advantages enjoyed by keiretsus. The keiretsus are ideally prepared to conquer the microelectronics markets because of their size, their network of interrelated companies that act as users and suppliers of semiconductors and electronics, their internal system of risk sharing and patient bankers, and stockholders who are willing to take a long-term view. In particular the network of users and suppliers that share common affiliation through keiretsu banks and interlinked equity holdings provides a superior way to share technological information and spread the risk of developing low-margin, capital-intensive process manufacturing technologies that are critical to supporting higher-margin electronic products.

The most extreme version of the latter view holds that markets work efficiently when governments do not distort them. These analysts argue that U.S. industry is undergoing a natural restructuring as efficient markets propel withdrawal from commodity manufacturing markets. A milder version of this thesis emphasizes competition and diversity, holding that large, complicated industries yield many potential comparative advantages for firms. Some firms, like Toshiba, will win because of component specialties; other firms, like Apple, may triumph because of their software expertise; and still other firms, like Hewlett-Packard, will build their advantage on their reputation for robust reliability and service. Sources of advantages may be created by firms or reflect special properties of their home national markets. At the same time, there is vigorous domestic competition in Japan: there are many more competitors in key Japanese markets than in most other industrial countries; public policies promote generic research support open to all firms and improve the skills of work forces; and sophisticated government buying policies help large and small companies.

A narrower interpretation of Japanese advantages is sufficient. We believe that Japanese firms had a financial edge for two reasons. First, Japanese policies built a high national savings rate and for a long time cut off the rest of the world from easy access. Thus, the cost of capital for Japanese firms was lower than elsewhere, and it sank even lower for a few giddy years of the Tokyo stock and real estate booms. Deregulation of financial markets and the end of the speculative boom have suddenly eroded this edge. Second, Japanese government policies and industrial structure reduced the risks to capital and at the same time fostered competition. This is not an argument that U.S. capital markets are inefficient. U.S. companies are not short of capital, and their financial backers are patient. If semiconductor firms have trouble attracting funds, the industry must be less attractive than other opportunities. Why? Perhaps the dollar is fundamentally overvalued, and U.S. capital markets view other opportunities such as biotechnology firms as more rewarding than manufacturing projects that face stiff foreign competition.[17] But cross-national variations also may be a consequence of different styles of industrial organization that manage risk differently. Firms seek greater returns to justify riskier investments. Keiretsu members usually pay more for funds raised within the group, in essence paying a premium for an ensured credit line.[18] Nevertheless, U.S. projects are riskier still, so U.S. semiconductor firms must pay an even greater premium to attract financing. Explanations based on the size of Japanese firms do not explain their lower risks. Although it may be easier to attract funds on more favorable terms to smaller projects because a firm is not "betting the company," this does not explain Japanese investment patterns. Large, diversified industrial groups have large, diverse investment needs. If a firm invests in risky, low-return projects, other priorities will suffer. Indeed, Toshiba and other booming chip producers were not particularly large and did not have guaranteed outlets for their chips; Toshiba gambled on chips to create a competitive advantage in end products, such as laptops.

If Japanese ventures are safer, they are justifiable on a lower rate of return than American ones. To what degree is their risk diversified and thus reduced? Japanese firms enjoy four big advantages: (1) they benefit from their protected domestic market; (2) they benefit from a stable home market, which over time experienced lower inflation and higher growth than the United States market; (3) they usually are well positioned in a wide range of markets partly because of Japanese success in exporting consumer electronics. This spreads their exposure to exchange-rate risks and to downturns in individual national markets—a macro advantage that never appears on a financial balance statement; and (4) Japanese law permits banks to hold equity in firms, so they know more about their clients and are more likely to finance them in bad times than to foreclose.

Certain micro advantages also assist Japanese firms in managing their risks. The Japanese government's emphasis on uniform process technologies and its use of technical standards to level the playing field of systems integration reduce risks and risk premiums by narrowing the range of competitors for leadership. Japanese firms prosper if they emphasize price and performance and innovate incrementally. They usually can afford to wait for their chance to win at systems integration and architecture.

To illustrate, based on the amount of money committed to R&D, U.S. firms should have retained their early lead. Until 1985 U.S. firms' R&D spending was larger and more diversified than their Japanese counterparts.[19] But U.S. firms did not share a common vision that might have helped them define the building blocks needed for the new technologies. By contrast, according to U.S. industrial engineers who have had access to advanced Japanese electronics technologies, years after a MITI-led Japanese research project, the process techniques used by Japanese firms remained much more similar than in the United States. In short, research projects define a set of process paths that allow small- and medium-sized suppliers to achieve economies of scale because all major customers are shopping to meet similar needs.[20] This effect is reinforced because Japan pays greater attention to launching complementary research consortia that will collectively foster generic technologies, like CMOS integrated circuits. Many of these consortia are pinpoint efforts that disband after achieving a narrow, specific task.

Until recently Japan enjoyed one other advantage: the contracted base of production in Japan permitted close integration of design and production skills. But today the Japanese firms are moving a portion of their production overseas, partly in response to rising costs and partly in order to satisfy U.S. and EC trade demands. In short, in the 1990s Japanese firms will have to pay the adjustment costs of having to learn how to globalize.

THE U.S. RESPONSE TO THE JAPANESE CHALLENGE

The 1986 and 1991 U.S.-Japan Semiconductor Agreements

The U.S. government response to the Japanese challenge in semiconductors is revealed in the goals and achievements embodied in the U.S.-Japanese semiconductor negotiations, which often are cited as an example of dangerous bilateralism. Talks began in 1973 when Japan took two steps toward multilateral liberalization: it agreed to phase out quotas on imported semiconductors and to abolish mandatory technology transfers previously required of U.S. firms wishing to invest directly in Japan. The 1973 agreement did not address preferential purchasing links among keiretsu members, government subsidies, Japan Development Bank financing, benefits for products using Japanese chips under Japan Electronic Computer Company leasing programs, or NTT support for Japanese firms' research and production programs.[21]

The appointment of the United States–Japan High Technology Working Group in 1982 launched a new round of negotiations, just as U.S. semiconductor manufacturers started to stumble under the pressure of Japanese market advances. Under an agreement reached in November 1982, data on monthly chip sales were gathered. Prices, however, were not surveyed because of opposition based on antitrust grounds from the U.S. Department of Justice. The next agreement signed in November 1983 included a confidential note from MITI promising to encourage Japanese firms to buy more U.S. chips and to enter into long-term relations with U.S. firms.

U.S. industry and portions of the U.S. government were still concerned that conventional dumping cases were always resolved too late to help industry in a market with short product life cycles. In October 1985 the Department of Commerce forced an interagency agreement through the U.S. government to proceed with a self-initiated antidumping suit. The Semiconductor Industry Association (SIA) also charged Japan with unfair trade practices and brought a Section 301 case against Japan.

These initiatives set the stage for the July 1986 U.S.-Japan agreement. This pact had three basic features: (1) the Japanese government agreed that American firms would have a 20 percent share of the Japanese chip market (including everything from DRAMs to microprocessors) (the now famous side letter that promised U.S. producers a 20 percent market share was not included in the official record, in part because the U.S. interagency process prevented U.S. negotiators from pushing to make it part of the record); (2) Japan agreed to hold prices of DRAMs and EPROMs above floor prices consistent with the costs of individual Japanese firms; and (3) the Japanese government agreed to monitor production capacity to reduce the incentives for dumping created by massive excess capacity.[22] Japan also agreed to monitor costs and prices of exports to the United States and third markets in accord with GATT rules. In effect, Japan again pledged to help U.S. suppliers gain access to the Japanese market. Overall the agreement was geared to the variations of costs among firms, not on a floor price system that MITI preferred. In return, the United States agreed to suspend its antidumping cases.

When complaints about dumping continued, the United States eventually imposed sanctions in April 1987. The 1986 semiconductor agreement gave MITI new responsibility to ensure that prices did not violate antidumping agreements, thereby crystallizing the potential capacity of the Japanese industry for strategic pricing. The pact covered EPROM and DRAM chips. Japanese firms argued that the purpose of the pact was to bolster price levels and professed puzzlement over U.S. price cuts on EPROMs.

The SIA credited its antidumping provisions with saving U.S. EPROM producers just in time while being too late for DRAM producers. The price path of the two technologies diverged sharply through 1990: EPROMs experienced sharp price competition, while DRAM prices were substantially above levels required by the pact. The SIA concluded that a healthy American industry undercuts the potential for price collusion opened up by antidumping pacts, while sympathetic critics argue that straight subsidies to the firms may be better than price floors. There is no doubt that to the extent the pact boosted prices it injured U.S. users of semiconductors, who are used to steep increases in productivity (price per performance ratios) as a result of ever more powerful chips at low prices. There was a continual additional dispute about the true U.S. share of the Japanese market: Japanese calculations show that IBM's intracorporate transfers would raise the U.S. share by two points; U.S. firms point out that Japanese measures of the market cover only 80 percent of the major customers.[23] Critics contend that Japan manipulates prices to discourage competitive entry. Japanese DRAM prices jumped as soon as U.S. computer companies rejected the creation of a consortium for DRAMs.

The trade pact's impact on U.S. chip sales in Japan is more complicated. Foreign firms achieved less than a 14 percent share of the overall Japanese market by 1990, but approached a 20 percent share in sales to the six largest Japanese firms. The process built some stable business relationships between key U.S. firms and Japanese giants. But even if the United States succeeded in supplying 20 percent of the chips purchased by Japan's nine largest firms, overall

U.S. market share would climb to only 13 percent, a marginal improvement since 1986. Many of the new sales to the first-tier Japanese firms also were squeezing the rest of the market. Hitachi bought more U.S. chips for its internal operations and then pushed harder to keep up its volume by fighting U.S. firms in the rest of the domestic market.

A more encouraging sign is the pact's cumulative impact on learning by U.S. firms, which now have access to the most sophisticated users in Japan. The semiconductor industry reflects the von Hippel effect: enormous gains in innovation and efficiency can come from learning from sophisticated customers. NEC and Hitachi already have said that they can meet their targets only by better consultation with U.S. firms at the design stage. There also is a growing commitment by Japanese automobile makers to boost the use of foreign components, a crucial breakthrough because automobile makers are traditionally among the world's most sophisticated users of microelectronics.[24]

At the same time the chip agreement was a subtle disservice because it provided DRAM makers with an incentive to move more aggressively into systems integration. Kenneth Flamm argues persuasively that the trade pact makes it easier for Japanese firms to collude on price and production capacity while the U.S. government continues to approve limits on production capacity. It is easier, therefore, for Japanese firms to earn substantial rents on DRAM production, and industrial organization theory shows that firms with high rents on inputs to production are better off claiming them as part of a move into the downstream product. In short, Japanese firms have even stronger incentives to move into systems-integration products as a result of the DRAM agreement's effects on pricing and production capacity.

However, on the international level the semiconductor negotiations also clarified several debates between bilateralists and multilateralists. The agreement showed why multilateralism does not deal effectively with these issues of industrial organization. The negotiation hinged on determining what constituted a fair price for semiconductors. One commentator noted, "Pricing questions are extremely technical and intricate. The arcane law, regulations and administrative practices applied by the U.S. Commerce Department are relatively obscure to people in the United States, even those closely involved in their application. It is difficult to imagine negotiating cost and pricing questions in a multilateral setting. The general rules found in the GATT and in the Antidumping Code are about as far as one can go multilaterally."[25]

Two options were open to make the agreement compatible with the GATT, both of which were taken. First, to comply with GATT rules concerning most-favored-nation (MFN) treatment and nondiscrimination, Japan's commitment to market access was made to "foreign-based," not U.S., semiconductor producers.[26] The agreement was inclusive, not exclusionary. However, it has rankled the EC that its companies are not on the verification and market certification committees set up under the agreement. Second, the parties acknowledged that the GATT was competent to review whether particular solutions conformed to GATT rules. The Japanese restrictions on shipping product to third parties to avoid leakage to the United States were subsequently ruled GATT-illegal. (The GATT did not specify whether the quantitative bans or the pricing rules constituted the illegal restriction.) It appears that trade diplomacy involving intricate problems of industrial organization is much like the law: it is easier for courts to examine the principles underlying a particular contractual agreement after it is signed than to determine how the contract should have read in the first place. The GATT can review a variety of intricate issues, but initial resolution is beyond its capabilities.

The complexity of these matters was demonstrated by the debate over its renewal. There were three striking features of the process. The first feature was the degree to which Japan implicitly pinned its hopes on limits imposed on the pact by the American computer industry, the biggest consumers of chips in the United States. The computer industry formed the Computer System Policy Project (CSPP) (its founding members were Apple, Compaq, Control Data, Cray Research, DEC, Hewlett-Packard, IBM, NCR, Sun Microsystems, Tandem, and Unisys) because it did not want to pay twice for a semiconductor agreement. Its principal architect, IBM, also had taken numerous initiatives (including a temporary minority stock position to shore up Intel) to keep the U.S. semiconductor industry healthy. Lengthy bargaining between CSPP and SIA finally led to agreement to support a new agreement on October 5, 1990. Japan had opposed renewal, but this unified front by U.S. industry made a new deal inevitable.

Reflecting the CSPP-SIA bargain, the 1991 pact reaffirms the 20 percent goal for foreign access to the Japanese market by the end of 1992. The two sides did not, however, agree on the extent to which this goal should be binding, and foreign suppliers were almost certainly going to fall at least 5 points short of the goal by the pact's end date. They also compromised on how to count market share: the United States insisted that Japan not count the sale of chips from IBM in the United States to IBM Japan as well as some other firms' transactions; the Japanese won some concessions on small parts of these totals, which were equivalent to about 6 percent of the total market.[27] The pact also abandons Japanese control over export prices. Instead, MITI will maintain current data on corporate costs and provide the data to the United States within two weeks or to third-party governments when complaints arise (if a suspicion of dumping in their markets is raised). Washington is authorized to impose dumping duties without conducting a full investigation on EPROM chips. Washington hopes this mix will undercut a Japanese export cartel while still providing rapid enough action to protect the reinvigorated EPROM producers. DRAM makers must hope that no Japanese firm will trigger a price war to claim the United States' small remaining share of the market, especially because the pact embodies a strong U.S. political commitment to retaliate if the Japanese are imprudent. CSPP argues that antidumping calculations should permit forward pricing on high-technology items and not simply calculate against current costs because companies should include anticipated savings from expanded savings in current pricing. It also urged that users be given a larger role in the administrative process involved in dumping determination and that there be exemptions from antidumping if the product has no practical domestic substitute. The hopes of U.S. DRAM makers probably are shored up by the EC-Japan dumping agreements of 1989 (DRAMs) and 1991 (EPROMS). These pacts conceded that Japan was the low-cost producer in world markets and set reference prices that justified a substantial import duty on Japanese chips to sustain the European industry. These pacts suggest that Japan acquiesced to continued price stabilization, in part to protect its own massive investments. The 1991 pact also shows that Japan often thinks more aggressively than the United States about how to structure the future role of the newly industrializing countries. During this same period the United States largely dealt with South Korea by insisting on tariff cuts on semiconductors, improving protection of intellectual property, and threatening antidumping actions.[28]

The second feature of the debate over the renewal of the 1986 semiconductor agreement was the degree to which the United States rejected Japanese hints that there could be more global planning about production capacity, demand forecasting, and investment plans. Japanese executives pointed out that such an approach would help firms from newly industrializing countries enter the game without disrupting the world market. But at a point when the Japanese-dominated Asian market for electronics had just surpassed the size of the U.S. market, U.S. industry rejected this idea. This undercurrent illustrates the limits on management of trade. It makes little sense to even loosely legitimate market shares at a global level (as opposed to demanding specific market-access targets in a particular segment) when doing so rationalizes the potential dominance of one country.[29]

The third significant feature of the debate was that U.S. and European experts agreed that firms should continue to restructure radically. The National Advisory Committee on Semiconductors' annual reports repeatedly stressed the need for industrywide alliances to achieve these ends. Many of these measures also would require shaping new ventures in services infrastructure (such as broadband digital networks and intelligent highway systems) in ways that stimulate the semiconductor industry. Although conservatives and liberals differed on the details, important representatives in both camps have endorsed this close linkage of the structuring of service industries and hardware development—implying that the resolution of high-technology hardware problems would continue to pose major challenges for trade policies for advanced services.[30]

CORPORATE RESPONSES: THE ROLE OF ALLIANCES

The semiconductor trade agreements are symptomatic of the emergence of a new set of rules for international competition that assumes that global industry is being restructured. But trade pacts are limited. Firms are experimenting with ICAs as one way to supplement specialized trade agreements. Indeed, the latest SIA position implicitly links trade policy to alliance policy.

Motivations for ICAs

The strongest motive pushing Japanese firms is the desire to avoid trade friction. Other factors include the attainment of technological parity between U.S. and Japanese producers, the tremendous financial investments required to develop new process technologies and product innovations, and the evolution of new technical relations between integrated circuits and electronic system design.[31] Current trade realities will not permit continued Japanese autarky. Moreover, a combination of rising capital costs and declining margins may have moved some Japanese firms to conclude that sharing risks may be desirable in the high-volume markets. In customized segments U.S. firms particularly have strong technological assets. So Japanese firms in the first tier of semiconductor producers have decided to use alliances with foreign firms to obtain technology for customized products and design tools and to share risks. In return, the Japanese firm purchases foreign chips and transfers some Japanese manufacturing know-how to other companies (sometimes by operating joint manufacturing facilities). Newer Japanese entrants into the business have experimented with deals to become suppliers of specialized products to major U.S. producers. And large Japanese users have entered into alliances with U.S. firms as part of their campaign to alleviate trade tensions with the United States. The critical move on this front is the decision by automobile makers to include U.S. firms at the "design in" stage for semiconductors.

U.S. firms need to refurbish the support infrastructure for manufacturing skills, improve scale and scope economies, and share the fixed costs of research, and Japanese firms have much of what they need. Because U.S. firms believe that Japanese firms work better with long-term partners, all major U.S. chip producers are experimenting with alliances with Japanese partners. Perhaps the most striking feature of the alliances is the degree to which they emphasize newer complementary products for the U.S. firms. Firms are not sharing their core products, but they are building their product families to compensate for their narrow core strengths.

European firms recognize that no individual EC member government has the resources to make the financial commitment to a massive semiconductor support program. If the European Community is necessary as a catalyst for approval, then alliances are necessary. The question for Europe is to determine the degree that EC-based alliances should include U.S. or Japanese firms. There have been a few joint ventures linking European and Japanese firms, such as the International Computers Limited (ICL) arrangement for gate array technology with Fujitsu (which preceded Fujitsu's purchase of ICL) and SGS-Ates' somewhat broader tie-up with Toshiba.[32] Nonetheless, European firms probably will continue to concentrate mostly on intra-European, European-U.S., and perhaps some triad deals with U.S. firms as the pivotal members. Table 6.3 lists thirty important ICAs in the semiconductor sector. Most of these were announced after 1990.

U.S. Domestic Alliances

The existence of a larger competitive fringe of DRAM suppliers in the United States and Europe would keep Japanese suppliers honest in the same way that the Japanese fringe once kept U.S. suppliers honest. With rents of almost $3 billion in 1989, Japanese firms had a strong incentive to move downstream to collect them. U.S. firms needed to whittle down Japan's advantage, and market forces plus new Korean entrants have done so in the 1990s. (In an era of growing interdependence between components and systems U.S. firms will be disadvantaged if there is not enough competition at the components levels to make contractual alliances trustworthy. The alternative is doing most things internally. Its interest in a vital competitive fringe also means that the U.S. has a long-term interest in encouraging entry by other Asian suppliers and encouraging cooperation with European entrants.)[33] But the problem for U.S. producers goes beyond the volume or market percentage of chips. The range of products is important as well. There is no single chip

Table 6.3
Major Semiconductor Alliances

Alliance	Year	Agreement
IBM–Thomson-CSF	1992	Thomson-CSF will market IBM power PC microprocessor chips
IBM-Hyundai	1991	IBM to sell some advanced memory chips to Hyundai
IBM-Toshiba	1992	Cooperative development of SRAM
IBM-Siemens-Toshiba	1992	Joint development, not manufacturing, 256 megabyte chip in IBM labs in U.S.
IBM-Siemens	1990	Advanced DRAM cooperation; joint $700 million plant in France; cancel pact for 64 megabyte plant in 1992
AT&T-NEC	1992	Joint venture 51% owned by AT&T will sell AT&T chips to Japanese companies and some systems that use chips from both firms
	1992	Cooperate on 64 megabyte DRAM development
	1990	AT&T CAD technology for NEC advanced logic technology
AT&T-Mitsubishi	1990	256 K SRAM production capacity of AT&T for new SRAM technology of Mitsubishi; AT&T capacity in gallium arsenide foundry and silicon packaging for Mitsubishi. Expanded in 1992 to include microcontrollers.
Intel-Sharp	1992	Joint design, manufacturing and development of process technology of flash memory (.6 micron); includes Sharp factory in Japan to produce Intel chips
Intel-NMBS	1990	NMBS sources DRAMs and flash memory to Intel
TI-Hitachi	1991	Joint development of 64 megabyte DRAM
TI-Hyundai	1991	Hyundai manufactures 1 megabyte DRAM for TI
TI-Kobe Steel	1990	Kobe to build TI ASIC chips
Hitachi-Gold Star	1991	Gold Star manufactures 1 megabyte DRAM for Hitachi
AMD-Fujitsu	1992	5% cross-equity swap and joint development and manufacturing of flash memory chips in joint Japanese plant
Advanced Micro Devices (AMD)-Sony	1990	Sony buys AMD factory in U.S. and provides some technology to AMD
Sematech-JESSI	1991	U.S. and European research consortia agree in principle to develop memory chips jointly; implementation pending

Table 6.3 (continued)

Alliance	Year	Agreement
Sematech-Ultraclean	1991	Sematech becomes member Society (Japan) of Tohoku University research group, which works on semiconductor technology with 235 Japanese and 20 foreign firms
Siemens-SGS-Thomson	1990	Cooperation to develop and sell microcontrollers
Siemens-Toshiba	1988	Siemens licenses Toshiba 1 megabyte DRAM and CMOS technology
Integrated Device Technology (IDT) (U.S.)-Siemens-Toshiba	1991	RISC technology; IDT RISC technology to be jointly developed and some production cooperation among the firms[a]
Motorola-Toshiba	1986	DRAM manufacturing. Updated periodically to cover new generations.
Motorola-Philips	1990	Philips will sell Motorola's RISC's systems under an original equipment manufacturing contract
Motorola-Philips	1992	Joint investment to build semiconductor design facility for interactive multimedia products
NEC-MIPS	1992	To jointly develop 64-bit RISC chip
Paradigm-NKK	1991	NKK (a steel firm) buys 10% of Paradigm and licenses its SRAM technology
SGS-Thompson-Oki	1991	European DRAM manufacturing
Sanyo-LSI-NKK	1991	LSI commits to new Japan R&D center to cooperate on HDTV chips and will manufacture with Sanyo.
Advanced Computing Environment (ACE)	1988	Firms agree to use MIPS RISC technology as base for their computer systems[b]

[a] IDT is a 1980 startup that has sales of roughly $200 million per year.
[b] ACE members included MIPS, Compaq, DEC, Bull, Gold Star, and Epson.

technology that holds the key to the future. For the United States to succeed, trade pacts with Japan at minimum must lead to a growing diversity of roles for U.S. chips in Japanese products. The U.S. government sought MITI assurances of long-term relationships for U.S. firms, but this will work only if it leads to contracts covering a wider range of chips. Only a variety of products can ensure that U.S. chips are involved in more than one stage in end-product design, and only multistage involvement ensures constant interaction with designers. (Japanese firms complain that U.S. firms do not have appropriate products, a classic chicken and egg problem for foreign competitors in Japan.) The industry leaders will maintain broad, long-term relationships with the designers of key end products. The Japanese keiretsu system excels at nurturing this type of relationship; the U.S. industrial procurement system does not.

One U.S. response to Japan's success was to create DCAs among U.S. firms on the MITI model. Prominent initiatives have included cooperative ventures between the U.S. government and industry to provide R&D (Sematech and the Defense Department's effort on high-resolution displays and imaging) and a common venture of all U.S. chip makers and some computer firms to produce DRAMs. Only Sematech survives. The Pentagon's Defense Advanced Research Projects Agency (DARPA) proceeded with a much smaller program for high-resolution imaging than originally planned, and a variety of low-profile consortia are tied to universities. The most important initiative is the FCC's selection of the new HDTV standard: because of breakthroughs in digital technologies, the FCC may be able to choose a technology that leaps past Japanese and European designs.

Sematech is complemented by research consortia such as the Microelectronics Computer Technology Corporation (MCC) and the Semiconductor Research Corporation (SRC) as well as by the Corporation for Open Systems (COS). MCC began with twenty-one members and an emphasis on semiconductor projects and now nurtures startups as well. MCC distributes licenses to firms funding specific projects, other members are licensed after a three-year lag. The COS, which has counterparts in Europe and Japan, spends $8 million annually from four members to develop protocols in accordance with "open systems" design being advanced by the International Standards Organization and the CCITT of the International Telecommunication Union. Democrats favor increased funding for such projects, as the Omnibus Trade and Competitiveness Act of 1988's Advanced Technology Program showed.[34]

DCAs also are weighed down by cleavages within U.S. industry that hamper selective cooperation. Industry segments and different tiers of firms are divided. (By contrast, the concentrated structure of Japanese industries makes it easier for Japan to work out differences in interests.) Sematech has gone a long way toward reducing distrust between manufacturers of process technology and chip producers, but the failure of U.S. Memories, which tried to create a common manufacturing consortium for DRAMs, is a testimony to the gap that separates chip makers and computer houses. U.S. Memories would have entailed much greater financial risk (a $150 million investment even in its modified plan) than Sematech because it planned to enter into commercial competition. Although the U.S. government declined to offer financial guarantees large enough to eliminate the bulk of the risk, IBM and DEC stuck with the plan to the end. They had Intel, National Semiconductor, Advanced Micro Devices, LSI, and Hewlett-Packard as allies most of the way, but most computer houses refused to join.[35]

The U.S. Memories failure reflected the limited U.S. experience with consortia for manufacturing due to antitrust restrictions. U.S. political tradition and economic strengths will not permit a replication of the keiretsu system. U.S. government involvement could discourage restructuring if it concentrated on supporting a few firms rather than many. U.S. antitrust policy grew out of the fear that large firms based elsewhere would drive local businesses out of existence. Nonetheless, the Bush administration sought relaxation of antitrust law governing consortia for manufacturing.[36]

R&D policy is subject to an uneasy blend of meritocracy and distributional politics that achieves its worst outcomes when industrial restructuring is necessary. The U.S. government dropped one of its most successful civilian technological programs, commercial communications satellites, when the range of dominant winning firms became too small to sustain political support for funding in Congress.

Even though IBM invested in Intel in the early 1980s to sustain the company when it faltered (it sold out after Intel recovered) and IBM is now cooperating with Motorola to promote x-ray lithography expertise, small makers of chips and computers often wonder whether cooperative ventures will, in effect, legalize the sharing of knowledge and customer ties among a few insiders. Here, too,

Sematech has offered some lessons. It began by promoting applied research but has become an instrument that its industrial members use to share with the federal government the costs of financing specialized equipment of some smaller suppliers of production technology for the industry. Recently, Sematech was mobilized to provide additional support for the fortification of Perkin-Elmer. After Perkin-Elmer was nearly sold to Nikon of Japan, the U.S. government lobbied for a sale to a California group and IBM to keep its optical lithography technology under U.S. control. (IBM holds a minority share along with Perkin-Elmer; the Silicon Valley Group bought 60 percent of the business for more than $20 million.)[37] Sematech's efforts are still too narrow, however, and doubts persist about whether the best of the technologies of its members will be shared with the group. This problem is especially acute because many key technologies will flow to U.S. leaders from their new Japanese partners. Sematech also could flounder as a result of internal cleavages. LSI Logic left the consortia because of its support for process rather than end-product technologies. Protests over favoritism by nonmember firms have hurt its political base.

Similar questions surround intellectual property issues. In recent years firms like Texas Instruments have used their accumulated patent positions aggressively against U.S. and foreign firms to bolster their financial positions. But if patent balances move into greater balance in the future, and other forms of intellectual property become critical issues, more complicated alliances will emerge that bridge the software-semiconductor-computer nexus. One early example, noted in Chapter 3, was Sun's workstation strategy, which was based on the idea of permissive access to intellectual property to develop a standards community built around a specific technological approach.

Relationships with Japanese firms also are vital for sustaining diversified product development. U.S. firms need to provide a total line of products for consumers, ranging from DRAMs to microprocessors. But few U.S. firms can produce everything for themselves (and the same fate may soon befall Japanese firms). Even where U.S. firms are innovative leaders, they may not be large enough to finance new chips alone. For example, Intel, which holds about 80 percent of the booming market for flash memory (memory that does not require power to hold the information stored on the chip), overtook Toshiba, the original Japanese developer of this technology, through innovative design follow-up and improved manufacturing. But by 1992 it lacked the funds to do the manufacturing alone at a time when market volume is soaring and heavy Japanese spending to catch up is expected to lower margins. In a fine example of seeking complementary assets, Intel decided to partner with Sharp for the manufacture of flash memory chips. (U.S. firms can use Korean firms for low-end DRAMs, although Korea hopes for technological parity by the year 2000.)[38] As Michael Borrus notes, only alliances can teach U.S. firms about Japanese organizational practices that greatly boost their productivity. Strategic alliances to complete product families are commendable as long as firms manage their reliance on outside suppliers carefully.[39] The question is how to do this.

R&D agreements provide one partial vehicle for achieving cooperation to open doors. Although the Japanese have demanded that U.S. firms locate a lab in Japan if they want a piece of MITI's HDTV R&D budget, U.S. firms cannot afford to set up a lab for every new technology segment. Perhaps the U.S. government may ultimately fund a cooperative laboratory for microelectronics research in Japan for U.S. firms. This approach would avoid the trap of making access to Japanese technology solely through the channel of proprietary research institutes. (Two research groups—the Argonne National Research Institute in the United States and Japan's Institute of Computer Technology—agreed to collaborate on a fifth-generation computer project before the project faltered.)[40] The problem with such efforts is that they focus more on the technologies than the managerial processes that are shared in corporate partnerships.

A fundamental issue for U.S. trade policy is how its own policy on access to U.S. government-sponsored consortia will influence the policy of other countries. The Computer System Policy Project led by the chief executives of most of the leading U.S. computer firms has urged that the maximum restraint on foreign participation be a functional equivalent to "local content" for judging whether a firm is American. (CSPP prefers a lower barrier.) In this case it might be

U.S. production and research facilities. As U.S. firms increase their research facilities in Japan (eleven U.S. research facilities for electronics existed in Japan in 1989), this is a standard that U.S. firms could live with as a criterion for their own admission to foreign consortia. Table 6.4, for example, documents the active participation of European affiliates of U.S. companies in European collaborative R&D programs.

Increasing numbers of ICAs linking U.S. and Japanese firms seem inevitable. Strategic partnerships between U.S. and Japanese

Table 6.4

Participation by European Affiliates of U.S. Companies in European Collaborative R&D Programs, 1984 to Present

Esprit I and II	RACE	BRITE	Eureka HDTV Project
ITT[a]	ITT[a]	ITT[a]	ITT[a]
IBM	IBM	Donnelly	Captain Video
AT&T	AT&T	Ford	LTV
Digital	Hewlett-Packard	Rockwell	Covia
Hewlett-Packard	Texas Instruments	Lee Cooper	
Sybase	GTE		
Swift SC	DHL		
Moog Controls	Dupont		
3M	Ford		
Dupont			
Dow Chemical			
Honeywell			
Artificial Intelligence			
Babcock & Wilcox			
Cambridge Consultants			
Intersys Graphic			
Peat Marwick McLintock			

Source: Computer System Policy Project, 1991.

[a] ITT companies participating in one or more projects including Bell Telephone, SEL, Face Standard, ITT Europe, ITT Germany, and Standard Electrica. Controlling interests in many ITT companies have been purchased by CGE/Alcatel, so these ITT companies' participation as "U.S. firms" would predate such acquisition. An ITT company not controlled by CGE/Alcatel still remains active in the EUREKA HDTV project.

firms could work on research and product development and manufacturing. Keiretsu arrangements with a handful of U.S. and European firms could form the core of networks of firms that would try
to produce and market everything from process technology through
televisions and computers.

Currently, firms seem to use DCAs and ICAs to create a common technical infrastructure. They identify the most promising
paths of development, work out common process technologies
(sharing of software development tools is a critical component of
these partnerships), and undertake basic research. In some cases the
U.S.-Japanese efforts have evolved into sharing a family of products
for selected market niches.

Some arrangements are little more than licensing and outsourcing arrangements. National Semiconductor has licensed some NEC
designs. Sony has licensed some processing technology to AMD,
and it is leasing an AMD plant for Sony's U.S. production. On the
flip side, NMB Semiconductor of Japan is a minority partner in a
joint venture with Intel to sell DRAMs on the world market; Intel
controls marketing, supply allocation, and so forth. (NMB will add
a fourth plant in the United States in light of anticipated demand
and will transfer manufacturing process technology to Intel. NMB
is a 1984 Japanese start-up firm with no keiretsu parent although it
is partially owned by Nippon Steel.)[41] The NMB-Intel deal may
suffer because Intel was eager to find a partner better schooled in the
industry. Thus, it formed a venture with Sharp, a weaker DRAM
producer, to produce the next generation of the flash memory
market dominated by Intel. (Flash memory is a critical technology
for the next generation of consumer products.)[42] Other more ambitious deals involve U.S. sales to Japan and cross-technology exchanges. AT&T's relation with NEC provides that AT&T products
will be designed into NEC communications (such as cellular
phones) and computer products. In return, AT&T will provide
NEC with manufacturing technology for microcontrollers. Both
sides also will transfer national products and technologies for application-specific integrated circuits. The NEC deal will be further
bolstered by AT&T's selection as a development partner for NTT's
digital cellular technology system. AT&T also has an arrangement
with Mitsubishi Electric that covers SRAM. The relationships are

not a giant sales outlet for AT&T. Indeed, AT&T probably will benefit more from sales in the United States using NEC licensed technology than it will in Japanese revenues.

These Intel and Sharp deals also are the beginning of long-term relationships for sharing product designs and some specialization in production. All parties are trying to determine how much to bundle design and production. Consider the arrangements between Toshiba and Motorola and between Texas Instruments and Hitachi. In both cases the U.S. firm will share technology for their microprocessors with their Japanese partners, and, in return, will share in state-of-the-art DRAM technology. Motorola and Toshiba also own and operate DRAM plants jointly in Japan. The Motorola-Toshiba deal is controversial because Motorola made only 1 megabyte DRAM chips in its U.S. plant; it jointly produced 4 megabyte chips in a plant co-owned by Toshiba in Japan, but the European plant was canceled for reasons of cost. Critics wonder whether Motorola gave up too much technology for the manufacturing process know-how. (Toshiba estimated it has almost a dozen international alliances as key parts of its global business.)[43] In no case will any partner abandon its independent operations as a market leader.

Computer manufacturers such as Sun Microsystems and Hewlett-Packard also are experimenting with various alliances in the international semiconductor market. Hewlett-Packard is trying to rush its RISC computers to market by joint development of chip sets based on its architecture with the South Korean firm, Samsung. Samsung also will manufacture the low-end computers of the new line. Sun has built its strategy around a common infrastructure for technology and product networking. For example, it has signed an agreement to let Philips make microprocessors with its RISC chip technology, one of six such agreements in the United States, Japan, and Europe. The Philips deal was abetted by the two companies' then common ties with AT&T.[44] There are two dangers with such an approach: it sacrifices proprietary control of the technology and standardizes the product, an element that plays into the strength of Japanese firms.

European Alliances

European companies belatedly have turned to alliances to resuscitate their industry. Initially the emphasis of policymakers was on ties to other European firms, but by 1991, even before a number of new foreign-owned plants opened, European semiconductor makers saw their share of the European market drop from 39 percent in 1990 to 38 percent in 1991.[45] There are recent signs of more diversification. More ominously, the EC's active program for semiconductors has exhibited its first signs of trouble.

The biggest players in the European chip market, which accounts for about 23 percent of the world market, are U.S. firms. But European firms have tried several tactics to rebound. For example, European Silicon Structures was created in the 1980s through an elaborate legal structure that let it claim to be a local firm in several EC countries. This gave it advantages in procurement markets that were critical to its business plan. In short, it tried to be a pan-European firm specializing in custom-made microchips.[46]

Three more fundamental initiatives came in partnerships of Philips and Siemens, Thomson and SGS, and Thomson and Philips. The Philips-Siemens alliance represented a massive commitment by their parent governments to support the resuscitation of the DRAM industry. Eventually this alliance gave birth to many of the memory chip projects supported by the eighteen-country Joint European Submicron Silicon Initiative (JESSI), the EC R&D project for semiconductors. Philips remains the largest producer of semiconductors in Europe. Thomson and the Italian state-owned firm, SGS, created a 50-50 joint venture for semiconductors that is now Europe's number two producer. Thomson, the fourth-largest consumer electronics firm in the world, considers alliances indispensable for sustaining its semiconductor effort. Especially important is its $3.8 billion alliance with Philips for joint development of HDTV. The French government is contributing $500 million to the effort.[47]

The European Community has fostered broader alliances on all advanced semiconductor technologies, including supporting manufacturing skills, through JESSI. Its explicit focus is on commercial projects, not just research. JESSI is a $4 billion program (spread over eight years) under the Eureka initiative. Yet Eureka is not technically an EC project, and no EC regulations govern its membership. (Indeed, in early 1991 French President Mitterrand suggested that in the future the Soviet Union might be allowed to join Eureka.) Philips demanded European participation in Sematech as a price for U.S. participation in Eureka. IBM showed that corporate diplomacy can prevail by inviting European firms to enter into its own proprietary semiconductor research venture, forming a joint R&D deal for the 64 megabyte DRAM chip with Siemens. In return it gained admittance to JESSI. (Many key issues are influenced by the choices of firms over the placement of R&D facilities. Siemens did not have a semiconductor research facility in the United States, and Japanese firms have had none in the European Community. One question is whether R&D collaborative projects done in Europe qualify as local R&D for the foreign collaborators.)

But JESSI recently ran into trouble. First, Philips cut back greatly its corporate spending after years of poor financial returns. It withdrew from a major project with Siemens and Thomson that was the descendant of its earlier Siemens alliance. This cut its spending on JESSI by 30 percent (still less than 10 percent of JESSI spending). Second, Fujitsu bought 80 percent of the British firm International Computers Limited (ICL), a member of JESSI and Esprit. This immediately caused a problem because many JESSI members did not want to share technology with a Japanese subsidiary. ICL announced its intention to meet all budget commitments under Esprit but was eventually asked to depart.[48] Later it was quietly readmitted to some projects.

The dispute over the ICL was an extension of a previous disagreement over whether IBM could join JESSI when EC firms could not join Sematech. This issue ultimately was resolved by means of an alliance between IBM and Siemens for chip technology that indirectly gave the European Community access to Sematech technology. (They developed and produced the 16 megabyte DRAM jointly and will develop 256 megabyte chip with Toshiba.)

The ICL sale was a disaster from the viewpoint of firms like Thomson because it showed how easily reliance on Japanese components can lead to loss of autonomy. (The ICL began its relationship with Fujitsu by sourcing its chips from the company. Similarly, Apple is contemplating dependence on Sony and Toshiba for manufacturing all of its portable devices.) The ICL deal made Fujitsu second in the world computer market and the top vendor in Britain. European alarm led to renewed discussions of whether U.S. and European firms needed to form some type of informal keiretsu to meet the Japanese challenge. Doubtless this feeling of mutual need somewhat influenced the decision of the European Community in September 1990 to retract its most formidable demands for local EC content by Japanese firms because the rule also effectively hurt U.S. firms, which still are pursuing an activist trade policy to nurture U.S. industry.

Joint ventures between U.S. and European producers are numerous but not yet as significant as ICAs that bind U.S. and Japanese interests. During the 1980s numerous alliances were made in which U.S. firms acted as key suppliers to their European partners, but in most cases European firms did not have much new chip technology to contribute to the mix. For example, during the 1980s Siemens entered a deal to second-source (that is, manufacture) the 32 bit chip for Intel. Siemens agreed to help with the technical development of the chip, to use the chips in its products, and to develop complementary devices. By contrast, although Thomson second-sourced with Motorola on the 16 bit processor, after strenuous negotiations in 1986 it could not reach an agreement for Motorola's 32 bit processor because Motorola did not consider the chip technology for telecommunications uses offered by Thomson to be sufficiently valuable. This dearth of advanced technology to bargain with made clear to many in Europe that they needed to retain some indigenous capacity for chip technology in specialized design, production, and other areas if they hoped to gain access to "reliable" U.S. technology on a timely basis.[49]

Although Europe wants to press the United States to go beyond common technical infrastructure and work on joint product development and sales, it is unclear whether this will produce a big swing toward more integrated families of products. In 1989 European and U.S. trade associations for semiconductors agreed to support each other in setting their floor prices in memory chips and cooperating on HDTV initiatives.[50] Now, IBM is undertaking larger deals with European partners even as it plays a more active role in JESSI. Most dramatically, in early 1992 IBM agreed to purchase between 5 and 10 percent of Bull, the French computer firm. This purchase will move Bull into a deal for cross-sourcing of laptop computers, RISC chips, and other products. It also will diminish NEC's role as a supplier of technology to Bull. (The French government evidently also hoped that the European Community would object less to financial support to Bull if IBM rather than France Telecom was a shareholder.)[51] Simultaneously, Apple is assembling a global product team for the next generation of computing, including SGS-Thomson, Sony, and to a lesser extent Bull. The 1991 Apple-IBM technology cooperation agreement complements the relationship.

The 1990s could be especially appropriate for product alliances. There is general agreement that the next generation of computers and consumer electronics will converge: Nintendo games and pocket calculators were precursors to multimedia computing and much more powerful electronic organizers, for example. And the belated crossover of communications and computing may happen. This is forcing a fusion of new technologies ranging from special chips through liquid crystal displays and from software through CD-ROM memory. No single firm has the necessary resources nor can it hope to cover all fronts successfully. But Japanese firms have nailed down leadership in most of the key hardware components, the United States and Europe have selective leadership or parity in hardware, and the United States has a lead on software.

In response to both U.S. (e.g., Microsoft and makers of personal computer clones) and Japanese challenges, IBM and Apple agreed to joint development of computer operating systems and multimedia software. Motorola allied with IBM to create new chips to supply the projected systems, and Bull will participate via its IBM links. At the same time, Apple and IBM recognized the potential for tapping rivalries in Japan. They wooed the second tier of Japanese electronic suppliers (NEC, Hitachi, Fujitsu, and Matsushista are the first). Sharp joined with Apple to offer new electronic organizers, and Toshiba then agreed to produce multimedia computers based on Apple software while Sony manufactures Apple's laptop computers (a niche where Sony had not done well). Motorola and Sony each took 5 to 6 percent of an Apple venture to produce new wireless personal communicators. Toshiba and IBM had already set up a joint factory using Toshiba liquid crystal display technology. Toshiba then joined with IBM for joint develop of SRAM, and the two added Siemens to a collective project to create the 256 megabyte DRAM chip. And IBM tried to set up an alliance on multimedia with Time-Warner (which itself has minority Japanese holdings).

No one knows if the effort will work. Certainly some of the potential circle of firms will fall out. And the biggest question may be what role Europe will play in international alliances.

Four key questions face the United States and the European Community:

- Does the European Community want to encourage substantial Japanese sourcing of Europe through U.S. plants with high levels of local value added? To the extent that such plants strengthen the U.S. production base, the European Community may prefer them to Japanese imports.

- Does Europe want to pursue the Asian market on its own? Asian firms seem to expect that most sales to and from Europe from Asia other than Japan will involve U.S. firms with EC operations. EC firms have few sales or design operations in Asia.[52]

- Does the European Community want to integrate its R&D more with the United States? If so, it will probably have to accept some rule that admits Japanese firms as well. Although the European Community could demand something akin to strict reciprocity (such as access to equivalent Japanese projects), this would still represent a major shift in EC policy.

- Does the European Community want to encourage partnerships with the United States for production capacity? In particular, is the European Community interested in extending the concept of R&D to the creation of common "flexible" manufacturing plants that could serve as common production capacity for cooperating firms? This would require a new framework for antitrust law for both the United States and the European Community.[53] A related idea, endorsed by EC Commission, was a pan-European venture involving the three largest European producers. Philips rejected the idea in follow-up talks, while Siemens and SGS-Thomson had a limited pact for microcontrollers, a market controlled by U.S. firms. The big three had 10.5 percent of the world market.[54]

SEMICONDUCTORS AND THE EMERGING
MARKET-ACCESS REGIME

The global market for semiconductors is less open than it used to be. The EC's policy of fostering champions is more vigorous than before and its limits on Japanese activities more overt. The United States has imposed more conditions on access to its market. Japan, however, has cautiously liberalized. Japan is much closer to an open industrial policy than it was in the mid-1980s. At the same time, the globalization of firms has increased sharply. This has opened up new opportunities and challenges. Firms are turning to ICAs to build common, global infrastructures for the next generation of technologies. Alliances also allow firms to reduce the cost and risk of fielding extensive product lines. This is necessary because customers are reducing the number of their chip suppliers, and the ability of even large firms to offer a full menu is weakening. The widening international distribution of technology also is forcing experimentation with ICAs. This effort is reinforced by cautious efforts to unbundle design and production and allow more flexible strategies. But firms in all the triad countries are nurturing their supply base. It is not yet evident whether this is possible without international partners. Thus, as with automobiles, the fate of chip makers is integrally linked to the fate of their specialized suppliers. This may foreshadow the coming globalization of smaller suppliers to the semiconductor industry.

These developments correspond to the substitution of new pillars of a market-access regime for the old free-trade pillars. The pillars that describe the structure and governance of the emerging market-access system are evident in the fast-changing semiconductor regime. The Japanese model of industrial organization swept through the semiconductor scene, evoking responses from U.S. and European firms. The new structure of the industry is a hybrid of the U.S., Japanese, and European models (pillar 1). The semiconductor market is too important and too global to be dealt with by purely domestic policies. International agreements are getting extended jurisdiction over new areas of policy that change procurement policies by private firms (pillar 2). The mix of hardware and software that results in the creation of chips is now available on a worldwide basis. Trade agreements covering R&D policies of telephone companies and delivery of new global networks for computer-assisted design are central to the successful execution of trade and competition policies for high technology (pillar 3) (see Chapter 7). In addition, since 1986 there has been a rapid movement to specialized industry codes that ultimately should blend bilateral, minilateral, and multilateral elements (pillar 4).

The semiconductor market also conforms to the new pillars that lay out rules for a market-access regime. Where once chips were traded freely, but there was not much foreign investment, there are now webs of interconnections based on international alliances. To meet both the technological and trade policy challenges they face, semiconductor firms have gone global to survive (pillar 5). Indeed, to thrive firms are trying to build regional and global advantages in part of the market that will give them leverage over the entire semiconductor market at home and abroad (pillar 6).[55] Alliances are accelerating these changes and may blunt some forms of protectionism. Thus after chip makers, system providers, and specialized suppliers to chip makers enter successful alliances, the cries of even strident corporate protectionists are muted. Product and technology flows become too vital to close regional markets.

CHAPTER SEVEN

International Telecommunications Services

Telecommunications is at the heart of the emerging world information economy. It is central to the continued vitality of other service sectors and to advanced industrial sectors. We define telecommunications services to include (1) network facilities (the equipment that permits the provision of services over networks open to all users); (2) basic public services (services that involve no manipulation of the content or format of a message and that are delivered over networks that are available to all customers); (3) value-added and information services (also known as enhanced services) (services that may be offered by public or private networks and can include data, video, and voice); (4) mobile and radio facilities and services (also known as overlay services); (5) integrated services digital networks and integrated broadband communications networks; and (6) private networks operated by firms or more rarely by a consortia of firms.[1]

International telecommunications traffic has expanded rapidly as globalizing companies and ICAs integrate their far-flung operations.[2] As a result corporate traffic between countries "is spurting at an annual rate of 15% to 20%, about double the 7% to 9% corporate domestic rate." International revenues from corporate traffic are expected to rise from about $5 billion in 1991 to about $14 billion by the end of the decade.[3]

Telecommunications services are distinct from automobiles and semiconductors. From the start, telecommunications services, like other services, were not handled by trade officials or the GATT. Not until the early 1980s did trade officials begin to suggest that free or at least freer trade and competition in telecommunications services was possible and desirable. Since then, regulators and trade officials, supported by large users of telecommunication services, have pressed once secure telecommunications monopolists to allow more competition and freer trade in telecommunications services. Just as governments moved selectively to protect their key manufacturers, they pushed to liberalize trade in services, particularly trade in telecommunications services.[4] Telecommunications will never conform to classic free trade, but it is undergoing a period of remarkable liberalization. Ultimately, a market-access regime is likely to emerge in place of the old system of cooperative national monopolies.

The traditional national telecommunications administrations cooperatively managed international telecommunications on a monopoly model. The old pillars of the free trade explicitly placed telecommunications services outside the realm of the regime. Technological, regulatory, and economic pressures, however, are forcing rapid change in the way telecommunications services are provided in the face of demands for global service. Unlike the situation for automobiles and semiconductors, the major forces for change emanated from the United States. Although the United Kingdom and Japan provided early support for greater competition in the provision of domestic long-distance and international telecommunications services, Europe and Japan basically followed the U.S. lead on telecommunications services. Indeed, the marketplace of the United States was dominant. Five of the seven international routes with the largest volume of international traffic involve the United States. Moreover, in 1990, Kokusai Denshin Densai (KDD), Japan's international carrier, was only the eleventh-largest international carrier and was not gaining.[5]

As the old bargain for the provision of telecommunications over public networks fragmented, new forms of global competition in telecommunications arose,[6] but with sharp disagreements about how to structure the rules for a more competitive global industry.

The common denominator is a shared belief in the need for an increased role for investment-led commerce and extensive internationalization of domestic regulation. International telecommunications services were traditionally the product of national monopolies operating through stable ICAs to collaborate in the monopoly provision of a single international product. But the companies themselves were national in scope and operations or were owned jointly by national monopolists (for example, the Intelsat satellite system). Today, new ICAs are emerging in response to competition, and three emerging alliance patterns correspond to three different economic and political visions of the industry. U.S. telephone companies, in particular, are experimenting with all three options. The relative success of the alliance strategies will strongly influence the precise international rules for the sector. Regardless of which one wins out, telecommunications services, which once were distinct from the free-trade system, now are converging with the emerging market-access system prevalent for automobiles, semiconductors, and other industrial sectors. Even though sectoral agreements are likely to persist, officials may be able to manage diverse sectors under the umbrella of a market-access system.

TELECOMMUNICATIONS MONOPOLIES AND JOINTLY PROVIDED SERVICES

The global market for telecommunications services traditionally was characterized by national monopolies shielded from foreign competition. Telecommunications services were organized under an international regime that was served by the International Telecommunications Union (ITU). Efforts were made to collaborate on technical standards within international organizations to develop a common technical infrastructure, which could interconnect at international gateways. The work of these standards organizations was dominated by the national telephone companies acting as cooperative national monopolists. Specifically, key standards were worked out within the ITU's International Consultative Committee for Telephones and Telegraph (CCITT), which usually followed the lead of the Conference of European Postal and Telecommunications Administrations. Idiosyncratic national standards were permissible so long as international connection points (gateways) met world standards.

Each national telephone system was a monopoly, and international telephone services were provided by a shared monopoly of the national monopolies. The telephone companies viewed international calls as jointly provided services. National telephone companies argued that telecommunications services did not constitute trade; rather, they were the product of a joint investment by two or more countries in a common infrastructure (such as transoceanic cables) connecting the countries. Monopolistic communications providers simply extended the assumed economies of scale and scope from the domestic network to the international arena through joint investment. In theory, the messages carried over the cables were handed off at the midway point between the sending and receiving country.

The accounting rate system provides a contractual mechanism for sharing revenues among two legally distinct entities that are jointly engaged in providing international services. Three distinct rates are used. The *accounting rate* is established between two carriers to be used as the basis for international settlements. To set an accounting rate, each pair of carriers negotiated a rate per paid minute of traffic that they would use to settle any imbalances of traffic flow between them. Accounting rate revenues were then divided between the two carriers, usually on a fifty-fifty basis. The carrier sends the traffic and reimburses the carrier receiving the traffic by a fixed proportion of the accounting rate—an amount known as the *settlement rate*, usually 50 percent of the accounting rate. By contrast, the *collection rate* is the amount that each carrier charges its own customers. Each national telephone company was allowed to charge its own customers whatever rate it wanted for the international message. The collection rate may or may not be tied to the accounting rate.

To illustrate, a call from the United States to Madrid might cost customers $2.00 per minute from the U.S. side and $4.00 per minute from the Spanish side. If the two telephone companies declared the official settlement rate to be $1.00, both companies would receive at least 50 cents per minute for the call. Thus, a call from New York would yield AT&T a revenue of $1.50 per minute

($2.00 minus the 50 cents payment to Spain). But Telefonica would receive $3.50 per minute for calls from Madrid to New York.[7]

The rationale for monopoly in telephone services was essentially that (1) monopoly would increase reliability in the performance of tasks central to the public order (such as the provision of communications); (2) monopolies could tap economies of scale or scope in the provision of services; and (3) monopolies could advance considerations of equity expressed in the idea of "universal service." Most countries gave authority over communications to a single monopolist and made no distinction between the telephone company and the government. In short, most countries had no separate regulators for communications. Indeed, as a rule, telephone operations subsidized national postal operations; long-distance services subsidized both telephone services and the post office; large business users subsidized residential and smaller business users; and the telephone company services subsidized national monopolists that made telephone equipment. In addition, labor was guaranteed substantial job security and received relatively lucrative wages.

Telecommunications equipment has three market segments. Central office switching equipment is the largest segment and is the most expensive to develop and produce. Transmission equipment was traditionally the most traded equipment because it tended to be purchased in one-time procurement packages. Terminal equipment (faxes or handsets) was the easiest segment to enter but long remained a telephone company monopoly. Telecommunications equipment was exempt from GATT coverage because it was considered part of government procurement.

Monopoly telephone companies relied heavily on a handful of equipment suppliers that were familiar with the idiosyncratic technical features of the national network. In theory, monopoly control over services and equipment boosted technical integration and reliability. The market for telecommunications equipment featured firms organized around multination domestic strategies (such as ITT). The equipment firms were multinational in their production and sales, but there was little integration among their national operations. Traditional electromechanical technology was highly labor intensive. Equipment that was too expensive or complex to produce locally was imported, but companies emphasized as much local production as possible even if the cost structure was not entirely efficient.

Rising R&D costs, increasing economies of scale needed to cover the costs of switching systems, and shrinking subsidies from telephone companies made it harder for the manufacturers to maintain business as usual. Moreover, digital technology drastically reduced the employment needs of an efficient manufacturing operation. Since 1970 the major manufacturing firms consolidated. Today, the only first-tier suppliers of network equipment left globally are AT&T, Northern Telecom, Ericsson, Alcatel, Siemens, and the NTT supply family (Fujitsu, NEC, Hitachi, and Oki). This number will shrink.

Virtually all advanced countries have opened the terminal equipment market to competition. Most suppliers of network equipment still are protected, but they too face more competition. Major shifts in terminal equipment trade account for most shifts in telecommunications equipment trade balances. Thus, fax machines, key telephone sets, and cellular telephone equipment account for the bulk of the large Japanese trade surplus on telecommunications equipment.

The first real challenge to the arrangement for international services came with the introduction of communications satellite technologies in the 1960s. Communications satellites made it easier to provide international long-distance calling capacity compared to the undersea cables of the day. They also allowed point-to-multipoint service, making satellite television broadcasts practical. Overnight, the market for transoceanic services exploded. The question was how to organize this market. The solution was to create an unusual ICA, Intelsat. Intelsat was, and is, a public international corporation owned by national telephone companies (and thus by governments) that produced a joint product for the world market. It was an early example of the extreme globalization of the firm, but for the most part it acted as a monopoly. Its chief competition was the international cable system that also was owned by telephone companies. (The case was somewhat different in the United States where Comsat, not AT&T, was the U.S. representative to Intelsat. To make certain that AT&T did not send all its transoceanic traffic by cables in which it was a part owner, U.S. regulators unilaterally promulgated what was called the balanced-loading rule. Until the late 1980s, this rule forced AT&T to send half of its transoceanic traffic through Comsat and Intelsat.)

In short, by definition the telecommunications service industry was not covered by the six pillars of the postwar free-trade system. The framers of the free-trade system explicitly excluded services and telecommunications services from their calculations, making pillars 1, 4, 5, and 6 irrelevant to telecommunications. Thus, although AT&T was a full partner in the global environment, it had no incentive to destabilize the cozy, cooperative system of jointly provided services under the international settlements system. The U.S. model of industrial organization applied, but only in the sense that the United States accepted the concept of regulated markets for major services at home and abroad. Trade officials were excluded from the arcane world of communications regulators (pillars 1 and 2). International traffic, all agreed, was jointly provided, not traded, so telecommunications were not part of the general, postwar free-trade system (pillars 3 and 4), and free trade and investment to provide telecommunications were never considered in the advanced industrial countries (pillar 5). Thus, debate about national comparative advantage with regard to telecommunications services was absent (pillar 6).

FORCES OF CHANGE IN TELECOMMUNICATIONS

By the late 1970s it was apparent that monopoly was going to be severely eroded in the most important market, the United States. By 1982 when the decision was made to break up AT&T, it became clear that the logic of changes in the domestic U.S. market would prompt the United States to demand a reorganization of the global industry.[8] The liberalization of the U.S. markets for equipment and services opened the United States unilaterally to foreign competition in the newly liberalized market, but U.S. firms did not gain equivalent access overseas. To obtain new opportunities abroad for U.S. firms, the United States had no choice but to redraw the contours of the international landscape. Luckily for U.S. firms, the stagflation of the 1970s had opened the door to politicians favoring privatization of state companies and competition in regulated markets as a growth strategy. Moreover, many of the economic and technological incentives that precipitated the regulatory revolution in the United States also were at work in other countries.

Technological Pressure for Change

The first impetus prompting competition was the digital electronics revolution. The creation of the information-processing capacity of digital electronics altered incentives about both the equipment and services markets. Although computing and communications have not merged into a single industry as quickly as some analysts expected, the underlying technological base is more closely integrated and was revolutionized by the ability to deliver more bang for the buck at astounding speeds of innovation. For the equipment industry this has meant that electromechanical equipment for telecommunications is rapidly giving way to equipment based on digital electronics and software.[9] The cost of installing fiber optic lines has fallen rapidly so that today it costs only marginally more to install than copper.[10] The head of strategic planning for Cable & Wireless predicts that customers soon will expect multimedia terminals on every desk and in every home, voice instructions and responses, a mobile telephone in every pocket, global broadband (the capacity to transmit voice, video, and text all at once) networks, and very-small-aperture satellite terminals as cheap as today's transistors. Moreover, software and service advances are even more impressive than these hardware breakthroughs and will have vast consequences for telecommunications and other sectors.[11]

In many countries almost the same companies dominated computing, electronics, and telecommunications manufacturing because economic conditions or government policy led to a concentrated national market of electronics suppliers. Elsewhere, especially in the United States and Japan, the electronics industry was more varied in its structure. Many firms outside the circle of privileged suppliers of telephone companies wanted to extend their product line to telecommunications and tap the technological expertise of the large research laboratories maintained by the largest national telephone companies. These innovators sought competition in telecommunications equipment. The transformation of the services market is being matched by the restructuring of the equipment market.

Growing competition, reduced subsidies, and technological changes increased the need for economies of scale, scope, and customized product design. The rising fixed cost of R&D also was significant. The next generation of traditional central office switching systems will cost at least $1 billion for a company to develop. It is estimated that it will take about one-seventh of the world market for a firm to recoup its development costs. At the same time, firms remain subject to political pressures to have significant local production and content. Therefore, they are building more sophisticated global manufacturing and design networks and trading among the various affiliates. One way firms are supplementing their resources is by allying with major partners around the globe. These efforts to develop strategic partnerships are not yielding dominant multinational consortia (as happened in jet aircraft engines). Instead, alliances are pushing firms to invest more in common technical infrastructure, to explore developing complementary families of products with other firms, and to make cross-investments in holding companies to promote global cooperation for development.

The entrenched suppliers of central office systems are facing competition because the private networking industry uses a different mix of equipment and suppliers. Traditional telecommunications equipment manufacturers are refocusing their efforts on new niches, such as wireless, or rethinking their product lines to accommodate the overlap between computer and communication equipment. For example, IBM mainframe computers may switch private voice and data networks instead of an Alcatel switch.[12] The political success of rival suppliers also opened the way to revolutionary breakthroughs in distributing "intelligence" in the communications network to the offices of major customers. Moreover, as intelligence moves outward from the network to the customer, the bargaining position of customers toward carriers is improving; indeed, the carrier business may become a commodity business.[13]

Pressure from Customers and Potential Market Entrants

The digital revolution gave business an incentive to integrate backward into communications services to harness new technologies to help them integrate their global business and to deploy telecommunications equipment and services in ways that would permit them to offer innovative new services.

The classic example of a customer going into new services is the success American Airlines enjoyed after creating Sabre, its computer airline reservation system, which now makes about $150 million annually. Today if American Airlines sold Sabre, which handles more than 40 percent of computer reservations in the United States, it could receive about $2 billion. Sabre usually is more profitable than the airline. (IBM and American Airlines, which created Sabre, have agreed to help Aeroflot to build a computer reservation system. This deal should generate substantial revenues and improve Sabre's penetration into the international computer reservation system market).[14] Similarly, Wall Street firms, which spent almost $7.5 billion on new technology in 1991, are trying to integrate their businesses and offer customers new services. For example, in November 1991 Merrill Lynch launched its Advanced Order Entry system, which allows all of the firm's 10,500 brokers to enter orders for listed stocks directly from their workstations. Not only is the speed and accuracy of doing business improved substantially, but the system may lead to new, as yet unrecognized, business opportunities.[15]

Other large users of communications services wanted to offer communication services as an adjunct to their established lines of business to enhance the value of their products. In addition, they wanted to be able to purchase their own telecommunications equipment on a competitive basis. These developments made it logical that the terminal equipment market was the first part of the telephone monopoly to collapse in most countries.

The key to the political economy of these large customers was the concentration of purchasing power in the hands of the largest companies and government agencies. A rough rule of thumb is that about one-half of the use of the long-distance network in any given country is accounted for by less than 5 percent of all customers. Normally, the top 500 customers are the relevant market. Because their numbers are small and the significance of their purchases is rising for their bottom line, it is growing easier to organize these customers for political action. They have become the most important advocates of regulatory reform. Bankers and brokers are particularly heavy users of communications services: to manage its own communications fate Citibank, for instance, owned and managed what amounted to the thirteenth- or fourteenth-largest telephone company in the United States; in California, the ten largest banks may account for as much as 10 percent of the business of Pacific Bell; and in Germany, Deutsche Bank was a leading critic of the Bundespost's conservative policies and one of the triggers for liberalization.

The suspicions that large customers have of networks and network providers are revealed in their support of innovations such as open network architecture (ONA). ONA is a U.S. regulatory design that requires open and accessible design of the underlying national communications network. ONA is meant to ensure that all the major functions of the U.S. public network are available to all specialized services companies that wish to use the public network to help deliver their specialized services. ONA often is treated as a technical issue, but it is fundamentally a political issue. The terms for using the network (including pricing and physical access) are negotiated among regulators, network providers, large customers, and major competitors to the dominant national network. In effect, ONA represents the partial privatization of regulation. Private customers do not trust regulators to oversee the growth and development of the network and its services. ONA permits them to bargain directly about future network design and pricing. Thus, it serves as a technical grievance process for would-be competitors with the central public network. Critics of ONA argue that it also reveals the problems of relying on quasi-private bargaining when one participant can subsidize its participation by charging the costs to its guaranteed rate base. The regional Bell operating companies (RBOCs), critics argue, simply overwhelm the process by sheer numbers and a willingness to call endless rounds of meetings.[16] Most strikingly, ONA and its equivalents elsewhere have become a key trade issue related to telecommunications services because customers and new competitors no longer accept the traditional idea that the technical standards of domestic networks are not subject to international control. (Significantly, all major new Japanese networks are owned either by DCAs or ICAs. These alliances were formed partly to help break down the barrier separating telecommunications carriers and their customers.)

The dilemma facing the public network is captured by the development of electronic data interchange (EDI). To illustrate, Benetton, a largely hollow corporation, has two strategic assets—its brand name and a leading EDI network. Its sales of $1.2 billion per year of clothing products flow from a company that owns virtually no manufacturing capacity. Instead, it spends almost $13 million a year on information systems to tie together its supplier mills, headquarters, seventy-three worldwide agents, and 50,000 stores in eighty countries (many of which have point-of-sales terminals). Benetton developed a new set of standards to describe the colors of textile fabrics so that it could mix and match suppliers as needed. Its EDI system provides virtually all of the paperwork, ordering, and logistics of its network of suppliers and distributors. The sales information that comes in throughout the day allows for almost instantaneous ordering of new supplies and adaptation to the market. As a result, Benetton can be extremely responsive to market conditions and has cost advantages made possible by relatively speedy delivery, low inventory costs, and customized delivery services, which can preclear customs.

Who supplies the EDI system for Benetton? Benetton had to provide a set of industry classifications to make the system work. But the assembly and delivery of the network were done by General Electric Information Services (GEIS), which some analysts estimate has at least 30 percent of the global EDI market. GEIS displays many of the characteristics of the emerging specialized network. Instead of relying solely on the standardized technical industry protocols, GEIS opts for specialized protocols when necessary. (Public networks rarely adopt this approach, partly because it is expensive and time consuming and partly because they want to be in the business of providing universal standardized services for everyone.) Although software is a more important part of the cost structure than communications transmission and switching, GEIS also works to reduce costs of the basic communications component of the system. Although pricing is less important to its customers than reliability and security, customers will reject the system if it costs too much. Perhaps most important, GEIS has no conflict of interest as a business. As a descendant of the General Electric computer corporation, it sees its primary role as an advocate of its large business customers. It even will quietly represent them before government regulatory authorities. Such a posture would be impossible for a large telephone company with many stake holders representing a wide range of economic and political needs.

Economic and Regulatory Changes

The demands of would-be entrants into the equipment and services markets and the outcry of large customers could not force change if the underlying economics of the industry did not permit cross-subsidies to be reshuffled. During the late 1970s and 1980s it grew ever more obvious that subsidies to equipment makers and the post office could be ended without substantial impact on telephone services. The logic of separating regulatory functions from the operations of telecommunications also became clear. Another important question centered on the impact of competition on universal service and subsidies to local household telephones. It is striking that during the discussions of the divestiture of AT&T, Congress largely removed itself from the process once it made certain that subsidies to local households would continue under competition. Under this "access charge" method, competitive long-distance carriers have to pay the local telephone company for the delivery of long-distance calls to local subscribers. In addition, competition prodded telephone companies to rationalize labor and technology practices enough to yield enormous new efficiencies that could compensate for much of the lost benefits of monopoly.

More fundamentally, the digital revolution altered the economics of the network. Fiber optic transmission substantially raised the productivity of money invested in transmission facilities. Central office switching still is more costly than the most advanced transmission facilities (because it is so expensive to develop), but the cost of switching has declined per call and the number of tasks and functions a switch can perform has increased tremendously. Like much of the computing industry, of which it is a slow and clumsy part, central office switching also is becoming less centralized. Thus, the ability to process and switch the transmission of messages is moving to less centralized processing equipment. For example,

Daini-Den-Den, the most aggressive of the new Japanese domestic long-distance telephone companies, relies on DSC, a small U.S. switch maker, for central office switching that is only one step up in size and complexity from the switchboards that are found in major U.S. offices. It is possible that powerful desktop personal computers, like Apple's Quadra, that cost under $10,000 could be programmed to perform the same function as sophisticated PBXs. The seven regional Bell operating companies and the major U.S. long-distance companies are engaged in a technical struggle over whose switches will control the network and where local and long-distance services join together.

In addition, networks in most industrial countries are mature enough not to require special financial boosts to reach de facto universal service. The degree of universal service in the United States—over 90 percent when AT&T was dismantled—has increased since competition was introduced. Even if minor inefficiencies are produced by the duplication of equipment in competing networks, these inefficiencies may be more than offset by improved efficiencies in operational practices and pricing that are spurred on by competition. Eli Noam has observed that public telephone networks evolve from providing a solution to new customers, which in turn benefits all other customers (because interconnection is easier and cheaper for old customers as new customers are added).[17] Later, because the connection becomes more expensive for adding marginal customers, some large users prefer to drop out of the network's cost sharing arrangements. Moreover, any attempt to build one network that can serve all customers for all needs leads to a lower common denominator of tradeoffs concerning technical operations and pricing. It is the equivalent to offering only a Ford Taurus to all potential automobile buyers. It may be a fine vehicle at a fair price, but it is not the right vehicle or the best price for all customers.

In short, key questions, which still are being debated, include, Who should switch communications services? Who should add new functions to the network? Should the network of the future rely more on fiber or on new cellular telephone systems? If the network is opened to competitors, will innovation suffer?[18]

Thus, the governments of Japan, France, and other countries are seeking ways to provide everyone with advanced communications services as quickly as possible. In Japan, MITI believes that delivering high-definition television and other advanced communications services to the home will help Japanese producers of sophisticated home electronic gear to grow. Similarly, France Telecom argues that the provision of Minitel terminals and services throughout France has triggered a revolution in information services and provided the public network with the knowledge and expertise to supply new information services to small business on a flexible, inexpensive basis. (Many reject these claims.)[19] By contrast, countries like the United States, where industrial policy solutions are discouraged and the expertise for providing these services rests mainly with private networks and multiple private networks, have been slow to reach the technical agreements necessary to allow internetworking for advanced services. (The United States, however, has done well by funding working prototypes of new forms of networking. The most influential example of networking is the U.S. government's initiative to start what is now known as Internet.)

The other side to these arguments is that there are multiple sources of comparative advantage in any industry. For example, the cumulative learning of both suppliers and customers is a key economic characteristic of advanced communications and information services. The high price of services for large businesses and the rigid technical infrastructure for advanced services in Europe combine to restrain experimentation and slow the introduction of these services. Thus, the market for EDI and other new services developed more slowly in Europe, which could place European firms at a competitive disadvantage against the U.S. rivals. Moreover, networks not subject to full-blown competition resist changing internal managerial incentives sufficiently to refocus on evolving, unpredictable customer demands. Their incentives still favor building a network based on engineering blueprints, not customer requirements.

THE FRAGMENTATION OF THE PUBLIC NETWORK: NEW FORMS OF COMPETITION

Although debate about the optimal balance between competition and monopoly for telecommunications continues, there is widespread recognition that there will be more competition. Even countries intent on modernizing their monopoly through aggressive technical investments and on improving pricing systems are granting limited rights to competitors for specialized services. The ITU is rewriting its rules to make it easier to offer competitive value-added networks.[20] Although most countries are focusing on modernizing and rationalizing their monopolies, a small but growing number are introducing wide-ranging competition, even for telephone services. Most of the liberalizers are Anglo-American democracies—the United States, the United Kingdom, Australia, New Zealand, and Canada. They are joined by Japan, Sweden, and Thailand. A few other countries probably will follow.

These countries adopted different reforms. Japan manages total capacity and planned services of its telephone companies more closely than the United States. The other Anglo-American democracies share a "Westminster" model of government based on the British example. Arguably, this system makes it easier to execute a major shift in economic policy than other forms of democratic governance.[21] The European Community occupies a middle ground between monopoly and competition that may well be decisive for the future regime for the telecommunications industry.[22]

The U.S. approach to networking is completely consistent with the typical features of the U.S. industrial system. U.S.-based alliances are mostly ad hoc in nature: innovation is pushed by a plethora of specialized, boutique firms, and there is considerable market fragmentation. The procompetitive environment promoted by the U.S. government induced a wide variety of firms (electronic equipment, software, computer service, and specialized telecommunications services) to enter the market to provide telecommunications services or equipment substitutes for network services. Firms integrate when they need to, not because the government urges them to. When integration fails, they may enter alliances.

One aspect of the U.S. scene closely parallels EC behavior. Both regions are characterized by geographic monopolies for local telephone services and duopolies for cellular services. This structure produces DCAs and ICAs to help with R&D. This was the purpose of Bellcore, which is jointly owned and operated by the regional Bell operating companies, and of the new common approach to data networking announced by McCaw, GTE, and the cellular carriers of five of the seven regional Bell operating companies.[23] The European Community (and its European ICAs) is serving as the venue for similar efforts. On both continents customers and suppliers integrate forwards, backwards, and horizontally as they stumble into global partnering in combination with their own integration strategies.

In particular, efforts are underway in the United States and Europe to foster continent-wide common standards and technical and network integration. Specialized consultative bodies are setting standards for processes that traditionally have not been transparent or easily accessible to foreigners. To deal with this issue the United States and the European Community signed the Mosbacher agreement to improve consultations on standards, but the agreement is an imperfect shield. Although the American National Standards Institute from the United States will get "a seat at the table" in the two principal EC standards organizations, the Comité Européen de Normalisation (CEN) and the European Committee for Electrotechnical Standardization (CENELEC), many standards are vetted in more specialized industry associations before they ever arrive at these two organizations. These specialized groups often are closed. (In May 1990 France, Germany, the United Kingdom, and the Netherlands announced a proposed new standard for computer security that differed substantially from U.S. standards; IBM and DEC did not see the proposed standard until September 1990.)[24] Moreover, many EC firms support the use of unique European standards to deny Japanese firms the possibility of perfecting products in (allegedly) closed Japanese markets and then unleashing them on Europe.[25]

Except in the United Kingdom, most European countries still maintain monopolies for voice communications and basic communications infrastructure, but now they seek more flexibility and alliances instead of developing their own integrated networks. Most inter-European ICAs were efforts to reconcile quasi-national monopolies when the need for EC-wide integration grew evident. For non-EC firms, ICAs were a way to gain political entry and the use of local infrastructure.

Because network procurement and deployment still is based on a limited monopoly strategy, there is less cost rationalization and innovation in telecommunications products and services than in other segments of European industries. The most innovative applications are the product of special arrangements for sectors, like banking, which are economically concentrated and politically influential and seek specialized but narrow common telecommunications capabilities. These successes notwithstanding, by 1992 the European Commission became convinced that stronger rules for liberalization were necessary to reform underlying costs and spur innovation. But even if the European Community achieves more competition, it certainly will continue to strive for high interoperability among public networks and to keep learning by doing in sophisticated services offered by public networks. This contrasts with the U.S. willingness to rely on the growing expertise of private corporate networks. If the European Community achieves an appropriate mix, there will be high interoperability of the public network and high amounts of learning by public networks, not just private ones.

Japan has experienced innovation by suppliers and customers and some cost rationalization in the wake of network competition. Almost all the new telecommunications providers are organized as DCAs or ICAs. This form is preferred partly because of the politics of the situation and partly because these alliances provide a mechanism for bridging bargaining barriers that separate suppliers and customers.

The Ministry of Posts and Telecommunications (MPT) still oversees price competition and is loosely constraining network capacity. The MPT, for example, would not allow Daini-Den-Den, the most aggressive of the new long-distance carriers, to lower prices faster or further than other new entrants.[26] The success of the new long-distance competitors and the tense MPT-NTT relationship suggests that limited competition on all fronts already is forcing greater rationalization. This could accelerate. For example, MPT probably underestimated the size of the new market for mobile and cellular services, and NTT certainly was slow to recognize and back the development of increasingly vital digital signal processing chips. Indeed, despite its size and technology, NTT so far has not made a mark on the world market. As a result U.S. equipment and service producers may actually be stretching their lead in these areas. Some reports in Japan indicate that intriguing work is being done on routers and other specialized equipment for private networks, suggesting that NTT may no longer be guiding development.

The Japanese market is now more fragmented and specialized than MPT may have initially intended. So far Japanese public policy relating to telecommunications has focused on heavy investment in new infrastructure and new technologies, policies that arise from pork barrel politics (such as money flows to construction companies supportive of the LDP), efforts to buy off critics of Tokyo's intensive development policies, and experiments, like Teletopia, designed to advance new service applications for fiber networks. Slow but real penetration of the Japanese market has been made by foreign interests, and there are enough local Japanese competitors to open the way for new alliance possibilities. However, until it is clearer how the domestic network will interconnect with global networks, future structures will continue to be murky. When these connections are clarified, new questions about trade and regulatory policies for Japan, Europe, and the United States will abound. If U.S. firms are allowed to enter the British market, why not Japanese firms as well?

It is useful to compare the strategies of U.S., European, and Japanese firms. U.S. companies wanted to lower the costs of networking and rapidly diversify the range of technological experiments. U.S. customers accumulated a great deal of expertise, which worked to their advantage with new systems of technology. We have already noted that the U.S. approach also fragmented the range of competitive, diversified suppliers and the learning of customers, particularly private corporate networks. In contrast to the U.S. approach, the Europeans emphasized efforts at integrating knowledge and suppliers but have been unable to cut costs and diversify technological experiments as rapidly as their North American counterparts. One reason for this is that the politics of European policy produces strong support for lower prices and new entrants. Therefore the European Community tries to encourage greater sharing and integration of know-how of the suppliers' base along with incremental efforts at more competition. Japan has a hybrid strategy.[27]

New Domestic Competition

The European approach reserves certain services for monopoly, but an important innovation is that monopoly now requires a positive policy decision; in the past it was competition that required a positive policy decision. In the original blueprint for 1992 the European Community reluctantly agreed that the reserved services will mostly be basic public voice services. Although there has been considerable argument inside the Community over the fate of packet switching (packet switching converts computer data into digital packets, which encode the information into "blocks" that are accompanied by an address or checking code), the monopoly provision of this service will decline. More centrally, the combination of voice services with call-forwarding and voice message systems (or data exchange) probably will be placed in the category of competitive services. The European Community also accepts the principle of competition in the creation of new services such as cellular telephone and radio paging services, which involve selective new infrastructure for the network.[28]

In addition, some European countries may accept the British idea that cable television networks should be allowed to evolve into telephone networks. There was widespread debate in Europe in 1990 over the Hermes project when eleven national railroad companies brought in Nynex and Sprint to consult on ways to collectively modernize their private communication systems. Some viewed this as the beginning of a new international telephone service. (The Japan National Railway already owns a long-distance company, and France's giant electricity company is considering entering the business.) However, in the wake of a massive political counterattack by the telephone companies, these companies have stated that they only will modernize their internal networks, and Daimler Benz pulled out of Hermes, apparently under pressure from France Telecom and the Deutsche Bundespost Telekom.[29]

In economic practice, the EC had a strategy of "back-door liberalization." Table 7.1 shows the fate of the reserved markets and estimates the shift in the EC market between 1986 and 2000. The forecasts for services in 2000 represent a best-guess effort to turn the EC Commission's pronouncements on the consequences of its policy for the future into numbers. This table shows a great deal about policy strategy; it is less important whether the forecast is accurate. (To provide a perspective on the European market, baseline figures for 1986 for the entire world are included.)

Table 7.1

EC Telecommunications Market in 1986 and 2000 ($ billions)

Market Segment	World	EC-12	EC-12
	1986	1986	2000
Telecommunications services	360	84	277
Voice	n.a.	74	190
New services[a]	n.a.	6	88
Telecommunications equipment	108[b]	25[c]	47
Computing equipment[d]	150	30	138
Total	618	219	740

Source: Peter Cowhey, "Telecommunications," in Hufbauer, ed., *Europe 1992*, p. 165.

[a] Enhanced and overlay services, including software for specialized information services.
[b] Market size estimated at $130 billion in 1991; *Communications Week International*, February 3, 1992, p. 1.
[c] Figures for 1987 including telex and telegraph.
[d] Integrated office equipment and software (including typewriters, data terminals, computers).

The critical elements of Table 7.1 are straightforward. In 1986 communications services were significantly larger than the total of computing and telecommunications equipment. But there was little competition in telecommunications services because they were overwhelmingly voice services provided by monopolies. Over the coming decade the market for telecommunications equipment is expected to grow steadily but to lag behind the growth rates of computing equipment. Telecommunications services will still dwarf the equipment markets, but the critical growth in services will occur where there is at least some competition. Technological innovation (pump-primed by the European DCAs, Esprit, and RACE) and market competition would lead to a proliferation of new services that would swamp the traditional voice monopoly. In short, the explosive focus of the European market is at the intersection of new services and computing equipment. These markets will be dominated by the logic of competition, even though monopolies will continue to dominate a substantial chunk of the market. However, the behavior of monopolies will be constrained because dissatisfied customers can leave their networks. This is similar to what occurs with energy utilities: electricity and natural gas are partial substitutes; each may be a monopoly, but the monopolies compete with each other.

The big issue is whether pricing reforms and reconfiguration of the network infrastructure promote more new services and produce a new generation of European equipment to provide these services. By 1992 the EC Commission suspected that back-door liberalization would not suffice to spur growth of new services and check the resurgence of monopoly. The digital revolution makes hardware and software less distinctive and monopoly ownership of facilities is cleverly converted into limits on the software service packages of competitors. Therefore the Commission proposed new EC rules to permit freedom for providers of private networks to lay their own network facilities and toward granting providers the freedom to route as they chose over existing networks.[30]

New International Competition

The technological and political revolutions overtaking domestic networks also are at work globally. The traditional framework of jointly provided services is eroding, especially in major international markets. Concern over a scarcity of adequate public telecommunications facilities has lessened as, for more than two decades, the unit costs of international telecommunications services has declined on the average by 8 percent per year.[31] Simultaneously, interoceanic traffic shifted from voice toward fax and data, particularly between Asia and the United States, where the time difference means that the business day overlaps only slightly.

Once a substantial infrastructure of communications facilities existed in industrial countries, the falling cost of services started to undermine the system. If one country lowered its charges in response to internal competition, and a second country remained a monopoly, then traffic flows would be distorted. The low-priced country would send more messages than it received. If the high-priced country resisted substantial reduction in the accounting rate, it could reap enormous profits and increasing surpluses over time. This explains why by the early 1990s the United States was experiencing an annual balance-of-payments deficit on telecommunications services approaching $3 billion. It also explains why the Federal Communications Commission, the State Department, the

Commerce Department, and the Congress suddenly became interested in revamping the accounting and settlements process.[32] At the same time, two small organizations—the International Discount Telecommunications Corporation and Viatel—are offering customers ways to achieve substantial savings at the expense of high-priced monopolies. In effect, they make it possible for customers calling from overseas to connect calls as if they were calling from the United States. For example, if a customer in Rome is calling Tokyo, it is possible to call a number in the United States and have the call forwarded to the Japanese number. Instead of paying the rate for a call from Italy to Japan, the caller is charged, in effect, the sum of the wholesale rates for calls from the United States to Italy and from the United States to Japan. This total is noticeably less than the direct dial retail cost.[33]

The international situation shares the same dynamics with major domestic markets. Large users complain. New competitors in domestic long-distance services want to expand globally. There is a shift in government policies toward cost-based pricing, increased competition, global equivalents of ONA, and transparency in pricing and regulation. A few countries already have permitted competition in transmission facilities, introduced multiple international carriers, and substantially relaxed restrictions on the shared use and resale of leased circuits. They also are agreeing to allow these circuits to be connected to the public switched network. At the same time, the decentralization of the intelligence of the network means that there is more competition among service providers to collect fees for providing a particular element of a service package.

These developments did not emerge magically. Trade negotiations were a vital catalyst. U.S. negotiators demanded changes in local rules to accommodate the internationalization of its services and equipment industries. They succeeded partly because all large firms (including foreign ones) that had invested heavily in the U.S. market wanted to reap the benefits of new forms of networking and partly because many foreign manufacturers of telecommunications equipment wanted continued access to the now open U.S. market. The price for this access was accommodating U.S. demands for liberalization in their home countries.

The list of U.S. demands speeded the process and provided a focal point for discussions on what regulators should do in other countries. Local advocates of change quickly seized on U.S. proposals as a minimum platform for reform.

This remarkable series of events spotlights changes in the nature of international trade negotiations and underscores the problems being encountered in traditional GATT dealings. As regulatory change accelerated in the United States, major firms became more insistent that they be able to modernize their entire communications networks, at home and abroad. They started asking the U.S. Trade Representative for help with recalcitrant foreign telephone companies that refused to rent them leased circuits or charged exorbitantly for them. Traditionally, these matters were questions handled by domestic telecommunications regulators; trade rules did not govern them. But the USTR, although warned that it had no jurisdiction, proceeded anyway. Simultaneously, the unilateral liberalization of the U.S. telecommunications equipment market threw the United States into a significant telecommunications equipment trade deficit just when Washington was concerned about the U.S. trade deficit. U.S. firms complained that they could not sell abroad but that the U.S. market was wide open.

USTR saw an opportunity for good trade policy and good politics. It argued that the United States had to liberalize foreign telecommunications services markets in order to assist U.S. equipment sales overseas. Competition in services would boost competition in equipment and vice versa. At the same time, U.S. competitiveness in general would be bolstered if U.S. banks, for example, could reap the benefits of new communications technology globally. The icing on the cake was that national telephone monopolies often were used by their governments as cash cows to finance national programs to bolster the electronics competitors of the United States. If the USTR could break open national phone monopolies, it could undercut the industrial policies of America's economic competitors. Although nothing is quite this seamless in Washington, this logic clearly emerged from various ad hoc initiatives undertaken by ambitious, idealistic trade negotiators: the negotiators wanted to save free trade and please politicians bedeviled by trade problems.

The bilateral negotiations with Japan on telecommunications equipment and value-added networks that ensued were among the most tendentious in the relationship. Europe's program for 1992 provoked friendlier, but still tortuous, negotiations about their impact on U.S. businesses.[34]

The details of these negotiations are less vital than their general thrust. At a minimum, the United States wanted to secure four objectives: (1) total freedom to sell terminal equipment (such as modems) overseas, (2) equal access for bidding on the provision of network equipment (telephone switches), (3) freedom for its international value-added network suppliers to compete effectively, and (4) freedom for U.S. businesses to operate their own enterprisewide communications system on a global level. The first two objectives were unattainable without movement on the other two because service monopolies constituted an insurmountable nontariff barrier, and to achieve the third and fourth objectives required a revolution in trade negotiations. They could be achieved only by internationalizing domestic regulations, ending the separation of trade and regulatory authorities, and introducing the functional equivalent to rights of foreign investment. For example, before competition in services could be contemplated, foreign firms needed to be able to lease lines for a flat fee closely related to the real cost of the circuit and foreign firms needed effective access to the standard-setting process for local telephone networks. Fundamental changes in major ITU rules—such as an end to its prohibition of shared use by several customers of a single rented circuit—also were needed. Furthermore, foreign service providers had to be allowed to service the links between their customers' plants in, say, Paris and Marseilles (to handle their local national network for data) and to establish local groups for programming and customer support in local markets. In short, if they were allowed only to export their services, they could not effectively provide support for their customers.

Later the USTR agenda expanded, encompassing the rights of new competitors to provide specialized network facilities. The United States pressed for the right of new satellite systems to compete in the provision of transmission facilities for corporate networks with Intelsat, and it argued that U.S. companies should be able to invest in new cellular telephone networks being established in many countries. The logic was that if foreign firms, such as British Telecom, were allowed to buy (minority) shares of cellular carriers in the United States, U.S. firms should enjoy the reciprocal rights abroad.

This revolution in trade diplomacy spilled over onto the multi-lateral agenda. The United States made the introduction of services into the Uruguay Round a priority (see Chapter 8). In negotiating a general framework code for services, negotiators tried to combine traditional free-trade principles such as nondiscrimination, most-favored-nation treatment, and transparency with specialized annexes tailored to individual industries. The negotiators made progress toward ratifying the original U.S. objectives, even though the telecommunications annex had to be watered down to win the acquiescence of developing countries. (Even then, the goal of industrial countries was limited: they wanted to persuade a respectable cross-section of developing countries to become signatories and recognized that many developing countries would not sign the code.) This was acceptable to the proponents of an agreement because many of the deletions already had been handled in bilateral negotiations among the industrial countries (see Chapter 9). However, dealing with the frontiers of competition presented a problem. All the contradictions between the traditional pillars of the free-trade system and the logic of market-access systems moved to the forefront.

The service talks on telecommunications stalled over basic voice services. The United States, under fierce pressure from its carriers (particularly AT&T), declared that it would not permit foreign firms equal rights to compete in voice services. Equivalent problems arose in several other service sectors. AT&T feared that without this reservation the GATT code would allow foreign firms to establish their own long-distance networks in the United States without ensuring that American firms would have the same right elsewhere. Instead, USTR offered to undertake a subsequent plu-rilateral negotiation (building on exploratory talks between the United Kingdom and the United States) that would open its market for telephone services on a reciprocal basis. Other parties, led by the European Community, objected vehemently. They argued that the U.S. approach would undermine the most-favored-nation clause of

GATT (nondiscrimination and unconditional reciprocity) and that it violated the basic concept of equal treatment of foreign and local firms. Although a final GATT compromise would only come as part of a total trade package, the United States pressed to remove the worst irritants by unilateral regulatory action. In October 1992, it streamlined regulatory oversight of international services offered by U.S. subsidiaries of foreign telephone companies if their parent company grants U.S. firms equal treatment on settlement rates and other terms of service on their international routes. Presumably, this formula would satisfy the United Kingdom and other countries who were willing to meet U.S. demands for lower accounting rates, expedited resale of voice services, and nondiscrimination among carriers. Because the same rules would cover a U.S. carrier owning a foreign telephone company, it would not be discriminatory treatment against foreign firms.

In short, the GATT process worked best when it built on the groundwork of bilateral negotiations, even those that had yielded imperfect results. The GATT process was too cumbersome, and the constitutional requirements too unwieldy, to allow satisfactory crafting of hard, original solutions. This raises two questions: Are these weaknesses fatal to any attempt to govern this sector (the next section of this chapter examines three major alliance patterns), and how can the GATT process be modified to avoid these traps in the future? (The final three chapters of this book wrestle with possible answers to this question.)

THE NEW GLOBAL SERVICES MARKET

The liberalization of national markets for telecommunications services forced major telephone companies to reconsider how they develop and deliver services globally. It also opened the door to newcomers in the market. As customers demand more sophisticated global services, three main strategies for developing and delivering global services have emerged: global cooperation strategies, global overlay and portfolio strategies, and global carrier strategies. Each strategy requires globalization of leading carriers; all involve important alliances. Each alliance pattern implies a different form of competition in world markets.

Global cooperation strategies emphasize new forms of coordination among the major national telephone companies as a way to deliver new services in many countries at once. Such strategies also make it easier for customers to deal with a variety of telephone companies by making "one-stop shopping" possible. *Global overlay and portfolio strategies* are more eclectic. If the network of the future is, indeed, more fragmented, then different suppliers are likely to provide different services within the network. Firms that follow global overlay strategies often develop specialized capabilities by investing in new facilities and software that supplement and piggyback on the existing public network. Firms using an overlay strategy do not offer comprehensive communications services. Instead, they target selective functions and services over the network for delivery, if possible, on a global scale. Firms that adopt portfolio strategies attempt to acquire all or part of national telephone companies that are being privatized. Southwestern Bell and France Telecom bought 51 percent of common voting shares in Telemex for $458 million in 1990 and bought another 5 percent equity holding in 1991 for another $467 million. In an even larger deal a GTE-led group that includes AT&T, Telefonica, and two Venezuelan companies paid $1.885 billion for a 40 percent share of Telefonos de Venezuela.[35] Or they purchase licenses that become available for specialized franchises. For example, many U.S. telephone companies are rushing to buy cellular telephone licenses in Latin America, Europe, Eastern Europe, and the former Soviet Union. Overlay and portfolio strategies are closely related. Many firms enter ICAs to pursue both policies. The third main approach firms take is to follow *global carrier strategies*. A global carrier strategy involves the provision of comprehensive communications services under a single global management umbrella. This is similar to the way international airlines provide global service. They do not fly everywhere, but they try to offer, under their own management, route structures that cover the key international business destination.

Global Cooperation Strategies

Global cooperation strategies were the natural response of the well-established telephone companies to the introduction of competition at a global level. The established carriers recognized that they would lose market share to newcomers offering cheaper domestic and international long-distance service to business and the public. From 1986 to 1990 AT&T's share of outgoing international voice traffic from the United States fell from 94.3 percent to 78.4 percent, while the combined share of Sprint and MCI climbed from 5.6 percent to 21 percent during this period. Similarly, Mercury started with only 0.2 percent of outgoing British traffic in fiscal year 1986 to 1987 but captured 14 percent of the traffic four years later. In Japan, where international competition began later, the two new international competitors to KDD almost doubled their share of international business in single year, from 6.7 percent in fiscal year 1989 to 1990 to 12.0 percent a year later.[36]

The established carriers were particularly eager to maintain a large percentage of the fast-growing markets for new services. Alliances with other traditional carriers were a logical outcome. A prime example of a global cooperative approach was the effort by AT&T, KDD, and British Telecom to jointly offer global information movement and management (GIMM). This 1985 alliance was an early attempt to coordinate the service offerings of major national carriers for global customers. A typical GIMM package tried to coordinate the development of new services and the technical specifications for their delivery. In addition, without explicitly rigging the market, the cooperating companies tried to ensure that their prices were attractive and their price structures were harmonious. At the same time GIMM made an ambitious attempt to offer one-stop shopping for customers that would allow large international firms to order and link communications services from different countries and to receive a single unified bill for those services. If GIMM strategies worked successfully, the global customer could go to any of the national telephone companies and place an order for its needs in various countries. Coordinated service developments and cooperative pricing also should allow customers to select packages of services at affordable prices without extended negotiations. Obviously, customers would like the convenience of one-stop shopping. But what happens if offerings are à la carte or if each partner remains fairly rigid on its precise offerings on routing and terms of services? A crude analogy is the "kludge" in software programs (ad hoc fixes that are not well integrated into the main program): if there are too many kludges, the program slowly loses cost and performance advantages. The same is true for networking when customers are not free to optimize routing or buy the precise services they need. Customers may prefer to shop and bargain with each provider individually instead of relying on a telephone company as a middleman that has limited incentives to push for better prices or services. Apparently, telephone companies often resist working through middlemen.

A global cooperation strategy is a form of detente among the established telephone companies. There are striking parallels to the burst of arms control and political cooperation agreements that emerged between the United States and the Soviet Union after 1985. Although each side still was viewed as the main threat to the other, U.S.-Soviet agreements partly reflected an effort to reduce bilateral tensions so resources could be freed to deal with new competitors. Telephone companies have cooperated with each other for decades, and they all are experienced at being the dominant (and often the only) owner of facilities needed for offering services. Each one knows the political and regulatory loopholes and pitfalls in their own countries. Their top officials are members of what amounts to an international "old boys' club": they hold quite similar views of the world and their place in it. In short, these telephone companies hold mutual attraction for each other. They fear one another but also are driven by worries about the range of new competitors they face. Regional cooperation also is common. For example, in mid-1988 the telecommunications administrations of the five Nordic countries established the Scandinavian Telecommunications Service AB. This jointly owned company was designed to offer "flexible, tailor-made international telephone and data links to businesses in the Nordic area."[37]

Established firms also may use DCAs to enter new markets. For instance, in April 1992 IBM joined GTE, McCaw, Contel, and the cellular operations of six of the seven regional Bell operating companies (all except Bell South) to announce the formation of a new venture to provide wireless data transfer. One of the partners, Pactel Cellular, estimated that by the turn of the century wireless data transfer could account for 10 to 30 percent of their cellular revenue.[38]

Most prominently, each telephone company feared losing return traffic flows on international telephone calls. This seemingly esoteric issue was at the heart of the fabulous profitability of the international services business. As described earlier, national telephone carriers split the revenues from international calls based on an official accounting rate. The company in each pair that sends (and thus bills) more minutes than it receives pays the other company the settlement rate times the number more minutes it sent than it received. When the established national carriers face competition for international calls, as now occurs in the United States, the United Kingdom, and Japan, new problems arise. For instance, if AT&T sends 75 percent of all calls from the United States to France, it expects France Telecom to send 75 percent of its calls back to AT&T (with appropriate percentages to MCI and Sprint). If, for some reason, France Telecom wished to punish AT&T, it might send only 50 percent of its calls to AT&T and the rest to MCI and Sprint. The loss of return traffic flows would be costly for AT&T, which would find it difficult to retaliate in the absence of government intervention. If this occurred with British Telecom or KDD, AT&T might retaliate by sending more traffic to Mercury or one of the new Japanese international phone companies. Minimally, AT&T will lose some return traffic as alternate U.S. carriers establish their international networks. AT&T long held an advantage on international calls because it provided easier access to international calling cards, had more international operators, and provided international directory services. MCI and Sprint are beginning to close the service gap, and other long-distance resellers are entering the international business as well. Typically, when MCI or Sprint establishes direct telephone service with other countries, the contract includes some guarantee that the national telephone operator will return traffic in proportion to what it receives. Technically, France Telecom cannot demand better terms from AT&T for returning traffic to it, since the FCC forbids U.S. companies from acquiescing to such "whipsawing," but the rules are more ambiguous with regard to rapidly growing "private voice" networks. A conflict between AT&T and France Telecom might accelerate the tendency of France Telecom to switch discretionary traffic away from AT&T. Of course, every national telephone company also delivers services other than telephone services.

Although revenues from new services are dwarfed by telephone revenues, their market share will increase. No formal rules exist about dividing and sharing traffic on these new services, but all the established carriers see the benefits if the club cooperates to jointly develop these services and fend off interlopers. Thus, major carriers are trying to nurture return traffic flows and carefully enter the market to provide overseas services. Nonetheless, AT&T and MCI strongly support lower accounting and collection rates abroad because they fear they will lose major customers unless their major overseas partners reform significantly. Moreover, their bargaining position with their foreign partners is awkward as long as their partners are shielded by the old pricing system.

There are other constraints on countries that have allowed the most competition. AT&T has aggressively expanded its presence overseas. One crude but impressive measure of its international commitment is that at divestiture in 1984 AT&T had approximately 250 employees based overseas. By 1992 its overseas staff had expanded to approximately 25,000.[39] At the same time AT&T is hampered because, alone among major telephone companies, it also is a major provider of telecommunications network equipment. (Telefonica of Spain and Italcable of Italy are AT&T's main partners in the network equipment business in Europe; previous alliances with Olivetti and Philips were dissolved.) Its unique position makes AT&T reluctant to compete with potential customers to provide services, but other carriers worry about buying AT&T switches and giving AT&T, a potential international rival, important information about their service capacity. AT&T prefers to partner with others in providing services in the hope that this will generate good will for its equipment sales. In fact, AT&T has creatively used the settlements process to help finance equipment purchases by other countries. (AT&T can retain settlements due to other countries in lieu of payment for equipment.)

KDD's problem is that it is tiny compared to NTT (its major domestic counterpart). NTT also possesses formidable technological and financial resources as well as a strong, long-term interest in the global market. Under Japanese law NTT cannot easily provide international services, although unlike AT&T and British Telecom there are no restrictions on relations between its regulated and unregulated units. Moreover, although in 1990 plans were shelved to dismantle it, NTT faces ongoing threats of dissolution. NTT feels it must mute criticism that it is unwieldy but does not want to rock the regulatory boat too quickly. In this spirit, NTT established offices abroad and set up a separate data subsidiary. The sales of NTT International reached $100 million by 1989. In early 1992 NTT announced that it will set up a separate corporation for mobile communications with 1,800 employees and assets of 319 billion yen that eventually will have separate stock ownership. It is beginning to test international markets, frequently in partnership with foreign companies.[40]

British Telecom had another problem during the early years of competition. Its internal network was inadequate, so it had to invest to modernize at home to win a better standing with British authorities. Cable & Wireless had to build a domestic U.K. network for Mercury while relying heavily on the income generated by its Hong Kong base. To generate cash and prepare for the reversion of Hong Kong to China in 1997, Cable & Wireless sold 20 percent of Hong Kong Telephone to a Chinese company and joined AsiaSat, another ICA involving China, to provide satellite transmission capacity for domestic networks in several Asian countries. In short, although special problems hampered the international expansion of the major telephone companies in all three key countries where domestic telephone competition was permitted, a growing number of global cooperative deals were signed. However, no tight management integration of the services or pricing structures yet exists, which makes it difficult to make money from facilities that are subject to competition.

Global Overlay and Portfolio Strategies

A second range of strategies consists of global overlay and portfolio options. There are four basic niches:

- Firms may offer services, such as computer communications network services, that are relatively unregulated on a global basis.

- As countries offer franchises for new, specialized services, firms are becoming franchisers. In general, countries offer two or more licenses for most new services to promote at least limited competition. Foreign firms often are allowed to purchase these franchises and then invest in facilities needed to supplement the existing national network so the service can be provided.

- Firms may invest in supplementary transmission facilities on a global basis. In essence, investors develop underseas fiber optic cables or global satellite systems that compete with the established telephone companies to provide service. Motorola's Iridium is a new low-earth-orbit satellite, and as of March 1992 ten rival consortia wanted to build satellite systems that cover continents or the entire globe. Iridium would be operated as an ICA with national telephone companies as shareholders.[41] Regulatory policies are changing to accommodate entry of these private cable and satellite systems.

- Firms may buy part or all of national telephone companies as they are privatized and become available on the market.

Collectively, these global overlay and portfolio strategies raise a new problem for companies that must decide whether they want to create a portfolio of investments or to build an integrated global service network.

Entry into Unregulated Services on a Global Basis The first efforts to provide integrated global service were in the area of unregulated services, which are the descendants of value-added networks (VANs). The VANs—the earliest effort to create private international networks to serve the needs of advanced users of computers— were mainly American because the United States was the leading innovator in this field. Typically, a VAN leased circuits from national telephone companies and provided packet switching and advanced software programming for its clients' computer networks. VANs tried to establish nodes (or gateways) in cities that were central to their clients' operations. It was important to locate nodes close to the commercial operations of clients because charges for communications services are loaded on the "last mile" over the local network. As the distance between the node and the customer increases, the charge increases.

VANs provide a common point for customers to become providers and enter the market to offer communication services, often through alliances. First-generation VAN customers emerged in banking, airlines, and other sectors where there was a need to exchange large amounts of data. The advanced communications capabilities that these industries required led their industry associations to lobby for regulatory approval to establish specialized global networks to serve their industry. Together these VANs emerged as ICAs that operated in semiclosed markets. Second-generation networks emerged from customers when individual firms made networked applications available to third parties on a competitive basis. Sabre, the American Airlines reservation system, was just one example. In some cases, the purpose of these operations is to share costs (such as in Sears's provision of long distance and data services to third parties) as well as to improve the performance of their own company by being networked to suppliers and customers more closely (as is the case with electronic data interchange service). Typically, these VANs go "global" by incorporating regional partners. By contrast, third-generation systems integrators like EDS are building networks to assist their customers. These firms see communications as a form of product differentiation for their more general services of computer programming and information coordination for telephones. The communications function is not viewed primarily as a profit center; it also is a way to remove a bottleneck for customers and to provide a differentiated service product to demanding customers.

Global communications rules were not designed to accommodate VANs. VANs were exempted from established rules because ITU recommendations allowed alternatives to public telephone services when national telephone companies could not provide them. Local telephone companies have been racing since the early 1970s to establish their own VANs over public networks. Initially, the telephone companies hoped that providing the services would give them an excuse to deny regulatory permission to private VANs. But as the forces of competition won out politically, the telephone companies refocused on providing better services over the public network.

The old telephone company dream of a powerful public network displacing private services has lingered in two forms. France, Italy, Spain, and some other European countries argued that packet switching should remain a monopoly of the public network at least on an interim basis, but this monopoly will cease by the end of the decade. Other European countries already have abandoned this monopoly in favor of innovation of the public network, and AT&T and its competitors in the United States have championed virtual private networks. Using the new capabilities of central office switching, it is possible to provide circuits and services on demand for major customers. Virtual private networks privatize the public network by dedicating the resources of the public network to the specialized demands of private customers and by offering these customers customized pricing and service configurations. In the United States carriers were slow to provide virtual private networks to large customers, so many customers opted to bypass the carriers. Belatedly the carriers lured many of these customers back with virtual private networks. But most key customers still retain enough newly learned expertise to improve their bargaining leverage. They can credibly threaten at any time to bypass or threaten to bypass the carriers if they again become unreasonable. Many users retain control over selected network control functions. Providing virtual private networks on a global scale requires extensive coordination among national telephone companies. Some key questions regarding coordination center on who will provide the value added in this virtual private network and who will control the network nodes.

For all their efforts the traditional telephone companies found it was especially difficult to coordinate the introduction of advanced integrated networks across countries. One response was that European telephone companies innovatively opted to purchase U.S. VANs: British Telecom bought Tymnet; a group of European telephone companies plus NTT bought Infonet from the Computer Sciences Corporation; the Computer Sciences Corporation initially remained as a minority share owner and VAN operator, but ultimately MCI bought out its share.

It is illustrative to contrast Infonet's strategy with the purely cooperative cross-referral approach of GIMM-style ICAs. GIMM evolved too slowly. In contrast, Infonet provides a packet-switched network operating at a global level, which is jointly owned by its shareholders and is programmed with advanced computer services. However, Infonet was less successful in introducing a related venture for managed international data network services and other proposed common services because of the complexity of programming the network collectively and because the partners disagreed about commercial strategy. Customers were never able to get a single bill for services from the joint venture. Infonet lacks many of the capabilities of the originally discussed plans for managed data. While European carriers purchased U.S. networks, Japanese companies experimented with establishing their own networks and also with becoming partners in U.S. networks. For example, NEC worked to build a business partnership with GEIS, and both AT&T and IBM organized significant consortia with local partners in Japan to deliver VAN services. But cautious regulation in Japan still slowed the growth of all these networks, both purely domestic and alliances.

In 1991 British Telecom established Syncordia (based in Atlanta) to provide global network outsourcing services. To improve cohesion, British Telecom insisted on ultimate control. British Telecom tried but failed to bring France Telecom, the Deutsche Bundespost Telekom, and NTT into Syncordia. Instead, France Telecom and the Deutsche Bundespost Telekom formed Eunetcom, their own outsourcing operation. (Originally, British Telecom, the Bundespost, and NTT discussed establishing a supercarrier consortium called Pathfinder, ultimately renamed Syncordia, to offer managed voice and data network services.) Syncordia has recently won a contract to operate a significant portion of IBM Europe's network.[42]

Smaller carriers also are entering alliances. Unisource, unveiled in October 1991, is supposed to meld the international value-added business and international personnel of PTT Telecom Netherlands, Swedish Telecom, and Swiss PTT Telecom into a single firm. Unisource's announced intention is to offer pan-European private network services, with extensions worldwide. It will interconnect its networks with those of Sprint.[43] Similarly, second-tier U.S. long-distance and international carriers are looking to merge with each other or to find foreign partners. Telecolumbus, based in Switzerland, has agreed to buy up to 40 percent of IDB Communications, which owns World Communications, Inc.; Canada's Teleglobe also has a stake in IDB. Italy's STET is an equity partner in Orion Satellite Inc., France Telecom has a minor stake in TRT/FTC, and, although it backed away in late 1991, Italcable had agreed to take a 20 percent stake in LCI International.[44]

VANs open the door to global networks at least for selective communications services. In theory, a VAN could represent the partnership of many national telephone companies, but it is far from certain that telephone companies could cooperate on such a venture. For example, AT&T created the JENS network in Japan in partnership with Japanese trading houses and banks and then purchased the ISTEL network in the United Kingdom. AT&T could link these two subsidiaries together through its own U.S. network, but European telephone companies are worried about AT&T's ability to go it alone. Similarly, Tymnet, which is solely owned by British Telecom, is rapidly expanding the number of its nodes in Europe and elsewhere to try to provide one-stop shopping for its customers globally for VAN services. Tymnet also claims it will provide a single integrated global rate structure.

As producers and consumers experiment and learn about VANs, the introduction of new VANs with differentiated products is accelerating. The VANs are often built on alliances. Groups of major firms often use specialized industry VANs in the global market, as in the auto and airline markets. The broader political mandate for competition will also inevitably result in complicated infrastructures for VANs. Public networks in major countries have improved enough to permit customers to rely on them more than in the past, but customers also want assurances that public network operators will not use their control of the infrastructure to unfair advantage.

Licenses for Specialized Services A second approach to overlay and portfolio strategies is to purchase licenses for specialized services. Most commonly, firms purchase licenses to provide mobile telephone and data services, paging systems, or cable television systems.

For example, PacTel Cable, Southwestern Bell, and US West have interests in cable television in the United Kingdom: Bell South is involved in cable television in France, US West is in ventures in Sweden and Norway, and Southwestern Bell is involved in Israel. Most often countries offer two licenses: usually the public telephone company gets one license, and the other is put out to bid. (Many countries, however, do not permit their telephone company to own cable television systems.) These services are growing rapidly, and digital technology—which allows more service to be provided over the same amount of radio spectrum and radically reduces the cost of the equipment—will permit even faster expansion. Digital technology also permits these new services to be combined in new ways. One handset can now serve as a cellular telephone and a pocket pager. Wireless data networks capable of handling large data flows will emerge in the 1990s. Technology is increasing capacity so rapidly that overlay services as a group collectively soon will pose a challenge to the core monopolies of the public telephone network.

Significantly, many governments have started to license consortia of local and foreign companies. Motorola, Bell South, Bell Atlantic, and GTE each are part of Brazilian cellular consortia; AT&T and Ameritech are both part of a fifth consortia. Bell South has cellular operations in Mexico, Argentina, Uruguay, Venezuela, Chile, and New Zealand.[45] In a few cases the national telephone company is so suspect that countries are setting up new competitors for basic telephone services. Bell South is part of the Optus consortium, which bought Aussat and is now the second carrier in Australia, and Nynex now owns 10 percent of the new telephone provider in Thailand, where a backlog of orders exists for more than 2 million lines. Pacific Telesis owns a share of Mannesmann Mobilfunk, the second German cellular franchise, and US West owns a 10 percent share in Lyonnaise Communications, a major French venture. Numerous firms, led by US West, are rushing into Eastern Europe and the former Soviet Union. Foreign telephone company expertise is needed, particularly when the local telephone company faces viable competition. Inclusion of U.S. firms also allows host countries to claim reciprocal access to the U.S. market.

When digital radio ventures truly challenge regular telephone systems, public authorities have responded in an ad hoc manner. In some countries bidders for cellular telephone licenses were told to deemphasize price competition in their business plan. Authorities do not want cellular services priced so low that large numbers of customers abandon the public telephone network for plain old telephone service. So far public networks have assumed that mobile services will continue to be heavily dependent on the public network for switching, billing, and the completion of many local telephone calls. But new technologies may allow a significant share of mobile traffic to be fed directly through independent facilities that can bypass the public network. Germany has let its cellular competitor build its own fiber network to connect its radio cells. There are no absolutes, but the degree of reliance has crucial economic impact on the division of revenues.

Many companies have tried to assemble a portfolio of new franchise licenses, but this strategy has hidden snares. The value of any individual license that a company holds depends on the characteristics of the territory under license and on the extent to which that territory can be interconnected with other territories under licenses by the same company. In other words, the value of four licenses in California is greater if one firm owns all four licenses than if four different firms own one license apiece. Roaming plans that allow customers to travel are easier to establish when firms control more territories. The same is true internationally. Potential synergies exist among radio services in individual countries. If a company cannot easily interconnect with other attractive territories and their operating companies, the value of its individual license is lower. As a result a tardy, but fervent, pursuit of cellular standardization in Europe is underway so travelers can use the same instrument throughout Europe. Scandinavian countries were the early cellular leaders, in part because they all adopted the same standard. The United States overtook Europe because France, Germany, the United Kingdom, and other countries insisted on their own idiosyncratic standards that made it impossible to use the same mobile phone in different EC countries. (The same problem plagued the European television industry.) The European Commission probably will propose new rules for common numbering systems and for making it easier to share data bases. If this occurs, continentwide roaming will be made easier. Moreover, for a company to provide attractive price and service plans that encourage long-term use of the system, some management coordination of pricing and service strategy, such as GIMM strategies, is needed.

Another problem is that because countries issue only a few licenses in specialized markets, companies pay a premium for them. However, as the distinctions separating specialized market segments disappear, if new competitors can enter related markets, the value of the original licenses will decline. It is as notoriously difficult to identify future competitors as it is for governments to pick winners and losers. In the early 1980s, before the divestiture of AT&T, a client asked Kas Kalba, a leading telecommunications consultant, to evaluate the strengths and weaknesses of five telecommunications companies: AT&T, Exxon, IBM, ITT, and Xerox. The client assumed three or four of these would be significant telecommunications competitors during the 1980s. Ten years later only AT&T is a prominent telecommunications sector player.[46] The United Kingdom established elaborate distinctions between different forms of mobile voice systems, but these divisions have failed to work. In the United States "enhanced cellular" services are being discussed that presumably would create new opportunities to bypass official licensees just as enhanced data services made it possible for competition with the established public network. Moreover, new competitors may come from anywhere, including manufacturing sectors. In 1991 Daimler Benz bought 34 percent of Sogeti of France, the parent of Europe's largest software and systems integration firm.[47]

Global Transmission Facilities Adding overlay facilities to the equation further compounds the difficulty of valuing licenses. Overlay facilities are the joker in the deck of international cards. Governments now are authorizing groups other than major telephone companies to buy shares of new international transmission facilities, particularly in the so-called private transatlantic and transpacific fiber optic cables. For example, US West has applied for permission to build a trans-Siberian fiber cable, and Nynex announced in May 1992 plans to lay a submarine cable from the United Kingdom to Japan. Other newcomers have built satellite systems that compete with Intelsat. In 1992 they won agreement that all aspects of Intelsat's monopoly will end by the end of the decade. The age of services provided jointly by a monopoly of monopolies is over.

The significance of these new facilities cannot be overestimated. The new submarine cables provide new market entrants like Sprint with an opportunity to be first in line to reserve transmission capacity to carry international services. By partnering in new cables, Sprint acquired the massive additional capacity it needs and can buy capacity on more favorable financial terms. Moreover, the huge volume of new capacity increases everyone's incentive to discount prices and offer new services to fill the cable. Each time a new transoceanic cable is announced, critics suggest that there is not enough traffic to fill it. So far, however, every cable has been sold to capacity by the time it was ready to enter service.[48] At the same time, new satellites often are legally constrained not to carry certain types of services, particularly services that will be connected to the public switched network. But the provision of customized private networks is more than enough for most large, private customers to operate their internal networks. These new transmission facilities make it possible to connect national franchises in new ways and open ways to deliver global service packages by bypassing much of the traditional network. For example, new transoceanic fiber optic cables land near New York City, only a short hop from the national loop. Using the New York Teleport, British firms can serve British and other customers in New York without ever dealing with Nynex. Similarly, if universal telephone numbers emerge that assign a customer a single number that can be used anywhere, a company could link its employees within a global private cellular network that would tie together local cellular services and private fiber optic cables. AT&T is experimenting with individual global 700 numbers that could be kept for a lifetime. When the owner of the number dials a location into the network, incoming calls are forwarded to that number anywhere in the world. (This raises the question of whether the customer or the telephone company owns a telephone number; the answer to this question is likely to have profound public policy implications in the near future.)[49]

Buying National Telephone Companies A final wrinkle in the global portfolio strategy arises when foreign firms are allowed to buy part or all of national telephone companies. In every case to date the purchasers were ICAs, not single firms. All or part of the national telephone companies of Chile, Argentina, Venezuela, Mexico, New Zealand, and Gibraltar already have been sold. Numerous additional telephone companies could be put on the auction block. The national companies in Czechoslovakia and Hungary, the Netherlands and Portugal, Australia, Brazil, Malaysia and Singapore, Puerto Rico, and Uruguay all have been mentioned. Typically, offers do not provide for 100 percent foreign control. (The most dramatic case was New Zealand, which sold control of its telephone company to Ameritech and Bell Atlantic for more than $2 billion. As a result of the sale New Zealand raised enough money to pay off 10 percent of its national debt.) Significant local ownership remains, and the government still regulates the privatized firm's behavior. For enterprising firms, buying national telephone company purchases opens up a variety of possibilities for new forms of global networking. Only a few firms will acknowledge these opportunities, but the record is clear. In addition to an equipment deal with AT&T and an agreement to cooperate on technical and marketing studies and personnel exchanges with Bell Atlantic, Telefonica, the Spanish national telephone company, bought large shares of the Chilean, Venezuelan, and Argentine telephone companies, and after failing to win control of Telefonos de Mexico and the Puerto Rico Telephone Company, it bought Telefonica Larga Distancia de Puerto Rico (presumably as a hemispheric hub).[50] Telefonica proclaims no ambitions to be a global carrier, but its lineup of major franchises is impressive. Its record at home is less impressive. As one financial writer suggested, Telefonica "is most popular with investors and stock analysts who use its services least."[51] The master of this game is Cable & Wireless, the telephone company that tied together the colonies of the old British empire.[52]

Although the merits of each deal vary, in most cases the purchase of these national telecommunications carriers will improve local services. But one perverse incentive is their impact on trade liberalization. Foreign investors will not buy the carriers unless they are guaranteed more access to the national market, but their revenue plans depend heavily on passive profits from international traffic. Investors expect to stimulate international traffic to finance their heavy new investments in the network. (Most purchase agreements set minimum investment and performance targets.) Thus, some of the new owners became alarmed when the Uruguay Round service talks introduced the possibility of competition in international voice services.[53]

Global Carrier Strategies

The final new competitive strategy—efforts to become global carriers—follows from the purchase of national telephone companies. A few companies hope to provide services to their customers on a worldwide basis under a single management structure. Global carriers have no wish to operate exclusively through their own facilities or to market their services on a global basis. They will operate through a mix of local joint ventures and ICAs for common infrastructure to supplement their own network.

Global carriers function more like the operations of major accounting firms. Most accounting firms operate their own international offices and partnerships and also rely on local accounting firms, which serve as foreign affiliates. National regulations and the lack of business volume make it impractical to maintain offices everywhere, so accounting firms channel business to local affiliates that meet their standards of service, pricing, and customer cooperation. Such a strategy of affiliates alone would not produce a distinctive global client network. A core global organization to coordinate operations and to market and provide service also is needed.

In the telecommunications sector Cable & Wireless, British Telecom, PanAmSat, and perhaps Motorola are exploring global service strategies along these same lines. Cable & Wireless has the most explicit strategy. It controls major telephone companies in the United Kingdom and Hong Kong, has extensive fiber holding in the United States, and runs telecommunications in many former British colonies in the Caribbean and the Middle East. It also is a partner in AsiaSat and now is trying to expand into Russia, as well.[54] These national franchises provide the anchor for its global network. In general Cable & Wireless develops local facilities enough to allow local citizens and firms to connect with advanced international facilities that make it easy and affordable to call relatives or headquarters in the United Kingdom and the United

States. Profits flow from high volumes of traffic, not from high prices. The experience of Japan, where prices dropped dramatically after the introduction of competition, and of other countries suggest that the elasticity of demand for international communications services is high. Calling volume expands in proportion to falling collection rates. A global fiber network complements national franchises, which, in effect, gives Cable & Wireless and its partners first call on this nearly "global digital highway."

Where possible, Cable & Wireless prefers to own subsidiaries, but it also uses local partners in a new way. After Prime Minister Thatcher intervened on its behalf, it also took a minority position in International Digital Communications, one of the new Japanese international carriers. Local partners blend with global pricing and a service guidelines system established by Cable & Wireless. Cable & Wireless needs a firm footing in the United States and has a commercial relationship with Sprint. Because Cable & Wireless and Sprint both rely heavily on Northern Telecom switches, they can move beyond general international standards. Cable & Wireless also bid for FTCC, a long-distance carrier in the United States with revenues of $200 million per year. This company is not a Sprint rival, but it allows Cable & Wireless to directly connect to its key European customers located in the United States. This has led to important U.S.-U.K. negotiations on the terms of reciprocity. In 1992 Cable & Wireless sold 20 percent of its British operation Mercury to Stentor, the Canadian long-distance consortium, to raise investment capital.

Other firms are repeating the Cable & Wireless story. In 1989 British Telecom purchased slightly more than 20 percent of McCaw Communications, one of the two largest U.S. cellular telephone companies, for about $1.5 billion, but it never learned how to use McCaw to its advantage. AT&T bought out its holdings in 1992, thereby creating a base for its own global radio strategy.[55] British Telecom still also owns Tymnet, one of the largest VANs, Syncordia, and a group of smaller paging and air telephone service companies. It has announced plans to build another transatlantic fiber optic cable in partnership with MCI. British Telecom appears to be positioning itself to build on its U.S. cellular holdings to create a

Euro-U.S. private voice and data network. For example, British Telecom has pursued smaller companies owning fiber optic networks in major U.S. business centers. This effort reportedly was part of a $1 billion investment strategy to own switching and transmission facilities in twenty-two major cities around the globe, which would allow British Telecom to provide complete telecommunications services for its global customers by 2000.[56] From time to time rumors circulate that British Telecom also would like to buy Sprint. Sprint is the weakest of the three major U.S. long-distance carriers, but if it failed, it is unlikely that AT&T or MCI would be allowed to buy its all-digital network. It is unclear why AT&T should want to push Sprint out of business if that resulted in the sale of the network to a stronger national competitor or, if laws were changed, to let British Telecom or Bell Canada buy Sprint at 60 or 70 cents on the dollar. The new operator would be able to undercut the prices charged by AT&T and still be profitable.

Certainly, British Telecom joined Cable & Wireless in advocating reforms in U.S. rules that would allow British and other foreign carriers to own U.S. common carriers. Indeed, now that the British Telecom–Cable & Wireless legal duopoly essentially has ended, the United Kingdom is allowing foreign firms to enter the wide-open British market. Sprint already has announced that it will build its own national network in the United Kingdom. When the Major government largely abolished the duopoly of British Telecom and Mercury, a flurry of new companies sought market niches. But only two companies, Sprint and National Network (a private U.K. group of electric power companies), have so far announced plans to build their own networks. Sprint has announced plans to invest about $350 million to begin building its own British network; National Network plans to spend about $265 million on its network.[57]

Similar stories are emerging in satellite communications. Intelsat faces competitive satellite systems, which are authorized to provide voice and data services to private networks.[58] For example, PanAmSat, one of the key new entrants, provides the daily feed of programming from the BBC in England to its U.S. affiliates. Orion, the satellite venture that prompted the U.S. to support competition in the sky, has joined forces with British Aerospace. Another new venture will specialize in providing private data and voice services for the internal operations of the large global companies. Although these "private" services are not now interconnected to the public switched network, Intelsat has agreed to phase out these restrictions and allow them to interconnect to the public network. If this occurs, Intelsat and its competitors would be part of a market characterized by active competition. PanAmSat already has satellites that compete with Intelsat (but are not permitted to connect to the public network) for services to most of western Europe and Latin America. It now proposes to launch additional satellites to obtain global coverage that would not need to rely on local connections for many of its services.

Similarly, Motorola has proposed the Iridium satellite system for global cellular telephone service. Customers would carry dual-mode handsets that could connect with conventional cellular systems at home and with the Iridium system overseas.[59] Many skeptics doubt that a global cellular network is feasible at present because of differences in regional standards. However, as chip technology improves, telephones that are universal may contain more than one chip set. Another question likely to plague global cellular networks bedevils land lines: Where should the intelligence reside? Iridium plans to put most of the intelligence into satellite switching. Others plan to rely more on terrestrial and other parts of the system. Iridium has courted the national telephone companies, which fear that it will bypass them and cost them revenue, to convince them that they would be better off with Motorola as a partner. More generally, the launch of new global systems expands the options for global interconnection and increases the incentives for arbitrage for customers. It is likely that as new systems proliferate, there will be more conflicts among rival carriers over how to divide revenues.

Just as profoundly, the rise of new forms of global carriers implies a severe reshuffling of the rights and prerogatives of local carriers. Although countries still may limit competition in their local markets, it is getting more difficult to determine what constitutes the local market. National and international long-distance carriers have an incentive to bypass local service providers to serve their customers more directly, saving their customers money and reducing the technical complexity of their task. In Canada, for example,

Teleglobe, the international long-distance carrier, has lobbied for the right to establish service nodes closer to major Canadian cities than in the past. The nearer the node, the less Teleglobe has to rely on the local network. The same applies to switching services. Simultaneously, Bell Canada is threatening to do a deal with a U.S. company to bypass Teleglobe unless Teleglobe brings down its overseas rates sharply to attract international traffic from U.S. businesses.[60] ONA significantly unbundles switching services. Who should perform what part of the switching function? Germany, for example, reserves for the monopoly only real-time switching of plain voice services. But the growth of multimedia communication sessions will make this function less important in the future.

REFORMULATING THE RULES

The international communications services market always has been an industry of alliances, but the nature of those alliances has changed radically as the fundamental dimensions of competition and globalization shifted. For decades, national telephone companies were partners in a restricted international market arrangement: a monopoly served each country, and the monopolies shared services and some limited technical infrastructure together. Major technological challenges prompted some innovation, most notably creation of the Intelsat system to act as a single global provider of satellite communications services that were then resold by the national monopolies. But the satellite market was basically closed. Planners of the original system believed that entry costs were so high that only governments could afford them, so it made sense to sponsor a single integrated system. As the cost of launch services dropped, it became possible for private firms to enter this market.

These changes in the world market require reformulation of the rules governing the global market. The most significant sign of changing rules was the entry of trade authorities into the domain of communications regulators and monopolists. Until the late 1970s telecommunications equipment was not covered by GATT surveillance because it was a form of government procurement. Trade authorities also are examining how restrictions of the provision of communications services hurt would-be service suppliers and customers that need sophisticated service to operate globally. Uruguay Round negotiators tried to create specialized new trade codes to cover telecommunications and information services. And, after long ridiculing the notion of GATT intrusion, the ITU belatedly reformulated its rules to accommodate greater competition and agreed that greater coordination with the GATT was needed.[61] The ITU recognized it was getting so rigid it could lose its clients.[62] The ITU, in effect, argued that it should remain the primary vehicle for regulating global telecommunications markets but agreed that trade authorities might assume a role equivalent to national antitrust authorities. (European Commission's DG-IV, for example, claimed the right to review the decisions of member states with regard to telecommunications to ensure that minimum standards of competition are maintained.)

Dramatic policy reformulations also are evident at the regional level. For example, in 1992 the European Commission proposed a competition directive to end monopoly on inter-European long-distance telephone networks in the name of improving social cohesion and European networking, both of which were endorsed in the December 1991 Maastricht Treaty. If the Commission overcame stiff French resistance, additional orders might address access charges and grant new entrants permission to invest in infrastructure as necessary. The outcome would likely depend on whether proponents could build significant European industry pressure for the move and on whether a formula could be found that did not appear to make AT&T the big winner if the EC sanctioned the establishment of European telephone companies to handle long-distance voice and data traffic.

Although such a move to give the market more dynamic properties would be propitious, R&D policy is still adrift in Brussels. The commission continues to explore the possibility of focusing more on applications and on refining its own version of the Maastricht priorities. It is looking at R&D for rural telecommunications networking to help services spread to rural areas (in part to help rationalize European agriculture). It also is exploring the prospects of using telecommunications applications for other forms of networking, including the establishment of "smart highways."

How does the emerging international regime for telecommunications services conform with a market-access regime? Unlike automobiles and semiconductors, the market for telecommunications services is moving from a closed-market system to a significantly more open market. Although Intelsat remains the dominant provider of global satellite services, real competition in satellite services is on the way. Other traditional international services are being opened to competition, and new services markets such as computer networks were imperfectly open from the beginning. Moreover, the traditional framework of regulation for the global marketplace is eroding. At a minimum, there will be more in the way of shared global oligopoly, especially if national telephone companies create more common commercial instruments like Infonet that dominate global service markets. But it is more likely that a market-access regime will arise that combines open industrial policies and new forms of global carriers. This will require new ways to manage obligations for reciprocity under the GATT. In short, industrial policies will still apply to telecommunications services, but domestic and international services, as well as equipment markets, will be far more competitive than they were a decade ago.

The political economy of the fast-changing telecommunications services sector conforms quite well with the six new pillars of market-access regimes. A competitive model of industrial organization that is not dissimilar to the hybrid model described in the previous two chapters is replacing monopoly control as the dominant model for managing domestic and international telecommunications (pillar 1). The globalization of services and the internationalization of domestic policies, mainly emanating from the United States, the United Kingdom, and Japan, characterize the emerging telecommunications market. It is no longer possible to operate domestic telecommunications monopolies without considering the consequences of pricing and bypass for national development and international competitiveness (pillars 2 and 3). Although telecommunications has moved closer to the norm of other sectors, it still retains its special position and independent institutions that oversee its operation (pillar 4).

Trade and investment in international telecommunications services are more vibrant than ever before. Changes in accounting rates promise to bolster international voice and data traffic. At the same time, new competitive possibilities have boosted international investment in telecommunications infrastructure (pillar 5). All of this is happening because it is clear to countries that there has been an internationalization of the local loop. To be competitive in telecommunications and in other sectors in the future requires that information providers, carriers, and customers all be linked in extended regional and global networks (pillar 6). In essence, the new telecommunications services sector fits nicely within the realm of market-access regimes.

"Market access" is not a magic mantra that dispels all problems. The telecommunications negotiations expose the shortcomings of the current system for managing the world economy. Detailed, difficult bilateral negotiations will be needed to develop shared policy assumptions to fill in the gaps in any GATT agreement. Even if agreement emerges, it could quickly be made obsolete as a practical guide to policy. It will function adequately only if the market patterns implied by global cooperation alliances and overlay alliance strategies triumph. But the growth of complex portfolio strategies intermeshed with overlay network alliances may spur significant realization of the international carriers model, including complex alliances between integrated individual carriers (such as AT&T) and specialized alliance groups (such as in the JENS venture in Japan). If substantial competition in international voice and facilities networks becomes the norm, all parties may seek more nuanced international rules than those available though a GATT pact.

One solution may be to use the ITU to reach specialized regulatory agreements that do not require GATT approval. (The ITU recently adopted a new provision to allow "mutually consenting nations" to enter into specialized pacts for liberalization.) But the entire purpose of the GATT venture into services is to make sure that such venues as the ITU are held accountable to basic trade principles. "Cheating" on most-favored-nation obligations of the GATT via side deals in the ITU could provoke justifiable protests by developing countries. In the end, the world trade system is in trouble as long as the management of world trade and investment remains rigidly divided between multilateralism and bilateralism.

PART THREE

Recommendations

CHAPTER EIGHT

The Implications of Emerging Market-Access Regimes

Boundaries are eroding. The line separating U.S. and foreign models of industrial organization, domestic and international policies, goods and services, and trade and investment all are blurring. In the words of OECD Secretary-General Jean-Claude Paye, "The globalization of activities requires a rethinking of the rules which are needed. . . . In a growing number of domains the possibility of having effective action by the government no longer lies at the level of the state, but requires cooperation among governments and collective implementation by them."[1] Governments should expect that policies aimed at narrow, domestic sectors will spill over into other sectors and abroad. But this does not mean that governments will stop trying to create competitive advantage for their firms, to bolster employment, and to guide world commerce in directions they find desirable. World commerce and the roles of governments and global firms are changing, as are the implications of these changes for policymakers. Market-access pillars are being recast in terms of implementation.

What can and should be done? The floundering Uruguay Round negotiations, U.S.-Japanese bilateral efforts, the EC 1992 negotiations, and the U.S.-Canada Free Trade Agreement all present precedents for new possibilities. These cases might form the foundation of an efficient, equitable market-access regime. The principles, rules, and decision-making systems needed to make market-access systems function are influenced by the conduct of global firms and ICAs.

THE URUGUAY ROUND

In September 1986 GATT trade ministers meeting in Punta del Este, Uruguay, launched a new round of multilateral trade negotiations.[2] The Uruguay Round attempted to continue the process of liberalization and also to initiate major reforms in the GATT and the world trading system. The round was scheduled to conclude four years later. Within months, fifteen separate negotiating groups were established and negotiating plans were formulated for the round. Fourteen separate negotiating committees were set up under the Group for Negotiations on Goods. These committees focused on tariffs, nontariff measures, natural resource–based products, tropical products, agriculture, subsidies, safeguards, GATT articles, trade-related aspects of intellectual property, MTN agreements and arrangements, dispute settlements, the functioning of GATT, and trade-related investment measures. In addition, in the wake of a political compromise at Punta del Este, trade in services was addressed by a separate Group for Negotiations on Services.

U.S. Trade Representative Clayton Yeutter proposed and others agreed that GATT trade ministers should assemble in Montreal in December 1988 to conduct a midterm review. At Montreal preliminary agreement was reached "to liberalize tropical product markets, improve dispute settlement procedures, improve the functioning of GATT, settle the framework for a services agreement and to aim for a 30 per cent reduction in tariffs."[3] But the midterm review ended when U.S.-EC differences on agriculture could not be bridged, prompting Argentina to lead a boycott of all negotiating groups, not just agriculture. In April 1989 lower-level trade officials regrouped in Geneva and kept the round going by agreeing on negotiating objectives for agriculture and other unresolved issues such as intellectual property, textiles, and safeguards.

The round was first scheduled to close amid strenuous all-night negotiating sessions in Brussels in early December 1990. Nobody expected that all its objectives would be satisfied. If half the initial goals had been achieved and some progress was made in all or almost all negotiating committees, the round could have been called a success by politicians back home. Indeed, many participants including the United States saw the Uruguay Round more as a rule-making exercise than as a barrier-reducing effort. They wanted the round to begin a process of trade reform and never expected much more. Instead, Brussels was a replay of Montreal. The United States and the European Community deadlocked on agriculture when France and Germany refused to allow the European Community to agree to large, politically difficult, reductions in European agri-cultural subsidies. American negotiators were unwilling to uni-laterally disarm by reducing U.S. agricultural subsidies alone. When it became clear that no breakthrough was possible, Argentina led an angry group of countries out of the negotiations, unwilling to allow any progress in any other area without progress on agriculture. In important, controversial areas like services, no serious negotiations took place at Brussels.

Efforts to resuscitate the dying round were interrupted on January 16, 1991, when the United States–led assault on Iraq began. Neither the United States nor France, on the same side in this conflict, wanted to ignite a trade war while real war raged in the Persian Gulf. U.S. Trade Representative Carla Hills announced plans to begin a series of far-flung bilateral negotiations. President Bush announced bold plans to open trade negotiations with Mexico that ultimately led to the North American Free Trade Area. To force Congress to vote up or down on a GATT accord without amend-ments under "fast-track" legislation, President Bush needed to no-tify Congress no later than March 1, 1991, of his intention to submit an agreement by June 1, 1991. When it became evident that this deadline could not be met, the administration was forced to ask Congress for more time to conclude a GATT agreement. Senators Fritz Hollings (D.–S.C.) and Kent Conrad (D.–N.Dak.) introduced a motion to deny fast-track consideration to Uruguay Round agree-ments. The motion failed to win approval, and the Bush administra-tion received its extension, but senatorial dissatisfaction was shown when thirty-four senators agreed to cosponsor the motion.[4] This time U.S. fast-track negotiating authority is scheduled to run out in March 1993. President Clinton will decide whether or not to spend political capital to try to gain yet another extension. Unless a compromise is reached, the negotiations could collapse.

Throughout 1991 agriculture stalled the talks. The United States and many other countries were unwilling to accept a compromise agreement that excluded agriculture. Recognizing that his electoral mandate was deteriorating badly, President Mitterrand refused to budge. German Chancellor Kohl, who alone among world leaders may have had enough leverage to move France, was unwilling to push his beleaguered colleague into an agreement and was under pressure from his own farmers not to allow lower grain prices. In December 1991 trade ministers met once more in Geneva to prepare to conclude the round. They deadlocked once more, despite a strong push from GATT Director General Arthur Dunkel, who tabled an important compromise document (discussed in Chapter 9).

April 15, 1992, was selected as the next deadline for concluding the talks. That date came and went in part because in late March 1992 in elections for France's twenty-two regional councils the ruling French socialists suffered their worst defeat in twenty-three years. "They won just 18.3 percent of the vote, down from 36.4 percent in the 1988 parliamentary elections and 23.6 percent in the 1989 European Parliament elections." For similar reasons Chancellor Kohl was reluctant to discuss trade matters even at summits.[5] To justify its unwillingness to budge, in early 1992 the European Community began pushing "to link agriculture to services so it could blame the United States for seeking broad exemptions from free-trade rules for its telecommunications, banking, maritime and aviation industries."[6]

To try to salvage the round before the U.S. presidential election, in the spring of 1992 Europe hinted it might reform its internal farm program on agriculture but the United States was not satisfied. There was no deal at the economic summit of July 1992. During the 1992 U.S. presidential campaign the White House pressed for closure, but the closest it came was a tenuous agreement with the EC on agriculture. Despite business pressure for an agreement and although a successful end to the round could boost world trade by almost $200 billion a year within a decade, there is growing doubt that a deal can be negotiated before U.S. fast-track negotiating authority expires in March 1993.[7] Even if the U.S. negotiating authority is subsequently renewed, it will probably only be a short grace period which will not permit a major restructuring of the round.

In retrospect it seems clear that getting more than one hundred countries to agree on a package of compromises covering a wide range of complicated trade issues overloaded the negotiating mechanism. Incremental progress toward liberalization on a series of issues may be within reach, but creating a comprehensive new market-access regime to manage the world economy through multilateral negotiations is not. It therefore is likely that governments will need to find other ways to build multilateral agreement to form new market-access regimes. Globalizing bilateral and minilateral agreements between key players may prove a more promising approach.

THE CONSEQUENCES OF ALLIANCES

Many claim that the GATT is dead and that the Uruguay Round was its funeral. Others remain steadfast protectors of the multilateral free-trade faith. If the Uruguay Round does not achieve closure, the supporters will call for a new round to begin immediately. This book is our attempt to redefine the debate. Most of Parts 1 and 2 and the recommendations in Part 3 question the adequacy of the GATT approach, but our prescriptions are offered as ways to restructure the GATT, not to curtail it.

We share many of the assumptions of critics of the existing trade system—that the industrial organization models of the European Community and Japan are quite different from the U.S. model, that this requires a recasting of the rules for world commerce, and that the traditional principles that guided government oversight of global commerce in many sectors are no longer adequate. Even when unique economic characteristics of an industry do not require specialized guidelines, political realities may demand them. Moreover, multilateral negotiations are now so unwieldy that progress at resolving major problems grinds to a halt.

Nonetheless, we disagree with advocates of a mixed system for trade in which free trade and open markets are a "default option," employed when detailed rules for managing trade in an industry are absent.[8] Neither do we support modeling future world trade rules on the MultiFiber Agreement (which conducts global negotiations over import and export quotas for textiles) or on existing guidelines for air services (where governments supervise negotiations among airlines over reciprocal rights of entry, amount of services, and pricing for competition in world air markets).

These approaches were devised for a world without global industry when governments could still micromanage markets reasonably well. This world no longer exists. World trade arrangements change when either the globalization of firms changes in important ways or governments shift the conditions for opening of their markets to foreign competition. In recent years both changes have occurred, producing a competitive situation under which established regulatory solutions no longer suffice, nationally or globally.

Alliances, Globalization, and International Policy

Firms, including Japanese firms, are becoming more global in their production and sales, and TNCs from all countries are redefining the role of foreign subsidiaries. The experience of the U.S. automobile industry, for instance, shows that foreign subsidiaries are becoming sources of innovation for the global firm, not just the local theater of operations. As Chapter 3 demonstrated, staggering amounts of international production and sales are flowing through intracorporate sales of TNCs, as a percentage of world trade.

Firms are entering into numerous ICAs to develop knowledge, designs, standards, components, and products that are essential to their competitive success and are upgrading foreign marketing by customizing more products. This requires stronger subsidiaries (with their own research and design capabilities) or upgrading traditional joint ventures into strategic alliances.

The revolution goes beyond production and marketing to the consumption and intermediation sides of the market. The market revolution began when large, global users decided to change the rules of the game: customers became better organized and sought coordinated global changes in what suppliers provide. In this context, global alliances can be viewed as experiments aimed partly at reformulating the relationships between suppliers and customers. A good example comes from Japanese telecommunications, where all the new networks have major customers as shareholders. In the semiconductor industry, by contrast, an important consequence of the trade pacts was the proliferation of new ICAs linking U.S. producers and Japanese customers to redefine the bilateral market relationship. The new ICAs (and DCAs) also demand the creation of new links among partners. Thus, firms as diverse as Boeing and Ford are spending heavily on specialized global design and communications systems to tie together their corporate partners. Firms such as Benetton, which is primarily a name brand plus a specialized information network for coordinating small suppliers and a marketing system, are at the forefront of a revolution in the intermediation of production and consumption.

Thus ICAs are part of the experiment in how to manage fundamental changes in global competition. Many alliances will fail; most successes will eventually go out of business. ICAs are hard to create and sustain, but they are restructuring the fundamental competitive options open to firms everywhere. Sometimes they are strategic buyers, as when firms cooperate to develop common standards and act collectively to force them on suppliers. At other times they are strategic producers. At their most daring they permit firms to focus on the development of more tightly focused, specialized strengths and strategies while sharing risks and common resources with others. This results sometimes in complementary product development, as in Fujitsu chips designed for Sun workstations, sometimes in a common product, as in aircraft engines, and sometimes in limited product swapping and shared ownership of production facilities, as between Ford and Mazda.

As Chapter 6 noted, IBM, Toshiba, Motorola, and Apple are working to agree on shared resources and technical standards, some shared products, some product specialization (by market niches), and some product rivalry. This grouping could also have a larger set of secondary partners (e.g., Sony, Sharp, Time-Warner, and Bull). Whether or not this nexus emerges, it highlights how alliances have become a complement to intraindustry trade (specialized trading within an industry, as in exporting bumpers and importing steering wheels). As investment becomes a peer of trade and the Japanese model of long-standing ties to suppliers becomes more widespread, some investment equivalent to intraindustry trade is likely to emerge. Alliances facilitate a specialized sharing of the unique competitive resources of individual firms. Refocusing through alliances, then, gives firms new ways to specialize.

The policy implications of these alliances go beyond the important one of making firms more committed to the global market. They also change the incentives about the role of the public sector and protectionism.

Alliances open the way for a redefinition of what companies can do collectively and subvert desires for blanket protection. European alliances sponsored by the EC during the 1980s and 1990s were a European experiment to deal with globalization. Stagflation and the growing Japanese challenge were the triggers. Europe's key insight was its recognition that national policies alone could not support national firms. However, policies to support firms from multiple countries force national officials to explain why their taxpayers should subsidize citizens of other countries. In addition, established protectionist formats were too rigid. Thus, member governments somewhat reluctantly agreed to concentrate funding for Europe-wide projects with the European Community so that each country could pay its share of the bill. These programs encouraged private firms to work together in new ways and keep programs more oriented to commercial results.

Through alliances firms could alter the mix of public and private responsibilities. Previously, individual firms might not develop a new technology because they could not make money before others could replicate their efforts and break into their markets. As a result, governments had to fund projects to develop the technology or promise monopolies to firms that made breakthroughs. ICAs make it possible for private firms to pool know-how and costs instead of or in addition to public research.

Production and product development alliances also open up new options for dealing with risks. For example, until recently if Ford built a large new factory, the "salvage value" of the plant if the product failed was low. Alliances make it easier for firms to work together, sharing the risks by coinvesting. Global economies of scale are made possible without every firm needing a giant success in the market to justify the facility. Risk sharing allows firms to be less rigidly protectionist. They do not need as much government support to defend their giant specialized investments.

But the growth of ICAs does not mean that global dynamics have triumphed over local loyalties. DCAs, as pioneered by the Japanese, are as important as ICAs. One of the striking developments in the past decade is the renewed interest in the collective capabilities of U.S. industry by American firms. Advocates of domestic alliances argue that the domestic "supply base" is essential to the health of even global firms. Significantly, this was the position of both IBM and its midsized high-technology rivals. The preference for local partners has many sources—shared languages, similar corporate traditions, long-standing relations among local firms, and better opportunity to obtain government funding (it is more difficult to tax nationals to support foreign firms). DCAs often entail public-private partnerships; sometimes they occupy a quasi-policymaking role. The European Community has deliberately used various EC-wide partnerships to sift through much of its policy for high-technology industries.

In theory, DCAs are to some extent a substitute for international partnering. This was the case for Japan. But in the future DCAs and ICAs seem more likely to complement each other than to substitute for one another. Siemens is an anchor of electronics alliances for Europe, but its exchange of technology with IBM is far more profound than its European alliances. Similarly, nonmembers question whether the U.S. government should subsidize Sematech, because several of its key members are sometimes as involved in exchanging technology with Japanese firms as with their partners in Sematech. This frustration will become commonplace as governments and firms acknowledge that all firms need access to global technology (which requires ICAs) but can only gain this know-how on favorable terms if their domestic supply base is yielding technology vital to foreign firms. DCAs are vital for the domestic supply base.

The European experiments with EC-based alliances, the spreading Japanese production and trading networks in Asia, and the U.S. promotion of a free-trade area for North America and the

Americas suggest a final dimension to alliances. Firms have concluded that more significant parts of the business must move overseas. But they have vowed not to repeat the early mistake of American TNCs of outsourcing production indiscriminately. In an era of accelerated product development they plan to retain a core competence in production close to home in order to keep headquarters informed and a friendly supply base in place. Strength at home is the key to successful decentralization globally. But the home supply base has to be redefined on a broader regional basis in order to include less expensive labor and specialized complementary resources (Singapore and Mexico have lots of engineers with language skills not in Japanese and U.S. firms) with closer geographic proximity to headquarters. Many new alliances will emerge. (This is not simply a matter of moving low-grade production out; many of the activities will be quite sophisticated.) At the same time, this strategy improves market position regionally.[9]

The regionalization of the home supply base will accelerate the growth of more intricate regional trade and investment arrangements. Agreements in the Americas or Asia will not be as elaborate as in the EC. But regional supply bases provide ample incentives for specialized economic agreements. The trick for managing the world's economy is to ensure that these agreements also are open to third parties. As was argued earlier, regional arrangements are potentially good for foreign access because they open wider markets for local production subsidiaries.

Open Industrial Policies and World Commerce

The tensions between DCAs and ICAs are part of a deeper shift in the global role of governments and business toward open industrial policies. Free-trade critics rightly point out that other triad centers do not play by U.S. rules. The Japanese and European traditions favor more interventionist policies. This mattered less when the United States was the effective center of production and consumption. But although the United States remains the pivot of the world market, its relative power and influence has waned. Europe and Japan want to and will exercise greater influence. If this global power shift had occurred thirty years ago, its consequences might have been different: industrial policy was more closed then, and emphasis was placed on controlling and structuring competition among domestic firms and on market entry by foreign firms.

Consider the case of Europe. Industrial policy has changed, partly because the influence of organized labor has declined throughout Europe and partly because the costs of traditional industrial policies became prohibitive. For example, France liberalized its financial markets in the 1980s because it could no longer afford to subsidize the financial needs of French industries at costs acceptable to voters. Liberalization promised to raise new monies through stock offerings and to give the French middle class the same financial options as their counterparts in the United States or the United Kingdom.[10] At the same time, French firms insisted that they needed the scope of a single European market to be fully competitive.

Achievement of a single European market was made easier because its member countries agreed to accept less overt industrial policies. Countries like France could continue to assist their firms, but through new methods such as greater emphasis on harmonization of European assistance and integration of European technological assets through EC alliances. But the alliances themselves posed important questions about the relations between Europe and the world.

European governments have debated whether non-European firms should play a role in European alliances, and with some hesitation the Europeans have answered yes. Although Europe prefers Europe for Europeans, the European Community has found ways to declare U.S. firms to be European. Had it not, major European companies probably still would have sought American partners. Whether Japanese companies will gain similar standing depends on how Europe interprets Japanese government policies and how the United States responds if "Fortress Europe" excludes Japan. To date, the United States has played its hand cautiously.

As Part 1 discussed, Japan's closed industrial policy once made it effectively impossible for most non-Japanese firms to compete in sectors of the Japanese economy that MITI deemed strategic. (Some, like Detroit, failed because they also underestimated the market.) But Japanese government protection and assistance were only part of the picture. Japanese firms also introduced new approaches to design, production, and sales that resulted in perhaps the most important major breakthrough in the organization of firms since multidivision, multiproduct firms went transnational. Japanese policies gave their companies the latitude to experiment, and the innovations introduced by the firms revolutionized the market. Government ministries encouraged the formation of DCAs and fostered their success by encouraging members to deal with each other in good faith.

During the past twenty years a maturing Japanese economy has led the business constituency of the LDP government to resist many restrictive forms of market regulation. This internal discussion over how to restructure industrial policies to accommodate less government control over entry, pricing, and investment priorities became entangled with international commercial policy. Since 1970 Japan has been locked in a heated dialogue with the rest of the world over which Japanese policies need to change for Tokyo to meet its international economic obligations (see Chapter 9). The internal and external policy debates often were interlocked as foreign trade negotiations became intertwined with reform of domestic policies.

Japan remains committed to an administered market, but its control over that market is loosening. Just as significantly, a fundamental part of the new oversight tasks of the ever ambitious Japanese government ministries is the internationalization of the Japanese economy. The three case studies examined in Chapters 5, 6, and 7 clearly indicate that the Japanese government has accepted that foreign firms will play a larger role in Japan. The ministries are currently trying to blend the foreign firms into the administered market system. And Japanese firms are looking toward correcting national trade imbalances by exporting from their overseas subsidiaries back to Japan, as the discussion of automobiles showed.

The real question is whether Japan will accommodate a larger role for foreign firms on terms conducive to an open world economy. If openness is construed as traditional free trade, the answer is no. MITI is using international negotiations to increase foreign imports and investment in Japan as a tool to refurbish its administrative oversight over industry. The special trade pacts for automobiles and semiconductors are cases in point. However, this practice still may prove consistent with open industrial policies.

Any fundamental readjustment of policy provokes deep policy debates, and in Japan some officials and policy advisers seem to favor moving toward what might be called "cooperative mercantilism," a system not unlike the one that long prevailed for international telecommunications. Our case studies noted several trial balloons on behalf of cooperative market management schemes, including quiet Japanese proposals for capacity management for semiconductors and horizontal divisions of labor for automobiles in Asia.

Other countries treated these suggestions skeptically, and the failure of these initiatives highlights problems of cooperative mercantilism. These proposals contained several weaknesses. First, deals like the multifiber agreement are possible because of asymmetries in strength. They almost are take-it-or-leave-it bargains between strong and weak countries, although the developing countries finally were able to force an agreement in principle to eliminate them at the Uruguay Round. In contrast, in the past airline and other services agreements were, for the most part, handled as bargains among equals that depended on a political consensus among all major countries that the objective was to protect every country's home markets. When this presumption eroded, as it did in telecommunications and airline services, the viability of the international arrangements was compromised.[11]

Second, the trend, even in Japan, is away from micromanaging markets. Policy formation became much more complicated in areas like telecommunications and finance when conflicting claims arose from firms whose market segments once were neatly segregated but are no longer. Moreover, as firms globalized, they have grown more independent of government direction and more likely to form alliances with foreign partners. These changes are likely to proceed and deepen in Japan as long as trade and investment initiatives by foreign governments remain properly focused.

Third, firms have grown more skeptical about the ability of governments to make collective arrangements to manage global markets. Companies are reluctant to "bet the company" on government promises to oversee capacity, pricing, or entry. For example, in the absence of international policy consensus to safeguard arrangements against gray markets, understandings with governments can collapse. Quasi-legal gray markets—such as Asian "bucket shops," which conspire with airlines to discount tickets in contravention of airline agreements—are common in regulated industries. Similarly global market-sharing arrangements can easily be undermined by the international dissemination of technology, cross-entry of firms into related markets, and increased organization of global customers.[12]

Both free trade and cooperative market management fit current markets imperfectly. By switching to a market-access regime, however, it is possible to have an open world economy. Such a regime would tolerate extensive government intervention but acknowledge that international surveillance should be extended to many government practices once beyond the realm of trade negotiators. By accepting that industry-specific codes for world commerce are necessary, market-access regimes point the way to making such codes consistent with general principles of market competition and nondiscrimination against third parties. The process and ground rules for negotiations are important because theories about bargaining show how the design of the institutions and decision rules can shape outcomes. We advocate decentralizing many international negotiations for troublesome markets away from GATT but believe that these talks must adhere to new principles related to process, competition, and consequences for other parties affected by specialized agreements. Making parties to specialized industry pacts accountable to broader international principles should provide the participants with incentives to solve their problems through trade rules and alliances without fragmenting the world economy.

Even more fundamentally, globalization and alliances changed corporate preferences. In sophisticated, capital-intensive industries, many firms now favor contingent closure strategies. They favor keeping their markets open, unless others close their markets. Companies also prefer "pinpoint protectionism." American automobile makers and semiconductor producers, for example, sought relief that left their alliances intact: Chrysler wanted to get tough on Japan but not to cut off its reliance on Mitsubishi; the Semiconductor Industry Association wanted price protection and funding for industrywide alliances at home and market access in Japan, not deals cutting off its own alliances with Japanese firms.

Table 8.1 summarizes our observations about the causes and consequences of corporate alliances. Throughout this book we have stressed that corporate alliances arise for many reasons and take many forms. ICAs are a consequence of changes in the world economy, but they also are causing additional changes in the world economy and are raining down new policy challenges on officials everywhere because they change strategic options for firms and thereby confound the traditional lines of policy debate over liberal or protectionist policies for world markets.

ICAs and DCAs are forcing a reorganization of industry in the United States, Europe, and Japan. They also allow firms to reshape trade advantages even as they convince firms to support open markets and liberal policies. These alliances limit the range and effectiveness of traditional multilateral cooperative policies, allow foreign firms to penetrate national decision-making processes more effectively, and are pushing policymakers to innovate. By raising new possibilities that firms may be creating unfair competitive advantages, they are forcing governments to reexamine established trade practices such as antidumping policies and VRAs and to experiment with new approaches such as rules of origin and global and regional antitrust efforts to maintaining openness in a glob-alized economy.

In short, ICAs and DCAs have become visible vehicles of global policies for firms that need to act globally, even if they do not have the financial or managerial wherewithal to do so. They are logical corporate responses to changing global economic circumstances. Corporations have responded more rapidly than governments to the globalization of the world economy and the erosion of boundaries at many levels, and corporate alliances will affect government efforts to develop cooperative mechanisms for managing the world econ-omy. Corporate alliances have given new urgency to the challenge to governments to organize and manage global commerce in a post–Uruguay Round, post-Soviet era. Their global structure and their reliance on markets in Asia, Europe, and North America make it likely that they will reinforce the process of globalization and work to increase openness and fight protectionism.

Table 8.1
Ten Reasons for and Nine Consequences of Corporate Alliances

Ten Reasons Why Firms Choose to Enter DCAs and ICAs

Product development tasks:

1. ICAs are *management experiments* by private firms trying to cope with the new structure of international commerce and adjust to imperfections in highly competitive markets. ICAs are an intermediate step between contracting and ownership in a foreign country that lowers costs, boosts revenues, spreads risks, and provides access to needed specialized assets.

2. ICAs emphasize rapid, global product positioning to earn the margins needed to cover research costs. They are enhancing *economies of scale and scope* in manufacturing by combining global and regional production platforms to keep core production skills in each parent and meet additional regional capacity needs.

3. ICAs help share the cost of research and product development. ICAs *share the risks and speed the process* of developing, building, and bringing expensive new products to market. As flexible manufacturing systems proliferate, tighter relationships between component suppliers, manufacturers, and final systems assemblers are becoming common.

4. As key competitive assets in research, manufacturing, and marketing spread among countries, companies rely more on international operations to *secure complementary resources and focus their competitive strengths*.

5. ICAs provide for *common technical infrastructures*. Firms individually pursue international standardization and customizing of their technologies by partnering with other firms. Firms also are collaborating to promote collective standards for entire classes of products (often in rivalry with other groups of firms) internationally.

6. Firms are investing in *global networking advantages by creating specialized common capabilities*, as in global stock market trading systems.

7. ICAs may permit *common products* or even families of products for specialized segments of the businesses of a group of firms.

Improving market-access tasks:

8. ICAs promise *market access by making it easier to be treated as a local company*. Firms use ICAs to hurdle barriers to sales imposed by procurement codes. ICAs may qualify for government contracts from which foreign firms are excluded or they may be allowed to purchase local firms if they take on a national partner in the venture.

9. Partners in ICAs have *better information* about *and influence* over the home government policies of their member companies.

10. ICAs between producers and customers are a new way to *bridge gaps* that separate them by reducing bargaining costs and allowing faster mutual learning and feedback.

Table 8.1 (continued)

Nine Consequences of ICAs for Policymakers

1. In Europe, Japan, and the United States, ICAs and DCAs are facilitating a *reorganization of industry.* Easier restructuring allows adjustment to changes in global commercial advantages and potentially *reduces pressures for protectionism.*
2. DCAs and ICAs alter the preferences of firms by deepening globalization and the collective capacity of firms to respond to collective problems (such as R&D externalities). They also allow firms to share risks for certain types of specialized investments. In general, they *strengthen preferences for market access rather than protection and for pinpoint rather than general protectionist measures.*
3. ICAs alter the political benefits of industry assistance for governments. ICAs *increase the chance that benefits will "leak" to foreign partners,* not just national firms, and make alliance partners less willing to back exclusionary industrial promotion policies.
4. DCAs and ICAs may have *competitive and anticompetitive effects.* Alliances permit some firms to become newly effective competitors, but they may also block market access. In particular, alliances highlight the need for global antitrust rules and trade rules concerning market access.
5. ICAs raise important, hard-to-resolve new issues about nationality, such as rules of origin. They are a rapidly growing part of the world economy that is not beyond government control but is not easy to control efficiently by any individual government. They further *blur the lines between trade and investment rules in such a way as to force innovations in the rules* and politics that govern international commerce.
6. ICAs are part of a process of regionalizing the home supply base of firms even as they devolve more activities globally. This will produce pressure for *specialized regional economic arrangements to integrate the expanded supply base.*
7. ICAs provide a local partner of stature that can mobilize its own government to *penetrate the decision process.* ICAs have an easier time tapping local production assets for the purposes of providing local content. In addition, by providing links to third parties, ICAs may be able to influence the outcomes of bilateral negotiations.
8. ICAs *influence the range of policy options on market-access agreements for governments.* ICAs are devices major businesses can use to set private covenants that govern how foreign firms will be treated in national markets. Accordingly, they offer new possibilities for resolving questions about market access.
9. Globalization and ICAs are raising new questions about *government oversight.* For example, they propel the *internationalization of domestic regulations.*

IMPLICATIONS OF MARKET-ACCESS REGIMES FOR A MANAGEMENT APPROACH

Acknowledging the scope and depth of the changes transforming the world economy leads us to the problem of what can and should be done. In the aftermath of the Uruguay Round negotiations, how should policymakers manage the world economy? How can we implement market-access regimes? What structures are needed nationally and internationally?

Government Obligations

Governments have obligations to support the world economy. Architects of the postwar order believed all countries should be bound by mutually consistent obligations because if contracting parties are subject to different obligations, political contradictions are unavoidable. When countries demand special treatment, all obligations are called into question. It is easier to amend the system if everybody starts from the same place. The Uruguay Round negotiations emphasized government obligations to allow market access: countries should retain the flexibility to design their policies as long as they permit the contestability of their market. But if governments pursue policies that mix intervention with increased global market competition, then they have an obligation to be sensitive to the adjustment costs their own policies of adjustment impose on other countries. Even Japan now is considering acceptance of this position. This is a key theme of the writings of many Japanese economists who defend Japanese policies to enter world markets even as they note the adjustment costs imposed by these actions on established leaders: they note that Japan probably has some obligation to assist with correction of these costs.[13] Today, the Japanese government is committed to limited promotion of adjustment in the world economy.[14] There are signs that Tokyo no longer sees protectionism that minimizes imports as essential to future Japanese economic success.[15] Adjustment is proactive (move Japan toward a high-technology industrial base), not just reactive (reduce the size of the steel industry).

Adjustment obligations do not stop at Japan's doorstep. The United States has obligations of its own. It cannot continue to rely on trade policy to fix its economic woes. A market-access regime requires innovations to ensure effective contestability of foreign markets and national measures to help firms compete when necessary. International obligations and national measures can be reconciled only if U.S. political leaders are more honest with voters. They need to acknowledge that the U.S. trade deficit is linked to the low rate of national savings and the U.S. budget deficit and act accordingly. More incentives for capital investment and greater investments in the skills of the labor force are also necessary if the United States is to respond effectively to global competition.

For reasons enumerated in Chapter 2, decision makers traditionally favored multilateral negotiations, but new economic and political conditions may push governments to oversee some industries differently. Thus, although economists usually argue that specialized trade agreements undermine multilateralism, recent studies suggest that under some circumstances they may reinforce the multilateral order.[16] If so, government officials might usefully study other institutions for clues about when to centralize and decentralize decision making. The key question for policymakers is whether governments should extend the mandates of global institutions or decentralize oversight of global markets.

Simple but Comprehensive Rules

Two axioms run counter to the trends toward globalization and complexity: governments can do only a few things well at any one time; and it is easier to solve narrow, sharply focused problems than sweeping ones. As boundaries blur, what should governments do? Governments need a few clear anchors. Efforts to micromanage markets have little chance to succeed except in the context of flexible, specialized instruments that are tied to the structure of multilateral governance. Even specialized rules should not be too detailed. Industry codes and other specialized subagreements should build a cohesive body of precedent for particular industries, not generate mountains of rule books.

Multilateralizing Minilateral Problems

Persuading more than one hundred countries to agree on anything is time consuming and labor intensive at best and often is impossible.

The extended Uruguay Round negotiations are just the latest example. As issues get complicated, negotiating problems increase.[17] Instead of complaining about the damage to multilateralism that minilateral negotiations might cause, governments should change their approach. If top-down multilateral negotiations usually lead to no more than marginal progress, perhaps bottom-up negotiations will work better. The goal, after all, is to improve all countries' situation, regardless of the path that is taken.

Some Sovereignty over Domestic Regulations Lost

Sovereignty and nationalism are heady concepts, but the globalization of firms and markets has proceeded so far that there is no returning to the old system. International developments affect national regulations and policies. Unless governments adapt to this reality, they will undermine their competitive positions. The European example is encouraging, but it suggests that more industry-specific agreements are likely. Even when there are no explicit rules, European states operate on the basis of mutual recognition of national regulations (what passes inspection in Germany is accepted automatically in France). This keeps international rules simple. But mutual recognition works best if minimum standards for national rules are implicitly or explicitly harmonized because then a country that agrees to mutual recognition can count on minimum acceptable results. The fears of some GATT critics that the Uruguay Round will destroy the integrity of U.S. health and safety standards illustrates the political challenge of making domestic rules subject to international review. It must be made clear that countries have a right to regulate, but an obligation to do so in a way that is fair to foreign firms.[18]

Continually Evolving Principles

The world economy changes rapidly, firms adapt more slowly, and governments are the laggards. To keep pace governments will need to establish and rely on a few, strong central principles mainly related to equity (such as trade diversion) and procedure that are flexible and continually evolving. Redesigning the rules that govern the international system is the crucial task facing governments (even more important than their precise substance). There are two components to this task. First, the sharing of tasks among international institutions needs to be restructured. This already is occurring. For instance, the GATT is poaching on the service industry territory of other institutions but may have to cede control in such areas as the environment and tax policies. Second, when a few simple, stable rules will not suffice, countries need to articulate, negotiate, and implement new disciplines and defend precedents created by ad hoc

Table 8.2
Pillars for Managing the World Economy

Pillars of the Free-Trade Regime	Pillar of the Market-Access Regime	Policy Instruments
Governance		
1 U.S. model of industrial organization	Hybrid model of industrial organization	More reliance on bilateral and plurilateral negotiating forums
2 Separate systems of governance	Internationalization of domestic policies	Transparency, specialized rights of appeal, and self-binding behavior
3 Goods traded and services produced and consumed domestically	Globalization of services; eroding boundaries between goods and services	National treatment and tiered reciprocity for services
4 Universal rules are norm	Sector-specific codes are common	Reforms of VRAs, antidumping, and subsidy codes
Rules		
5 Free movement of goods; investment conditional	Investment as integrated coequal with trade	Rules of origin and new investment rules to ensure market-access, global antitrust
6 National comparative advantage	Regional and global advantage	Fair trade rules for procurement, standards, and R&D

trade initiatives. In short, the purpose of general agreements on trade is to frame more specific ones. Experimentation is the order of the day. The semiconductor agreements contained one bad idea (price floors), one interesting idea (a market opening target for Japan), and one excellent idea (new procedures for prompt correction of dumping violations). Procedurally, they had one terrible feature (the secret side letter) and one terrific feature (attention to the interests of European parties). (See Chapters 7 and 9.) This mix is probably normal. The challenge is to find ways to generate incentives to rectify mistaken ideas and procedures while allowing the interesting and unproven ones time to show their merits. To help readers navigate the final two chapters and integrate our policy suggestions into the overall argument of the book, Table 8.2 presents a summary of our world economy policy recommendations.

CHAPTER

Restructuring the World Economy

To implement the four pillars that define the structure and governance of market-access systems, governments can negotiate new international economic accords and more broadly ensure widespread international commercial cooperation. Although the U.S.-Japan-Europe triad is at the core of the analysis in this chapter, the strategies examined here also could help reintegrate the developing countries, the states that formerly comprised the Soviet Union, and Eastern Europe into the global economy.

The first four new pillars—the hybrid model of industrial organization, the internationalization of domestic policies, the globalization of services coupled with the erosion of the line between goods and services, and the proliferation of sector-specific codes—address the structure of market-access systems. Governments can begin to recast the governance of international commerce by establishing and reinforcing these four new pillars.

IMPLEMENTING PILLAR 1: MORE BILATERAL, PLURILATERAL, AND REGIONAL BARGAINS

As hybrid models of industrial organization emerge in place of the long-dominant U.S. model of industrial organization, defenders of an integrated world economy claim that bilateral trade negotiations are counterproductive and indicate the decline of the will to cooperate globally. They are cautious about regional arrangements and minilateral negotiations.[1] We argue, however, that the new hybrid models of industrial organization require new ways of organizing bargaining. According to Sylvia Ostry, the former Canadian Ambassador for Multilateral Trade Negotiations, "a trend to bilateral or regional blocs and to more unilateral behavior by powerful trading countries is likely to accelerate should the Uruguay Round of the GATT fail to deliver an acceptable package."[2] We expect governments to rely far more on bilateral, plurilateral, and regional bargaining in the future even if the Uruguay Round ultimately achieves an acceptable outcome. This can be a positive development as long as governments make diligent efforts to multilateralize these agreements so that broad coverage is achieved in a bottom-up instead of top-down manner.[3]

Indeed, if multilateral talks prove inappropriate for solving new problems, they actually may increase the risk of trade wars. The spread of decentralized negotiations may, in fact, advance global integration better than centralized, multilateral negotiations. Bilateral negotiations involving service sectors were traditionally organized around multilateral principles; however, those principles traditionally supported restrictions on competition.[4] But new problems are raised when governments opt for minilateral bargaining. Policymakers need multilateral guidelines to facilitate bilateral, plurilateral, or regional negotiations where much of the problem solving will occur. Then policymakers will have to worry about how to implement their decisions in a globalized world of market-access regimes. Finally, they will need to find ways to ensure that the results of decentralized negotiations are extended to all countries. A major problem of the current system is that it drives bilateral and minilateral negotiations into the twilight zone of trade relations, thus leading to the creation of such undesirable devices as VRAs.

From Multilateralism to Minilateralism

Management experts recognized long ago that markets work better than hierarchical control because central decision makers cannot know all the preferences and information available to market participants. Centralized authority is more efficient only when decentralized bargaining is plagued by hard-to-resolve collective dilemmas and decisions. For example, under a free-trade system there are perfectly rational reasons for countries to cheat. To discourage cheating, countries set up global institutions with the authority to create rules, police them, settle disputes among members, and provide remedies to injured parties. Indeed, to work smoothly most markets require transparency of information, the ability to enforce contracts, and the availability of numerous buyers and sellers.

When firms opt for central management, wise executives still allow decentralized decision making for certain issues. Airline managements could set schedules for airline flight attendants by fiat, but it is more efficient to allow flight attendants to use a bidding system that lets them compete for preferred flights. Attendants know their own strengths, weaknesses, and stress levels and have information about their availability. All management needs is for all flights to be adequately staffed.[5] Similarly, most international sourcing and distribution of high-technology products still take place through licenses and conventional arm's-length sales contracts because this approach is cheaper than performing these tasks within the corporation or through an ICA.

Likewise, many ambiguous but important responsibilities for "fair trade," such as setting reasonable standards, are essentially good-faith obligations that demand bargaining among nations, not resolution by a binding GATT text. The GATT recognizes this point but always has had trouble acting effectively on it. A GATT Working Party in 1954 and 1955 stated that "reasonable expectations" were the key to deciding whether a domestic subsidy is a violation of the GATT.[6] In 1991, Karel van Wolferen, an author frequently critical of Japan, suggested that if GATT Article XXIII is ineffectual in its task of increasing the liberal exchange of economic opportunities, "a search must begin for a substitute: a new set of multilateral safeguards that will protect economies steered by economic rather than political purposes."[7] Any effort to resolve these issues simply by having everyone turn first to a binding GATT machinery for dispute resolution is likely to overload the system. Although it was appropriate to try to strengthen binding dispute resolution, it made little sense to reject bilateral and plurilateral alternatives. The real goal should be to make agreements reached under bilateral and plurilateral bargaining subject to scrutiny by third parties that believe that they suffered injury. Bilateralism and plurilateralism allow countries to set up specialized enforcement and monitoring institutions in support of international commercial agreements. They also create specialized procedures that can expedite consideration of difficult problems, particularly when those issues involve complex calculations (e.g., fair market value) or multifaceted problems that are not easily worked out by traditional dispute resolution means. As the U.S.-Japanese agreements make clear, these tasks are at the core of many agreements.

Bilateral economic treaties have a long history and need not violate the spirit of multilateralism. More than two hundred years ago the newly independent United States entered into a series of bilateral treaties of friendship, commerce, and navigation with its principal trading partners. Much of the unfinished initial business of the ITO was consigned to such treaties in the 1950s, including obligations related to the treatment of foreign nationals in domestic commerce and law, and in the early 1980s the United States negotiated bilateral investment treaties with a number of smaller countries. The United States–Israel comprehensive free trade agreement signed in April 1985 was even more ambitious. These efforts set the stage for the United States and Canada, the largest bilateral trading partners, to pursue a comprehensive free-trade agreement. President Reagan and Prime Minister Mulroney signed the U.S.-Canadian Free Trade Agreement on January 2, 1988, and it was ratified by the U.S. Congress and the Canadian Parliament.[8]

Lessons from U.S.-Japanese Bilateral Negotiations

Like many treaties of friendship, commerce, and navigation, the 1953 agreement between the United States and Japan provided for consultation and dispute resolution. Unless both countries agreed on some other forum such as the GATT, the treaty obligated both signatories to submit disputes to the International Court of Justice. The 1953 U.S.-Japan agreement also allowed the signatories to designate a bilateral arbitration or quasi-judicial forum to resolve disputes.

Significantly, bilateral negotiations do not automatically signal the decline of the multilateral process or of the United States. Quite the contrary, at the height of U.S. power and commitment to the GATT multilateral process, Japanese violations of GATT codes were not contested by the United States through the invocation of GATT processes. Instead, to shield Japan from broader diplomatic pressure and to get better results, the United States agreed to bilateral talks. Although Japan was subject to many reservations by other countries concerning its accession to the GATT in 1955, the United States was committed to making Japan a full-fledged member of the GATT.

The United States and Japan slowly became experienced at negotiating ground rules for economic competition in a bilateral context. Inevitably, these discussions often interfered with Japanese domestic affairs because Japan's model of industrial organization conflicted with the model implicit in the GATT regime. Indeed, the real issue underlying the long series of U.S.-Japanese discussions and negotiations was to find ways to adapt the Japanese model to the prevailing multilateral order. Except for the opening wrangles over textiles, the first significant negotiations concerned foreign investment.[9] They show how bilateral agreements can serve multilateral goals.

Investment disputes are best understood in the context of Japan's model of industrial organization. After World War II the United States crafted the Foreign Exchange and Foreign Trade Control Law of 1949 and the Foreign Investment Law of 1950 to speed Japanese recovery. These laws established many of Japan's restrictive policies. Under these acts "protectionism was accomplished by presumptively restricting all foreign exchange and foreign trade transactions [including investment]. . . . A release had to be obtained from one of the 'competent' ministries."[10]

The United States began serious bilateral negotiations to open the Japanese market only after Japan's slow implementation of its commitments under the OECD Capital Liberalization Code that it signed in 1964. The vigor of U.S. bilateral representations was consistent with global multilateralism because the OECD Capital Liberalization Code was the controlling international agreement and the OECD committee charged with oversight severely criticized Japan. This initial campaign to win Japanese compliance was ineffective because the Japanese model of industrial organization stressed ongoing informal consultation and administrative ordinances to guide markets. Japan retained numerous discretionary controls over foreign investment, including controls over technology licensing that were supposed to prevent antitrust violations.[11] These measures made it hard for foreign firms to compete even after they were allowed entry. Moreover, the negotiations never determined whether foreign investors had the right to buy local firms.

In the late 1970s the United States sought major revisions of the highly protectionist Japanese investment legislation dating from 1949 and 1950, and the Japanese Diet passed new legislation. The presumption of Japanese law shifted from a "prohibitive negative principle to a positive principle which would permit a transaction unless it was specifically prohibited."[12] The new law made it easier for outsiders to identify opportunities, but, ominously, most implementation was left to administrative guidance provided by the Ministry of Finance and MITI and was not subject to public review.

An examination of the U.S.-Japanese discussions on telecommunications services and semiconductors show how bilateral talks are redefining trade rules, including procurement rules, that relate to the Japanese model of industrial organization. In 1979, Japan agreed to extend the GATT Procurement Code to cover Nippon Telegraph and Telephone (NTT), the Japanese government monopoly for domestic telecommunications. NTT was the only public telecommunication authority that became a signatory to the Procurement Code negotiated during the Tokyo Round of GATT talks; it did so only because the United States brought massive pressure to bear on Japan. For decades NTT was at the heart of Japanese industrial policy for electronics. When Japan agreed to make NTT a signatory, the United States, in effect, won acceptance of a new, fundamental principle that obligations under government procurement codes should not exempt any sector that is central to competitive success in key free-trade markets.

U.S. and European firms (such as Siecor, a joint venture that links Siemens and Corning for fiber optics) still complained that they could not bid for NTT contracts because they could not obtain written specifications. After months of negotiations, NTT agreed to document specifications, marginally eroding the advantages enjoyed by NTT's family of long-term suppliers, which benefited from the Japanese system of industrial organization. The next hurdle, foreign companies quickly learned, was NTT's demand that foreign products meet its precise design specifications, which meshed exactly with what NTT local suppliers produced. The United States therefore began negotiations to convince Japan to adhere to GATT Procurement Code principles that specifications should be based on performance standards, not on design or appearance.

After Japan announced that it would partially privatize NTT on April 1, 1985, U.S. firms worried that Japan would claim that as a private company it was no longer obligated to adhere to the Procurement Code. (The European Community also faced a dilemma when deciding how to determine coverage under the GATT Procurement Code. Private entities, such as the Dutch telephone company, retain special licenses that grant them quasi-monopolistic powers, yet they are so important in key markets that the European Commission decided to include them. Indeed, had they not been included, the public utilities would have protested bitterly.) U.S. negotiators pressed Japan to acknowledge that the newly privatized NTT was still a quasi-official agency and would continue to abide by government procurement codes. However, subsequent negotiations permitted NTT to continue its policy of inviting firms to enter into long-term developmental projects designed to produce products that met NTT performance goals. The only condition was that the process would be opened to foreign firms in the future.

U.S.-Japanese telecommunications talks also focused attention on the legitimacy of imposing standards to foster interconnectable technologies if this process, by requiring uniform design standards instead of equivalent performance, also creates hidden trade barriers. To counter this possibility U.S. providers of telecommunications equipment and specialized services such as computer networks proposed a standard of "no harm to the network." This put trade negotiators into the business of setting technical standards, a messy albeit necessary exercise. Until the late 1980s the U.S. government continued to lobby Japan for a no-harm standard on behalf of IBM's computer network services. At the same time IBM was working with Mitsubishi to provide computer network services in Japan.

The implicit principle that emerged was that standards issued by accepted standard-setting organizations are legitimate; standards also are legitimate if they command a significant base of user support in the global market and do not unduly interfere with officially set standards. The more general lesson is that governments should take advantage of the explosion of standard-setting alliances among firms. If firms can point to a substantial ICA that actively supports a standard, this should constitute important presumptive evidence of a global market position that normally ought to be accommodated by national standards. This is precisely how ICAs can help to resolve complicated regulatory questions.

Bilateral trade agreements covering specific sectors such as steel, automobiles, and televisions also have proliferated since the late 1970s. The first major accord was the Strauss-Uchiba accords in 1977, which set up an orderly marketing arrangement to limit Japanese television exports to the United States. In 1981 Japan imposed VRAs on automobile exports to the United States. One idea, first advocated by the European Community in the early 1980s, was to set a general import target for Japan. In 1984 the U.S. Department of Commerce and the U.S. Trade Representative endorsed this approach, but it made no further headway after being branded as anti–free trade by most other U.S. government agencies. As one set of sectoral talks followed another, pressure increased to reformulate the U.S.-Japanese commercial framework under a broader organizing rubric. Both sides were forced into more comprehensive bargaining strategies involving all key government agencies. The U.S. Treasury succeeded in having its talks on the liberalization of Japanese financial markets become the model for future negotiations.[13] The Market-Oriented Sector-Specific (MOSS) talks systematically examined all governmental and nongovernmental barriers to market access in four sectors: telecommunications equipment, electronics, forest products, and medical equipment and pharmaceuticals. These were "good cases" that were prone to produce "good case law" because they all involved industries where U.S. firms had substantial competitive advantages. If intense exploration of these firms' problems could yield new principles of conduct, the relationship was likelier to prosper.

The MOSS talks gave way to the Structural Impediments Initiative (SII), which allowed each government to make suggestions about fundamental reforms that the other should implement to remedy the bilateral trade imbalance. While the MOSS framework is far more tractable for most trade talks, the SII was constructive because it addressed the entire relationship, particularly the linkage between Japanese policies that favored savings and private production over consumption and public investment. Increased public investment in infrastructure and more proconsumer policies would lower net national savings and thus lower the Japanese balance-of-payments surplus.[14] The first halting efforts under the SII to sort out what features of the keiretsu system were consistent with multilateralism began by identifying and adjusting the features of the evolving Japanese model of industrial organization. Unfortunately, the SII also gave the United States an excuse to postpone adjustments in its own economic policies. For example, in 1990 the U.S. pledge in SII meetings to slash its budget deficit, boost savings, and strengthen education was mainly window dressing for concessions demanded of Japan. It allowed the United States to sidestep needed macroeconomic policy actions. The entire negotiation also raised the awkward issue of linkages between trade concessions and macroeconomic policies. When the 1992 talks commenced, Japan chided the United States on its desultory performance but tactfully avoided a demand for U.S. fiscal discipline in return for new Japanese trade concessions on the industries in question (automobiles, automobile parts, paper electronics, and glass). The United States reciprocated by downplaying demands for Japan to accept specific import targets in key markets.

One criticism of bilateralism stresses that it is a seductive alternative to multilateralism because it is advantageous to participants and excludes nonparticipants. Bilateralism is dangerous because each market must be pried open individually, increasing the likelihood that cartels will dominate key markets or liberalization to third parties will slow. The U.S.-Japanese semiconductor negotiations often are cited as an example of dangerous bilateralism even though, as Chapter 6 argued, they were reasonably successful exercises.

In fact, as indicated in Chapter 6, the semiconductor negotiations demonstrated why bilateralism may under some circumstances be superior to multilateralism when tackling issues raised by new models of industrial organization. At the heart of the semiconductor accord was the determination of a fair price for semiconductors, an exceedingly difficult task. U.S. legal, regulatory and administrative practices are so detailed and opaque that it is hard to conceive of successfully reaching consensus on questions of cost and price in the context of multilateral negotiations.[15]

The semiconductor negotiations also indicate that bilateral negotiations do not necessarily result in the formation of cartels. If firms have no choice but to globalize their operations, then it is unlikely that special bilateral advantages will yield large payoffs. This is particularly true if bilateral strategies are incompatible with global operations. Furthermore, if products created under a U.S.–Japanese bilateral agreement cannot easily gain entry into Europe, then global production strategies of firms are likely to suffer.

This raises an important paradox. Often decisions involving precise trade and investment rules result in the best outcomes when they are customized through regional trade pacts or ad hoc corporate-government consultations. But in order to decentralize decisions about substance, policymakers require a more centralized framework for property rights and surveillance. This paradox can be handled. Thus, to make certain that the U.S.–Japan semiconductor agreement complied with GATT rules related to most-favored-nation treatment and nondiscrimination, Japan agreed to grant all foreign producers of semiconductors, not just those from the United States, access to the Japanese market. (Nonetheless, the European Commission objected that any side agreement would discriminate in practice against EC firms.[16]) In addition, both Japan and the United States agreed to allow the GATT to review that agreement to make certain that it conformed with GATT rules and practices and the parties subsequently altered the agreement when parts of it were determined to be illegal under existing GATT rules. When it comes to passing legislation the U.S. Congress often takes its lead from the White House. Similarly, the GATT sometimes is more successful holding hearings after the fact to determine how well a trade agreement is functioning than to conceive, negotiate, and implement an agreement to begin with. The GATT, like the courts, does a better job bringing into focus the principles underlying an agreement after it is signed than before it is created. The results of bilateral and minilateral agreements may actually improve the GATT's operation so long as the GATT is allowed to review and amend them as part of the process.

Can Regionalism and Multilateralism Coexist?

Plurilateral and regional solutions also may be superior ways to solve such problems as nontariff barriers (NTBs). (The potential for sector specific codes is discussed under pillar 4.) Beth Yarbrough and Robert Yarbrough suggest that technical standards and other nontariff barriers arise because countries do not expect that market contracts under free trade will provide reliable guarantees for their national firms. (See Chapter 3.) Governments sometimes adopt NTBs to regulate their domestic industry, but most often they are meant to protect national firms from the defective global market. The technical standards require specialized investment by foreign firms, which is forfeited if the country then closes the market in retaliation for trade abuses by the parent of the foreign firm. This gives foreign firms an incentive to get their parent country to fix trade problems.[17]

Regional arrangements offer two advantages: (1) they open the possibility of creating large enough regions sharing common rules and commerce to permit improved access through foreign investment; and (2) they permit side payments that are sufficiently complex to tackle the worst problems associated with nontariff barriers.[18] The EC's 1992 program can eliminate many NTBs because the European Commission will provide centralized enforcement of common regulations and commercial agreements. EC members will be able to rely on EC safeguards.

The European breakthroughs rest on an elaborate political deal. The Commission derives its power from a maze of delegated authority from its member states. The decision-making structure allows member governments to supervise the Commission's extraordinary powers without delaying decisions endlessly. For example, a qualified majority voting (a quasi-unanimity rule) is permitted on many issues to expedite agreements, but a veto system remains on certain key functions of the Commission; thus, a country disillusioned with the general conduct of majority voting can retaliate on other fronts. Part of the glue is a series of side payments that winners make to losers under market-unification schemes. The Common Agricultural Program, the regional policies, and various supports for bolstering infrastructure are crucial. Obviously, nobody seriously advocates extending the EC system to cover global trade, but expanded regional arrangements that complement global rules may be viable.

In short, regionalism can provide a superior solution to many issues as long as there exists a mechanism for plurilateral consultation to reconcile the differences among regions.[19] Regional expansion, of course, must meet sound policy criteria of a market-access regime. Perhaps the most vexing complication of regionalism is the question of trade diversion from nonregional countries. GATT analysts argue that trade groups rarely pass the tests laid down in GATT Article XXIV (the U.S.-Canada agreement got a nondecision) and have wrongly concluded that this is an economic problem and a sign of GATT's weaknesses. GATT Article XXIV imposes conditions for a regional trade block's acceptability—no internal barriers within the block and no tariff level on nonmembers that is higher than the average tariff level of members prior to the block's formation—but neither condition is supported by economic theory. John McMillan, in an important paper, has proposed a simpler, more powerful test: "a trade block [is] admissible if the volume of trade between members and the rest of the world, measured at some specified level of aggregation, is no lower after the formation of the trade block."[20] Although it is difficult to implement this test, the essential point is that the basic pattern of trade flows is what matters. Moreover, given the major role of investment as a form of access, any "passing grade" on trade flows alone is a doubly powerful statement about continued integration of the world economy.

IMPLEMENTING PILLAR 2: TRANSPARENCY AND A NEW APPROACH TO OVERSIGHT

As separate systems of governance give way to further internationalization of domestic policies under market-access regimes, ambiguity and issue linkages increase. To cope with the blurring of bureaucratic authority and the collision of domestic and international economies and regulations, governments need better ways to define and clarify issues. Institutional innovations are needed for market-access regimes to function efficiently. Mixed systems of governance will require new emphasis on transparency, a new role for the GATT, and a new approach to oversight. Specifically, governments need to ensure more transparency in their bilateral and minilateral dealings, provide more disclosure of strategic intent, adopt more rigorous self-binding behavior, accept tougher presumptive rules of conduct, and expand the number and scope of specialized administrative procedures that allow parties to respond to grievances. To accomplish these steps, the GATT needs to be reformed to include new procedural obligations covering bilateral trade talks and obligations concerning disclosure and interpretation of national policies. To sustain a new global order, it is crucial to develop and implement these changes.

Ways Politicians Influence Bureaucracies

Global commercial problems now are so intertwined that it is futile to write multivolume administrative codes to govern them. Even in democratic societies, legislatures do not rely solely on detailed codes to cover behavior. They prefer to use administrative procedures to protect their interests and provide appropriate incentives to implement codes in ways that promote their intended goals. EC experiments with a quasi-federalist system are moving toward U.S.-style oversight, particularly in an emphasis on legal and written administration rather than on informal bureaucratic guidance.[21]

To accomplish these goals, political leaders use a variety of devices to monitor and influence the behavior of the bureaucracies that write and interpret regulations. Three types of policy instruments are particularly noteworthy—police patrols, fire alarms, and the explicit delegation of authority. Police patrols are standing arrangements to seek out and find violations of intent. Periodic investigative congressional hearings fulfill this function, as do the newly instituted biennial GATT reviews of the practices of major trading powers. The GATT instituted a regular scheduled review process of member trade policies in 1989,[22] and in late 1991 Europeans and

Japanese officials finally had an opportunity to scold their American counterparts for their poor handling of the domestic U.S. economy. Fire alarms are methods made available to aggrieved parties, particularly those critical to a policy's success, that wish to complain. For example, some countries provide special provisions for complaints about environmental policy that make it easier for advocacy groups to intervene in the administrative process. U.S. and Japanese trade negotiators are inventing processes such as rules requiring foreign membership in standard-setting committees. Delegation permits various authorities to act on their own discretion as long as they act on behalf of public goals. Privateering was the extreme case in modern history; the Bundesbank is another example.

Two important lessons are highlighted by studies of these control mechanisms. First, however formidable and "independent" the bureaucratic authority, its powers rest on definable political missions. Some missions are designed to resist short-term shifts in political sentiment. Others are more far-reaching. For example, the Bundesbank's profound anti-inflation charge rests on the aversion of all the leading German political parties to being identified as indifferent to inflation. Trade arrangements cannot be depoliticized, but it is possible that the jurisdictions of once separate bureaucratic domains can be reshaped. Thus, the Uruguay Round negotiations on trade in services provoked heated clashes over bureaucratic turf within member governments and between international organizations. At issue is how to ensure that trade liberalization proceeds despite the need for significant amounts of technical regulation of these markets. Trade negotiators can delegate authority and rule making to other bureaucracies as long as clear channels of appeal and a strong political mandate providing some ultimate jurisdiction remain. For example, if banking eventually is covered by the GATT, finance officials still will retain most banking oversight functions, but trade officials would set new standards by which to judge conduct and would become a new channel for appeals.

Second, as long as adequate appeals procedures (fire alarms) are provided, it is best to delegate some responsibility for identifying and pursuing complicated problems to the private sector or other interested parties. To make this approach work, governments that take up complaints will need to articulate their claims in terms of general precedents and self-binding behavior (discussed below). By acting this way the world economic community reduces the temptation for "fortune hunting." Small interest groups will have less incentive to act solely to maximize their own narrow gain if countries endorse principles that reinforce aggregate commercial interests.

A New Role for the GATT

GATT reform is a popular theme, but it is difficult to accomplish because procedural reform requires agreement on substantive policies. The most critical need is not usually discussed—the need to fundamentally reorient the mission of the GATT. The GATT can no longer serve only the dual function of neutral broker at multilateral trade negotiations and tribunal to which contracting parties come to settle trade disputes. Instead, the GATT needs a new triple mission—as a facilitator of multilateralism, as a depository of trade agreements, and as a coconvener of trade negotiations.

Other organizations have undergone radical transformations of their missions. The IMF at one time was the titular focus of international monetary policy coordination. Today, the IMF remains influential, but many of its functions have shifted to the Group of 7 or the Bank for International Settlements (BIS). The IMF lost its mandate to manage the international monetary system with the two dollar devaluations in the early 1970s. Since the announcement of the Plaza Agreement on September 22, 1985, the United States, Japan, the United Kingdom, Germany, France, and later Canada and Italy have worked uneasily together to manage the dollar and the international monetary system.[23] Most IMF energy today is concentrated on working with individual countries to reform their domestic economic policies when their economies run into trouble. Similarly, the BIS was established to monitor German reparation payments after World War I but became the central bank for central banks in the 1940s and 1950s and emerged as a key player overseeing international bank regulation in the 1970s and 1980s.

The GATT is likely to remain relevant in the future mainly because it already exists and can be transformed to serve as the institutional anchor of a network of policymaking. Reforms in economic management require new forms of proactive interpretation and oversight. Already the GATT has begun to work with finance ministries on issues related to trade in financial services and on how they might share oversight of trade-related financial regulation.

A dramatic proposal—to replace the GATT with a new Multilateral Trade Organization (MTO) with equal standing with the IMF and World Bank—was tabled in December 1991. It had significant backing, but was criticized by environmentalists who worried about concentrating too much power in the GATT.

Only GATT contracting parties could belong to the MTO. Countries receiving GATT benefits would assume the obligations of all existing GATT agreements in order to eliminate the fragmentation that resulted from selective acceptance of the Tokyo Round codes. The MTO would put any new rules on trade in services and intellectual property protection from the Uruguay Round under the same institutional umbrella as the existing rules on trade in goods. A stronger, faster dispute settlement mechanism would give the GATT more teeth by letting the secretariat pick panel members if countries cannot agree, shortening the complaint process to no more than fifteen months, making it harder to block a panel finding, and allowing for cross-retaliation (service or intellectual property violations can provoke retaliation against manufactured goods).[24]

Some grumble that third party members on dispute panels can create more mischief than reconciliation. Still, to the degree that the MTO is achieved, it assists the reconciliation of multilateral and sectoral pacts because dispute resolution can reduce the need for detailed sets of specialized rules. But quasi-judicial processes are not a satisfactory substitute for basic rule making by governments. This means that a reformed GATT has to build on improved dispute resolution by concentrating on three key tasks.

First, the GATT should play a central role in ensuring that bilateral, plurilateral, and regional agreements are multilateralized. For example, in 1985 the United States, Japan, and Canada converted a trilateral understanding on computer parts into a multilateral one.[25]

Second, the GATT's role as a depository of trade agreements (under Article XXIV) and the existing notification provision that requires countries to notify the GATT of bilateral and other trade agreements, without prejudice to their consistency with the GATT, should be reemphasized. This seemingly innocuous function is more important than it at first appears. For all of their deficiencies the textile VRAs became fairer and more tractable when moved under the GATT auspices by agreement of the parties. Not all agreements can be moved so completely to the GATT. But at minimum there must be firm rules to prohibit such arrangements as the "secret side letter" in the 1986 semiconductor pact between Tokyo and Washington, which undermined the basis for international commercial diplomacy. Multilateral bargains are meaningless if countries resort to secret pacts to negate public collective accord. Discretion is admirable, but there needs to be international agreement that all trade understandings will be registered and made available, if necessary with safeguards, to interested GATT parties.

Third, the GATT's role as a depository should go even further. Regardless of what economists think, there will be more bilateral and plurilateral pacts in the future, creating new trade precedents and principles. To this end, GATT members should agree to a rule that obligates signatories of every new trade and investment pact to file a brief interpretative statement with the GATT of the principles and rules created by the pact. A brief "multilateral impact statement" would consider the impact of the agreement on third parties and contain a concise explanation of the general rules of behavior endorsed by the pact. If these steps were required before a treaty could be judged GATT-legal, numerous ad hoc ventures with negative spillovers would be discouraged. In particular, countries with truly global economic interests would think carefully about the costs of "double-standards" of conduct. Such declarations of understanding and strategic intent would encourage self-binding behavior so that countries would more carefully consider the precedents their actions created.

These changes are manageable. They require more tactical innovation than substantive changes in the GATT. Andreas Lowenfeld has noted that specialized trade pacts outside the GATT are legal; they usually are considered a violation only if injury is shown. Moreover, Article XXV(5) allows for a GATT waiver (by a two-thirds vote of at least half the members); this kind of waiver was retroactively granted for the original U.S.-Canada automobile pact.

According to Lowenfeld, in practice the process is permissive, but there is some danger that it could undermine the multilateral process.[26] We share this concern, which is one reason that we advocate such innovations as mandatory "impact statements." As a precondition to bilateral and minilateral agreements, parties should explain publicly what they have accomplished and agree to abide by the same precedents when comparable disputes arise. We do not, however, advocate active pursuit of the waiver process.

During the current period of experimentation, countries should be encouraged to see what works. Specialized industry pacts should be reviewed automatically after a short initial trial period, perhaps one year. Third parties should be invited to lodge formal objections, and if their complaints are not addressed by adjusting the pact, the GATT should be able to intervene when injury can be shown. Then mediation or retroactive invocation of the waiver process should begin. Industry codes could even include dispute resolution processes that take into account the GATT.

One reason it is so difficult to strengthen GATT mechanisms is that governments are reluctant to agree to binding jurisdiction when the fairness of a particular marketplace is unclear. It is possible for the European Court of Justice to play a powerful role because unless it is perceived to treat all parties equitably, decision making in the European Community could be paralyzed. Industry pacts might allow for specialized dispute resolution mechanisms, such as multi-member panels with limited binding powers, perhaps along the lines emerging from the North American Free Trade Area negotiations. (There is no binding arbitration for general disputes in the draft of the NAFTA pact released on September 8, 1992, but the approach for antidumping and countervailing duty cases—which supplants judicial review in the three countries and sets up panels to make binding decisions on whether each country has acted consistently with its antidumping and countervailing duty legislation—is built on Chapter 19 of the free trade agreement between the United States and Canada.) Such panels might be required to include other GATT members, perhaps nominated by a standing GATT committee. Parties to agreements could be asked to explicitly consider the multilateral impact of their agreements. In short, by taking a number of small actions governments could lay the groundwork for ensuring that future bilateral and minilateral agreements are consistent with broader, multilateral understandings.

Although trade rules cannot be written that way, countries could also issue declarations of intent about their approach to interpreting the practical meaning of rules. This is roughly akin to the "enforcement guidelines" that the U.S. Department of Justice maintains in the public domain as a guide to its approach to antitrust law interpretation and enforcement priorities. If others then complain about U.S. behavior, the U.S. declarations can be put forward as a standard for its behavior to either condemn or defend it. The Department of Justice guidelines do not definitively bind the department, but a defendant in an antitrust case may cite the guidelines as one line of defense. Elsewhere we have argued that the rules governing telecommunications network access and pricing should be treated more permissively by U.S. negotiators if a country allows significant competition at the level of the basic network (such as AT&T versus MCI).[27] This is an enforcement guideline that the United States can live by. More recently, Kenneth Flamm has suggested that Japanese trade management should be judged in terms of its administrative capacity. He reasons that absent a detailed MITI bureau to police an industry, it will be hard for Japanese executives to cooperate and for Japan to exercise detailed administrative guidance. His logic suggests treating such industrial bureaus as evidence of presumptively unacceptable behavior: Japan can retain them if it wishes, but then other countries should have a right to more detailed accountability about their operations.[28]

Ideally, industrial countries should coordinate their positions on statements of intent. One mechanism would be to create new OECD guidelines. After reaching internal consensus, the OECD also might initiate consultations with other groups, like ASEAN. Because such guidelines are technically unenforceable, OECD members might attach national self-binding statements to these recommendations and use the GATT and other dispute resolution mechanisms to add weight to these statements when mediating disputes. In the 1970s, for example, U.S.-Japanese negotiations showed that it was no longer acceptable for a major trading power to use a "prohibitive negative principle" to organize access to its markets. This reflected the implicit OECD consensus that states had a right to take special notice if they identified such a rule even then.

Extending Transparency and the Example of Japan

Transparency is just as crucial as other institutional priorities in a redesigned GATT. Transparency is a pillar of the GATT that now needs to be extended to national rule setting and oversight because the European and Japanese models of industrial organization have become more central to the functioning of the world economy. Transparency is particularly important because in its absence it is difficult for countries to bargain successfully in a complicated environment. The benefits of greater transparency are illustrated by U.S. efforts to open the Japanese market.

In the mid-1980s the United States government won the right of foreign firms to own value-added networks in Japan and up to 30 percent of networks that had their own transmission systems. These rights were roughly equivalent to rights of foreign owners in the United States. Japan also agreed to abolish requirements for detailed licensing rules for VANs, thereby reducing administrative controls over licenses. However, Japan adamantly resisted altering its basic approach of careful oversight. It continues to closely supervise the expansion of total network facility capacity and allows liberalization of interrelated items only on an item-by-item basis. To illustrate, in a series of sequential negotiations the United States negotiated to liberalize fax networks, new international phone carriers, and rules for licenses for cellular networks equipped by Motorola.

Clyde Prestowitz puts it well: "The Japanese cannot 'open' in the American sense. They think of openness as removal of restrictions case by case, as the bureaucratic giving of permission, and have not the generic Western concept of an absence of the need for permission."[29] Prestowitz describes an approach widely accepted in Europe as well as Japan that governments may choose to be permissive, but they retain the final discretion over which companies may enter their markets.[30]

Still, Japanese regulatory thought and practice were effected by the long string of negotiations with the United States. For example, the telecommunications trade negotiations underscored that the process of setting standards and administrative ordinances for the Japanese network was crucial for U.S. firms and a total mystery to them. There was no formal process or foreign representation; therefore, U.S. negotiators successfully pushed for a more formalized decision process and for representation by Japanese subsidiaries of U.S. firms on the key committees. But there is little prospect for a wholesale change. Instead, a combination of changing interests in Japan and foreign pressure in selected markets may slowly alter processes for the areas most sensitive for international commerce.

Fundamental changes in the mission of the GATT are likely to be needed, and developing extended transparency and specialized grievance processes are important, as well. Several mechanisms can be implemented for monitoring and several instruments for controlling abuse of the complaint system, but a crucial part of building decentralized oversight and administration of the market-access regime is a redefined role for the GATT.

IMPLEMENTING PILLAR 3: EXTENDING NATIONAL TREATMENT AND TIERS OF RECIPROCITY

As the distinction between goods and services breaks down and services, like goods, are traded actively, trade rules and mechanisms that once sufficed for goods are no longer adequate. In some cases trade rules and mechanisms can be extended to cover trade in services. In other instances new rules and mechanisms need to be devised and negotiated.[31] Specifically, the mixing of goods and services and the internationalization of services require extending national treatment and creating tiers of reciprocity.

Extending National Treatment

The hallowed GATT principle of national treatment holds that once a firm has overcome barriers at the border and established itself in another country, it shall be treated no differently than the national firms in that country. The right of commercial establishment—essentially, the right to invest in a country—was never covered under the GATT, but U.S. negotiators hoped to broaden the rights of foreign investors during the Uruguay Round. The case of telecommunications services suggests that national treatment and the right of commercial establishment are trojan horses. National treatment is not acceptable if it means that a country can simply avoid liberalizing altogether. To escape national treatment, countries can close their markets by imposing a domestic monopoly. National treatment is an acceptable standard only after a country has begun to liberalize. The right to commercial establishment also is a sound approach, but it is a form of de facto regulation of foreign investment: it allows restrictions on foreign investment if access is granted by other means. This is a slight wrinkle on the long-established implicit practice that countries can choose between trade and investment access in sensitive markets. As noted earlier, effective access in complex markets is moving to investment-related access because of service, technological innovation, as well as politics.

EC 1992 negotiations highlighted the limits on upgrading national treatment to mutual recognition as the global organizing principle for services. Mutual recognition implies that what is accepted by one country's regulators will be accepted by its trading partners: if you can sell Heineken beer in the Netherlands, you can sell it in Germany. The European Community adopted mutual recognition of national regulatory standards, but to be workable this principle demands some form of minimum common standard. Moreover, in some markets, such as telecommunications services, political sensibilities may require a cap on liberalization through mutual recognition.

The European Community decided in its efforts to create a unified internal market that mutual recognition implied equivalent access to non-EC markets. An EC-U.S. disagreement over banking rules flared when the initial version of the Second Banking Directive appeared to demand exemptions from the Glass-Steagal Act and McFadden Act for European banks in the United States. Equivalent access raised political warning signs in the United States and probably was not necessary to achieve EC banking goals. Therefore the European Community reformulated the goal in terms of "effective access" for non-EC countries. Building on the same logic, the United States seeks, for telecommunications and other services, GATT agreements that accommodate "tiered reciprocity." The emerging precedent appears to be that national rules cannot be used to block effective foreign competition in a market subject to international liberalization. Different national regulatory approaches are possible as long as their cumulative effect does not prevent foreign entry.

Tiered Reciprocity

Other lessons can be gleaned from the European march toward market unification. The European Community discovered that overall reciprocity has limited utility for services. It usually works better to approach specific service sectors on the basis of sectoral reciprocity. The big question becomes whether all sectoral issues should be lumped together. This would be a mistake: reciprocity should cover tiers of services. These tiers could be cut in various ways, but each tier should cover broad bundles of services. The case of Japanese infrastructure illustrates how tiers might differ. Japan does not permit foreign firms to own basic infrastructure facilities such as airplane maintenance facilities or fiber optic cables, but it promises them that they will be granted equal access to local infrastructure. A country could choose the levels of tiers and the specific mix of services within each tier it would commit itself to. Reciprocity would be specific: access to the tier would be available only to countries that offered comparable access to their service tier. The composition of each tier could be renegotiated from time to time to permit distinctions among tiers.

In some ways tiered reciprocity is the nontariff barrier equivalent to the traditional logic of tariff negotiations. The beauty of tariffs was that they were item specific. There was no need to offer low tariffs on all steel products or a single tariff level for all consumer electronics. Had this been the case, tariff liberalization would have been slower because each time a contentious item arose, general sectoral progress would have stopped. Similarly, tiered reciprocity helps negotiators sort, disaggregate, and bundle specific service market segments in the context of the myriad of nontariff barriers. The FCC and other regulatory agencies already act this way when dealing with their foreign counterparts. We propose that

negotiators should bargain for concessions in light of GATT principles and in forums responsible to the GATT.

In short, the eroding boundaries between goods and services
and the globalization of services are likely to force governments to
adapt old principles—national treatment and reciprocity—to a new
reality. A revised understanding of national treatment needs to be
extended to cover services. At the same time the concept of reciprocity needs to be refined to handle complex issues raised by trading
access to domestic service markets that were until recently served
mainly by domestic, often government-owned, monopolists and
oligopolists.

IMPLEMENTING PILLAR 4: SECTORAL CODES

The free-trade regime favored universal codes of conduct. Industry-
specific agreements always were considered exceptions and almost
always were deemed economic disasters. Inevitably, market-access
regimes entail more industry-specific codes because a combination
of specialized market structures and politics makes it hard to apply
universal rules without causing even more disruption. The questions
are whether these codes can avoid becoming massive administrative
tomes and how governments can formulate these codes so they do
not overly restrict market competition. There are no perfect answers
to either question.

We favor simple, short codes over complex, long ones. By this
criterion, the second set of U.S.-Japan semiconductor agreements
was superior to the first set. This approach is superior in an era
when firms are adept at using ICAs because a major goal of these
codes is to change alliance behavior. Consider the case of semiconductors. U.S. firms wanted a better way to enter into supply relationships with key Japanese customers and wanted access to
technology and production assets located in Japan. The pact called
for penalties if the Japanese market did not open on a timely basis.
These collective sanctions changed the bargaining end game between U.S. and Japanese firms: before the pact U.S. firms were
forced to accept alliances on Japanese terms or not at all; now U.S.
firms can credibly refuse poor offers because, unless there is acceptable collective progress, penalties will be assessed on all Japanese

firms. Details related to market access were worked out through alliances, not trade regulations. However, our interviews suggest that many of these deals are not just pro forma shells. Value is being added on both sides. (There is a collective-action problem for Japanese firms: because each firm would prefer others to pay for working out alliances with foreign firms, MITI acts as a Sherpa to prod all firms. Predictably, the firms with the most sensitive exposure in the United States usually are the most responsive.)

Although industry codes should be pursued only when market competition already is skewed, they potentially can restrict competition. Nonetheless, logical safeguards for such codes exist. Part of the answer is to make each code recapitulate and adapt the general anchors of market-access systems such as transparency and the right to commercial establishment. Another part of the answer is to ensure that third parties can join codes and accept their benefits and obligations. In the following section we address a few of the challenges raised by industry-specific codes—the particular problems associated with VRAs, dumping, and subsidies.

Voluntary Restraint Agreements

Industry-specific codes have a bad reputation because of the track record of VRAs. One central reform of the trading system should be to rule VRAs presumptively illegal. The VRAs are a product of the desire to avoid nondiscrimination and compensation rules under GATT's Article XIX. Our approach solves the problem of nondiscrimination. (The European Community has favored selectivity since the Tokyo Round, while the United States favors it but has had some countervailing considerations. Developing countries used to oppose it but may come to see it as the lesser of potential evils.)[32]

Specific exceptions for existing codes for automobiles or steel might be allowed to remain. All VRAs should be bilateral industry agreements that are subject to third-party membership even though some agreements probably will not attract interest from other countries. If government took this one step, it would go a long way toward cleaning up the VRA mess while recognizing the needs that impelled them.

Better yet, we favor ending export restraints and switching to tariffs (with an automatic phase-out calendar). For example, the

United States might impose a steep tariff on Japanese widget imports for ten years but agree from the start to reduce the level of the tariff 10 percent each year. Some proponents of phased-out tariffs favor a five-year life span. A longer period may be necessary to achieve the political purpose of the strategy, to allow substantial adjustment for domestic firms, and to provide incentives for local production by foreign firms. Given current lead times on new plants and products a five-year cycle is too short. Funds raised from the tariff might be used to help the widget industry adjust to competition. But countries would have to agree at the outset that firms and industries that failed to adjust would be allowed to take their chances in the market. Setting the tariffs correctly would cap imports, but this would produce a more economically efficient outcome than we have at present. (This system has other advantages. Tariffication is easier to work out than VRAs when there are more than two parties involved. Tariffication also would throw a spotlight on the costs of protection.)

One objective of VRAs and emergency tariffs is to shift foreign production to the local market. As we discuss shortly, it is not surprising that as new foreign-owned plants open in rapid succession, new disputes over rules of origin arise. The cat and mouse game that follows over what should count as local content is often unfair and inefficient. Therefore, we believe that the OECD should recommend that countries that enact VRAs and emergency tariffs also should submit a comprehensive review of relevant local content issues. If foreign suppliers must play this game, it is fairer to them and ultimately more effective for the host country if the ground rules for foreign plants are clearly stated and consistent.

Dumping

GATT codes that deal with dumping implicitly use home-market pricing as the yardstick for measuring fair pricing in foreign markets. But recent U.S. and European practices instead view dumping in terms of selling below costs. Should the cost standard be average cost, marginal cost, short-run costs, long-run costs, current costs, or anticipated costs (sometimes called forward pricing)?[33] Those making the choice should be sensitive to the nature of the industry, but often they are not. This issue underscores one advantage that industry-specific codes enjoy over universal rules. The Computer Systems Policy Project, for example, has urged that antidumping rules permit pricing below-average unit costs during the introductory period for a high-technology product. This allows innovators to start prices lower to win early product acceptance and to be rewarded for their leadership. CSPP also wants to allow the allocation of capital and R&D costs over the product life cycle; this obviously requires an industry-specific definition.[34]

In addition, how should dumping be determined when products and services are of transnational origin? The GATT makes antidumping duties the sole jurisdiction of the importer. Some critics accuse the European Community of manipulating the accounting that underlies dumping charges. For example, when comparing the underlying reference prices for determining dumping, the European Community deducts more marketing expenses from prices in Europe than it does in Japan.[35] The European Community also is inconsistent about whether to use firm cost or average industry cost to guide dumping determinations. The European Community and Japan reached an antidumping agreement in 1989 that effectively set a floor price on DRAMs rather than requiring each individual firm to sell at prices above its costs (as was the case with the U.S. agreement). This difference means that NEC might sell a chip in the United States at one price and be guilty of dumping in the European Community.

The GATT's consultation machinery also might be invoked to examine pricing formulas set by antidumping agreements. If too many countries participate in negotiations, it is virtually impossible to work out a pricing formula. But it is possible to make calculations transparent and subject to consultation because antidumping agreements almost always cover acceptable pricing behavior in third countries. Moreover, expedited dumping proceedings (as worked out in semiconductors) probably should be extended to all key parties.[36]

The more that firms are held individually accountable (judged on the basis of their individual costs and behavior), the faster firms will globalize their operations. If individual strategies matter, then firms have a greater incentive to experiment with alliances to reinforce their capabilities and political friendships. Group accountability reinforces group behavior. Although the complexity of the situation makes it impossible to make sweeping recommendations, the basic strategy is clear: future administrative codes that cover origin and dumping should emphasize the accountability of individual firms. The semiconductor case illustrates the limits of current rules: shipments and modifications of products to third countries hampered the agreement. Some firms proved harder to deal with than others, but the agreement focused punishment on Japanese firms as a group. The experience with this agreement suggests that the GATT might diversify the vocabulary of dumping, recognizing the right of countries to address different types of dumping. For example, if a shipment of semiconductors exported from Japan to Thailand at below cost was then transshipped to the United States as Thai product (diversionary dumping), a penalty might be assessed on the value added represented by the chip. This approach would simplify the kinds of third-country problems raised by the semiconductor agreement and would allow countries more flexibility in dealing with proven cases of repeated dumping by a particular supplier. Investigations could be focused on practices of specific suppliers.

The emphasis on the individual accountability of firms would reduce trade tensions because punishments could be more focused. In 1988, the Omnibus Trade Act introduced this idea, but with vague language. The core idea is that firms and their subsidiaries found guilty of repeated, serious dumping (of, say, transport equipment) during a set period would henceforward be subjected to special fast-track investigations and increased penalties.[37] Moreover, in the spirit of some EC exercises, dumping investigations should explicitly take into account the nature of the ICAs of the accused firms. If they maintain significant partnerships with local firms in the market in question, that might tip a close case in favor of the accused firm. One reason for proceeding in this way is that it could reinforce fragmentation among Japanese firms. Trade policy should reward mavericks in the ranks of Japanese firms to weaken consensus on industrial policy in Japan. When Japanese firms disagree among themselves on policy, it is more difficult for Japan to execute its industrial policy.

Subsidies

Governments subsidize their firms in many ways, including their basic research, development, production, and exports. Subsidies may be transparent or hidden, direct or indirect. ICAs dilute some of the returns on subsidies to national taxpayers, which may lead to new ways to distribute the costs of subsidies (such as the EC consortia) or efforts to exclude foreign firms from specialized assistance (the U.S. government tolerates exclusion of foreign firms from research consortia it funds). It is safe to predict that governments will continue to subsidize their firms. The challenge facing policymakers is to determine what constitutes fair and unfair subsidies. Once some semblance of agreement is reached among countries, what can be done to discourage governments from using the most disruptive, least fair (to trading partners) types of subsidies?

Export subsidies are illegal under the GATT Subsidies Code. But as a result of a last-minute compromise to reach closure on the Tokyo Round, the Subsidies Code was gutted. The code as it emerged in 1979 was so weak that according to one negotiator, "You could drive a truck through it." The code is ambiguous and open to alternative interpretations. Production subsidies are GATT-legal under the code as long as they do not cause injury to others. The code also exempts export subsidies for primary goods and financing below market rates if not in violation of OECD guidelines (the OECD export financing agreement has more teeth). In part to fill these gaps, the U.S. Trade and Tariff Act of 1984 banned both production and export subsidies. However, so as not to penalize U.S. consumers unnecessarily, the United States applies a material injury test to decide whether it will impose a countervailing duty.[38] In other words, unless U.S. firms are harmed by a foreign subsidy, no countervailing duty is imposed.

There is no indication that subsidies ever will be easy to handle. Determining fairness will be difficult, contentious, time consuming, and labor intensive. One problem likely to arise is deciding whether countries should be allowed to camouflage subsidies to producers by arranging brokered marriages between them. France is willing in principle to arrange marriages among firms in which it owns equity or in which the government is the major buyer. These marriages shore up the weaker partner. But if the French government dictates the terms, would that constitute grounds to object to the merger? Perhaps. It might, however, be harder for the United States to find good reasons for objecting to the subsidies that often exist within private keiretsu. In general the United States is more comfortable when local legislation and enforcement are adequate to tackle such problems. Thus, the European Community should handle France. But even responsible regulators hesitate to act on cases that become political hot potatoes.

Another question that arises is whether countries should be allowed to encourage exports or risk-taking by limiting or removing a firm's downside risk. Thus, was it appropriate for Germany to subsidize the German members of Airbus to cover possible foreign-exchange losses? A GATT panel found that Germany was in violation of the Procurement Code. The Subsidies Code may also have been violated. Similarly South Korea has encouraged its extremely competitive construction and engineering firms to bid on large overseas projects by making the cost of preparing bids—which can total $1 million on a large macroconstruction project—fully deductible from their taxes.

Finally, there is the question of whether certain subsidies, such as adjustment assistance or regional subsidies, are acceptable if there was no intent to cause harm to others. The Uruguay Round negotiators were divided on this one.

The best response would be to create a general GATT agreement that puts forward the basic principles, and then rely on industry-specific codes for the details. For example, it might be possible to work out which kinds of subsidies are positively accepted, which are firmly prohibited, and which are indeterminate in the context of an industry agreement. Countries then could negotiate or turn to a third party when they thought that a particular program fell into the forbidden or indeterminate categories. The case for the complainant would be stronger if the complainant had first issued an early warning and consulted with the offending country about the practice that troubled them. This procedure should encourage prior consultation capable of heading off some of the ugliest conflicts before parties became intransigent. Subsidy programs in the indeterminate categories might be made subject to review to determine their relative magnitude and be evaluated against specialized injury tests. The extent to which countervailing duties were applied might be linked to whether the program was forbidden or indeterminate, its size, and the types of injuries it produced in the indeterminate category.[39]

As the first new pillar underscores, if multilateral trade negotiations are too overloaded and complex to succeed, bilateral and plurilateral approaches may prove necessary. In fact, the Japanese-U.S. negotiations on telecommunications services, semiconductors, and other sectors demonstrate that such an approach can reinforce global regimes; they need not fragment them. The second pillar suggests that in a globalized world the first order of business is knowing the rules of the national game and the international game. To do this governments need to work together to develop mechanisms that help make the rules transparent, that allow participants to appeal decisions, and that provide a process for reviewing and reforming rules in a timely and orderly manner. As the globalization of services becomes pervasive and the line separating trade in goods and services blurs under the third pillar, governments will need to experiment with, review, and amend the principle of national treatment as it functioned under the GATT and experiment with new forms of tiered, sectoral reciprocity in the granting of access to national and regional markets. The fourth pillar points to the need for industry-specific codes to permit quicker action under clearer guidelines than even the toughest multilateral principles and general dispute resolution system could afford.

These codes also should clear the way to some reforms of pernicious current practices. One should be the replacement of VRAs with tariffs. Another should be the obligation to develop standards for acceptable subsidies in some way other than by lurching to ad hoc judgments. And antidumping practices need to provide venues to protect interested third parties plus to emphasize the individual accountability of firms when possible. The benefit of industry codes globally should be that more tailored solutions can rid the world of some of the more pernicious forms of protectionism under the current general codes of the GATT. One point should be underscored: no group of industry codes will end the Japanese trade surplus or the U.S. trade debit. The vast bulk of trade imbalances flow from macroeconomic policies (on government budgets and national savings, for example), not microeconomic policies for international commerce. But industry codes can correct the gamesmanship by nations that distorts markets and causes massive problems of structural adjustment for industries and their workers.

CHAPTER TEN

Rules for Managing the World Economy

The final two pillars of a new market-access regime focus on the ground rules that govern transnational corporations and government attempts to create new competitive advantages. The rights of investors, rules of origin, dumping, limits on unfair government intervention, and global antitrust approaches are issues applicable to the worldwide operations of TNCs and ICAs.

Our approach reaffirms the desirability of foreign companies playing growing roles in national economies and recommends that government programs to create competitive advantages not exclude foreign firms. This means toughening the international rules for government procurement, research and development, and setting standards. We also endorse measures to ensure that foreign firms fully contribute to the local economy before they claim the rights of local companies. And we want to expedite using antitrust policy to steer domestic alliances (including keiretsu) down acceptable paths and to shape national competition policies. A market-access regime is a response to changing models of industrial organization. It must accommodate these models and discipline them, or world economic rules will be irrelevant to the central dynamics of international competition.

IMPLEMENTING PILLAR 5: RIGHTS OF FOREIGN INVESTORS, RULES OF ORIGIN, AND ANTITRUST

The growing fungibility of trade and investment is pushing governments to improve their policies related to the rights of foreign investors, rules of origin, and antitrust.[1] Just as widespread attention was paid to issues of privatization and deregulation during the 1980s, we expect governments to concentrate in the 1990s on rethinking and rewriting their rules governing foreign investment. We expect officials in Europe, Japan, the United States, and elsewhere will focus attention on developing and harmonizing new rules covering foreign investment and market access. They also are likely to elaborate rules of origin to determine where value is added and how goods and services should be classified for trade and investment purposes and to reorient some rules related to dumping to take into account the globalization of origin of goods and services. In the years ahead, governments increasingly will grapple with the following key issues.

Market-Access and Foreign Investment Rules

As demands for market access increased, governments began to rethink their trade and investment policies. The key question related to finding a balance between the rights of foreign investors and the rights of governments to limit or control foreign direct investment is a negative one. The question of determining what guiding principles might legitimately be used by governments to limit access to their economies by direct foreign investors becomes particularly crucial given the growing influence of non-U.S. models of industrial organization. An important minimum principle, embodied in the U.S.-Japanese investment talks, is that foreign investors should be allowed into a country as long as their entry does not preempt significant entry by local firms that are themselves subject to domestic competition. We presume that restrictions on foreign entry to protect a national monopoly would not normally be acceptable, for example. But even this minimal rationale for exclusion should be subject to challenge for concessions.

The investment provisions in the U.S.-Canada Free Trade Agreement are one example of a shift in this direction. Except in cultural industries, Canada agreed to phase out the review of indirect acquisitions and to progressively raise the threshold for review of direct acquisitions of previously Canadian-owned enterprises by U.S. investors from $25 million to $150 million. The United States, traditionally more open to foreign investment than Canada, agreed to a national treatment provision that prohibited the U.S. government from imposing U.S. reviews on Canadian investments in the future. Both countries agreed not to impose trade-related performance requirements on the other's investors.[2]

Another step in this direction is the effort to negotiate new rules (to supplement existing trade principles) that would govern foreign investment policy and domestic regulation of industry when it is in conflict with principles of market access. Ironically, national laws restricting foreign investment are being relaxed in most countries, just when the United States has become marginally more restrictive. The Exon-Florio amendment gave the U.S. government power to block foreign purchases of U.S. firms for reasons of national security, broadly defined. The U.S. executive branch has used this power selectively. At the same time, the United States is creeping toward tougher rules of origin and local content in such industries as automobiles. So far the United States has not required any specific export requirements for foreign investments in the United States.

The United States chose an approach to investment policy where it largely has clean hands—trade-related investment measures (TRIMS)—along with services and intellectual property as the most important new issues of the Uruguay Round. (When the United States unsuccessfully pushed for a new round of trade negotiations at the November 1982 meeting of GATT trade ministers, services, intellectual property, and high-technology products were viewed as the three key new issues. Nobody ever determined exactly what high-technology products meant. By the time the Uruguay Round was launched in 1986, trade-related investment issues emerged as the third important new issue.) A successful TRIMS negotiation would lead to greater market access for investors. Eventually, it may persuade other countries to concur, but informal pledges probably still will abound, as they did in the U.S.-Japan bilateral negotiations on automobiles in 1992. Although we support the TRIMS initiative, we prefer to focus on the core question of what foreign firms can reasonably be asked to do to qualify them for treatment as local firms.

Rules of Origin

This last question goes to the heart of the rules of national origin and local content that define when a good is produced locally and when processing by a foreign subsidiary is treated as mere window dressing. To answer this question, governments are turning to regulations covering rules of origin. Rules of origin are closely related to government procurement. They are vital in an era of market-access regimes and alliances because they provide a way for governments to assess the net benefits of the most intricate details of alliances and to act accordingly.

The EC case is instructive. More than 700 national quantitative restrictions on imports into individual EC member markets exist under Article 115 of the Treaty of Rome. The 1992 program will render most individual national bans toothless, but some will be translated into Community VRAs or monitoring programs on imports, such as the one for automobiles. The European Community will protect other critical technologies by using specialized dumping safeguards and applying strict tests to certify when products manufactured in the European Community are exempt from dumping safeguards.

In general EC rules of origin judge a product to be local if local content is at least 45 percent and some technically complex processing is performed in the European Community. Screwdriver assembly plants do not meet these tests. If the European Commission determines that products are of foreign origin, foreign firms have no procedural right to appeal the decision. This can lead to perverse behavior. To meet EC standards, foreign firms sometimes are forced to discard some value added in the United States and replace it in Europe. Texas Instruments contends, for example, that it had to jettison some of the U.S. value added to its European-produced circuit boards to qualify them as European.[3] Traditionally the European Community followed the origin rule of "last substantial transformation." The European Community requires that this transformation be economically justified, not just a matter of convenience to avoid regulations.[4] But the Commission recently altered its standards for sensitive industries to go beyond value-added tests.

The EC's approach on semiconductors was based on a test of most substantial transformation. Any product containing a dumped good such as a printed circuit board also must contain at least 40 percent local or third-party content. When applying the local or third-party content rule, the European Community often substitutes tests involving critical components of EC origin, thereby creating an indirect web of barriers to U.S. components. Moreover, if an antidumping finding is lodged, the European Community reserves the right to examine plants operated by firms of offending countries in the European Community or third countries.[5]

(More worrisome is that when the EC decided to nurture an EC-based VCR industry, it determined that even when coupled with VRAs the value-added rule was inadequate. The European Community therefore insisted that Japan set a quota on total VCR exports plus local EC production. Pricing provisions also were part of the deal. Japan realized that if it did not comply, Europe would stringently restrict imports. In 1983 MITI entered into an extraordinary agreement with the European Community on videotape recorders: in addition to a VRA on exports, the pact set restrictions on Japanese sales and floor prices for Japanese firms' output in Europe; MITI allocated shares to Japanese firms of both exports and production in Europe.)[6]

Rules of origin tend to strengthen the role of ICAs linking EC and non-EC firms. In general ICAs are significant in regard to rules of origin and to local content for two reasons: (1) they provide a local partner of stature that can mobilize its own government to penetrate the decision process, and (2) the relationship makes it easier to tap local production assets for the purposes of providing local content. Controversies about rules of origin fall under the jurisdiction of the Commission, but they are subject to an elaborate decision-making process that requires validation by about a 70 percent majority (using the EC's weighted voting system) in either the Council or a special Committee of Origin. The formal system has been used only fourteen times, but the informal system where consultation occurs, but no voting, is much more active. There are no procedural safeguards and no method of direct legal challenge to the rulings. The procedural safeguards for appeals by suppliers of components to a product are better than the safeguards for the "system provider."[7]

However tortuous the logic or protectionist the intent in any particular case, the European Community does not want to hand down blatantly prejudicial rulings on origin. Obviously protectionist actions could backfire on EC firms abroad or create unwelcome precedents for other EC industries where consumers might fight back. In its 1988 ruling on VCRs, for example, the Commission counted any significant ICA with Japanese producers as local European production. It scrutinized direct, solo investment for production by Japanese firms much more closely.[8] (But the Nissan Bluebird production in the United Kingdom, where the local partner was much weaker, was not exempted.) The European Community also seems poised to demand that there be nearly 50 percent local value added in technologically complex production processes for manufactured goods. They are likely to ask that a majority of value added for parts be supplied in the European Community. In return, they probably will require fewer tests of complexity: "whether the manufacturing operation demonstrates some degree of technical complexity and sufficient local content . . . (about 45 percent, including in-house assembly costs and overheads), a parts investigation will primarily focus on whether more than 60 percent of the value of the parts (typically excluding in-house assembly costs and overhead) are provided locally."[9]

More generally, EC deliberations suggest several possible emerging principles for trade that could serve as a basis for negotiation among governments:

- Governments may classify the origins of goods according to the most substantial transformation made. If they elect to follow this principle, they may use some reasonable combination of percentage of value added and complexity of processing to establish the "most substantial" contribution.

- However, if governments use the transformation test, they should not be allowed to require as high a percentage of content locally as a pure content test alone might permit. Double jeopardy is never a good idea. By these standards the NAFTA agreement on computer origins was reasonable because it combined a transformation test (on mother boards) with a 50 percent content standard on the rest of the system. The NAFTA rule on automobiles (62.5 percent North American parts by 2000) may be acceptable on the face of it, but the secondary rules were too restrictive. A more formal recognition of ICAs might also help.

- The existence of an ICA involving substantial sharing of product technology or production know-how could be taken as powerful presumptive evidence that the benefit of doubt should be given when the "substantial transformation" test yields ambiguous results. There is likely to be debate about what constitutes a significant ICA. The local partner may have only a minimum role in management and a slight financial role. This is consistent with the strategy presented in dumping cases of encouraging the individual accountability of firms and the deepening of alliances.

Antitrust Considerations

The fifth new pillar also poses the question of how governments should respond as TNCs and ICAs become ever more central to the operation of the world economy. We argue that market-access regimes will greatly enhance the importance of intergovernmental coordination on antitrust law for the global market. The globalization of the firm and rival models of industrial organization pose difficult issues for efficient, fair competition. To successfully manage the world economy, governments will need to establish global antitrust rules that provide direct oversight of TNCs and ICAs.

Some form of antitrust or competition policy exists in all the OECD countries. But most countries traditionally did not enforce or rely on antitrust laws as a primary instrument of competition policy simply because they were more concerned with building economies of scale by combination or encouraging the sharing of key competitive assets among firms. As a result, the United States had the most prominent and probably the most influential antitrust authorities in the world. From the viewpoint of the global regime, as long as the United States was the pivot of world markets, American antitrust law provided de facto scrutiny of the system of world commerce. Today, this informal authority is weakening, and the standards for judging antitrust violations inevitably will differ. For example, the European Community considers the effect of mergers on European integration, not just competition. This means governments have a harder time coordinating antitrust policies.[10]

One particular appeal of antitrust policy for a market-access regime is that governments already are quite experienced at evaluating the impact of disparate, specialized market conditions on competition. But before global antitrust can be accepted, governments will have to develop general understandings about fair competition simply to orient and begin to harmonize their individual policies. Such talks also should allow participants an opportunity to modify policies prior to antitrust challenges and to explore how much they can rely on others' domestic process for antitrust enforcement. For example, the Strategic Impediments Initiative (SII) negotiations allowed U.S. officials to explore the intricacies of the Japanese model of industrial organization, without changing much. Even critics of Japanese policies agree that the keiretsu's preferential buying from its own members is efficient and is a legitimate model for organizing industry. Therefore, the negotiations focused on specific practices that cumulatively blocked imports without markedly improving efficiency or on "one-time" adjustment packages that would allow foreign firms access to the keiretsu system that at one time discriminated against them systematically. Examples of specific practices blocking import penetration include special disclosure requirements concerning import agreement under Japanese antitrust rules and the practices concerning vertical integration of distributorships.[11]

The United States particularly challenged the restrictive distribution system for import distribution (where keiretsu groups dominate) and general consumer goods in Japan. Small retailers and captive outlets of domestic manufacturers dominate at the expense of large retailers, which are more prone to carry imported goods. The retail laws even gave small stores a veto over entry by large ones.

The SII also tried to attack cartels and bid-rigging arrangements. The most notorious examples were found in public infrastructure projects where bid-rigging is a way of life, and firms are major contributors to Japan's ruling party. There is no more chance of systematic reform of the construction industry in Japan than in New York City. The United States, however, won a commitment to strengthen Japan's weak version of the Federal Trade Commission. The many weaknesses of Japanese antitrust authorities also led the United States to consider new extraterritorial claims for its own laws. To this end the United States is exploring the possibility of extending antitrust law to the operations of keiretsu in Japan. The Justice Department might be allowed to use U.S. antitrust law to attack anticompetitive practices in Japan of Japanese firms operating in the United States, or more generally, the Justice Department would attack anticompetitive practices in home markets of foreign firms operating in the United States. The Department of Justice might sue the U.S. subsidiary of, say, Sony because of antitrust violations in Japan that hurt U.S. exports to Japan. This is consistent with past U.S. attempts to protect American consumers from harmful foreign practices.

The Bush administration also suggested it might pursue formal antitrust actions if U.S. exporters lost overseas markets because of collusive actions or other anticompetitive practices that took place beyond U.S. borders.[12] Antitrust laws could, in theory, be used to attack the Japanese keiretsu for anticompetitive effects on the U.S. markets. For example, Japanese automobile firms are bringing part of their vertical keiretsu with them for the automobile parts industry in the United States.[13] The United States might target the purchasing patterns of the major Japanese automobile firms because U.S. firms rarely have access to the "design in" phase of the procurement system.

In the past, even limited U.S. claims to extraterritorial application of its law were exceptional international behavior; most countries make no such claims. U.S. claims occasionally created conflicts with other countries. One striking instance was the Reagan administration's insistence in 1982 and 1983 that foreign subsidiaries of U.S. firms incorporated in France could not assist in the construction of a gas pipeline from the Soviet Union to Western Europe. The French government insisted that contracts between subsidiaries subject to French law had to abide by their contracts. The United States eventually wrote bilateral treaties on antitrust cooperation with Canada, Australia, and West Germany, which all had special antitrust concerns.

But extraterritoriality is the wave of the future, as witnessed by the EC 1992 program. The EC approach will be "more regulatory than the American. . . . In most cases where two firms agree to forgo competition to the extent necessary to collaborate in a strategic alliance within an EC jurisdiction, they must obtain specific approval of the transaction or risk an antitrust violation. Under U.S. law . . . no specific governmental clearance is required."[14] Mergers and acquisitions involving European companies with sales or European sales over a certain size will be subject to EC review. Corporate alliances also will be subject to merger notification and review under Article 3.2 of the Treaty of Rome. The other side of greater oversight is that block exemptions also can be used to reinforce market protection. This is the case with the exemptions for automobile dealerships.[15] Although no agreement exists on how to evaluate the effect of alliances between large firms on competition, unless they qualify for block exemptions, less formal alliances will be analyzed under Articles 85 and 86.[16]

When regulating foreign firms, the European Community always has insisted in principle that all locally incorporated firms receive equal standing, even if their headquarters are located outside the European Community. But the European Community never has challenged the right of its members to discriminate for certain policy purposes, by using, for example, VRAs and government procurement.[17] Usually, local production, not ownership, is the criterion for setting policies, which can help or hurt foreign firms. Moreover, the European Community is likely to consider ownership when extending rights in newly liberalized markets for services. Competition policy is not likely to be used when member states are acting to protect key national firms from foreign purchase. Unless countries resort to unfair state subsidies, the European Commission and DG-IV will not intervene. To keep local ownership, the European Community will attack national subsidies schemes as anticompetitive, as happened in the Rover and Renault sales, but it will exempt EC programs. For example, Germany's quiet policy to protect Volkswagen—no takeover will be permitted, and foreign entrants will not be allowed to wipe out all major German producers—is unlikely to be challenged.[18]

The European Community has recently asserted its right to bring antitrust actions against foreign firms if their actions at home injure EC consumers. It demanded details on the Matsushita purchase of MCA and the AT&T takeover of NCR. It is uncertain whether the European Community will follow the United States in projecting antitrust policies on foreign policies that exclude EC entry into foreign markets. But Leon Brittan, the EC commissioner in charge of competition policy until the end of 1992, proposed a new U.S.-EC treaty for "consultations, exchanges of non-confidential information, mutual assistance and best endeavors to cooperate in enforcement. Disagreements should be discussed frankly and, wherever possible, *only one party should exercise jurisdiction over the same set of facts.*"[19] The responsible party would fully consider the other's concerns. If it did not, the other party might have a right to demand arbitration under such a treaty.

It would be surprising if countries quickly acceded to binding arbitration. The United States was reluctant to enter such arrangements on most items covered under the U.S.-Canada Free Trade Agreement. But a system of plurilateral consultation on antitrust has begun to develop at the OECD. One possible model might be the BIS code for banking reserve requirements or the recent agreements on international standards for financial accounting. These codes resemble the EC approach, which sets minimum standards for common regulations and allows parties to act on the basis of mutual recognition of the validity of each other's specialized rules. A few common antitrust rules could emerge on especially difficult questions for overlapping jurisdictions, and discussions could be held about various forms of extraterritorial issues. This approach could appeal to the EC. An EC–U.S. accord could then sway Japanese acquiescence, even though Japan otherwise opposes unilateral extraterritorial applications of antitrust laws. There is, after all, substantial support in Japan for toughening its antitrust laws.

Besides consultative agreements, a modified version of the U.S. idea of suing Japanese firms for violations in Japan might be effective. To further this type of policy, the United States might create Department of Justice attachés in key overseas embassies whose jobs would be to work with governments to establish antitrust actions based on their local standards. In Japan, for example, although reasonable, general statutes are available, adequate enforcement and regulatory guidelines are not.[20] If the local government did not concur and the Department of Justice believed that there existed a clear violation of Japanese statute, the United States could suggest fact finding and mediation by a third party. This approach gives priority to local antitrust laws and domestic authorities but still encourages vigorous enforcement. Presumably, the United States would instigate its own antitrust action under U.S. statute only after local authorities rejected mediation or failed to act.

IMPLEMENTING PILLAR 6: LIMITS ON UNFAIR GOVERNMENT PRACTICES

National comparative advantage is not dead, but national comparative advantage alone is not enough for firms or countries to compete today in world commerce. The sixth new pillar of market-access regimes is built on the increasing importance of regional and global advantages. To deal with these complicated types of advantage and make market-access systems successful, governments need to find ways to be able to differentiate between fair and unfair government intervention, to settle disputes about these findings, and to enforce decisions.

We reject the terms of the free-trade versus fair-trade debate. Free trade as an ideal is absolute: there either are barriers that need to be removed or there are not. Reality is not so simple. Governments do intervene in domestic and international markets for a variety of reasons, legitimate and illegitimate. They will continue to try to create advantage for their firms and citizens. Paul Krugman makes the case for a minimum industrial policy succinctly: "My own proposal is that we adopt an explicit, but limited U.S. industrial policy. That is, the U.S. government should make a decision to frankly subsidize a few sectors . . . where there is a perceived threat from Japanese competition. It is possible that the costs of such a policy would exceed its economic benefits. But the downside would be limited: Federal expenditures of, say, $10 billion a year to support industrial R&D consortia would produce at least some benefits. . . . It is important to emphasize that I am not advocating some form of managed trade."[21] The increasing use of government policy to foster national industrial advantage makes it critical for governments to decide among themselves what constitutes fair intervention and what sorts of intervention are deemed unsatisfactory. We expect that in the post–Uruguay Round period governments will spend a great deal of energy to define, identify, and limit what constitutes acceptable intervention and what does not and to begin to find ways to limit unfair government advantage.[22] The objective is to allow effective market access to foreign firms but not to curtail government intervention. This is what we mean by open industrial policy.

As was noted earlier, other countries are telling the United States that industrial policy is not the enemy of an interdependent world economy. To the contrary, the absence of useful industrial policies in the United States is forcing it to overload the trade policy mechanism to fix problems that require other forms of adjustment. Nonetheless, the United States is right to push for better understandings on what constitute unfair behavior because such agreements inevitably will give foreign firms better standing in local markets and more access to local government programs (including R&D). When foreign firms share the local honeypot, it weakens the protectionist temptation. Here we focus on three aspects of fairness—government procurement, R&D, and technical standards. Others, such as intellectual property, could be added.

Government Procurement

Governments are the largest purchasers of goods and services in all countries. In general, local, state, and national governments prefer to buy from their own nationals, even if the price is a little higher or the quality is slightly lower. This is one way governments can stimulate certain regions or sectors and redistribute benefits among various groups in their countries. When national security or national culture is involved, the push for domestic procurement is even stronger. But when foreign countries or ICAs can provide higher-quality products for less money, how big an advantage for local suppliers is too much?

A related issue is whether government pricing policies and ownership of industry constitutes unfair market intervention. Governments can use pricing and state ownership to manipulate who may ally with whom in emerging market-access regimes. For example, the Thatcher government intervened to keep one automobile firm "British" and shortly thereafter considered blocking a buyout of other British firms by French companies owned by the French government, arguing that the playing field for mergers and acquisitions was not level. Once the worry was that state firms would not act commercially and would dump goods. With the shift to greater emphasis on foreign investment, the new fear is that state-owned firms will act too commercially: they will buy others and still be sheltered from retaliation in the marketplace by the veil of state ownership. These issues already bedevil the European Community. They will grow in global importance as closer integration of the world economy makes them more vital.

The telecommunications procurement talks highlight several principles. First, *private entities may be subject to the same rules as public ones* if they have licensed control over a market or substantial government equity investment. For example, France has toyed with the idea of having state enterprises with strong cash flows (such as France Telecom) buy minority shares in troubled electronics firms (such as SGS-Thomson). The decision that quasi-public telecommunications carriers such as NTT and British Telecom also needed to adhere to government procurement rules leads to a second principle: *government procurement should be defined by special market-entry privileges*, not by ownership per se. Indeed, Brussels pressed Washington to include all major telephone carriers, especially AT&T and the regional Bell operating companies, under an international procurement code. Brussels also offered to count inputs from any signatory to an international code as local content for the purposes of qualifying under EC standards. The European Community preferred a GATT code, but it was willing to settle for a bilateral or plurilateral deal. The European Commission was prompted by Alcatel and Siemens, which had limited success in selling to U.S. telecommunications carriers until recent successes by Siemens. Competition for regional Bell operating company procurement contracts is reasonably open, but the RBOCs are close to licensed monopolies for their core services (although this monopoly is eroding). As such, the RBOC process of purchasing probably should be subject to the code. In contrast, in the AT&T case there is greater reason for skepticism about openness because AT&T continues to produce much of its own equipment. Yet AT&T is neither government-owned nor does it have a government-licensed monopoly.

Therefore, it should not be subject to the procurement code. In mid-1991 the European Community threatened to retaliate against AT&T (and Northern Telecom) by tabling a draft directive that would have required a high proportion of local content (including software development costs) for central office switches and PBXs sold in EC member countries.

A third principle was that within limits, *governments may protect long-term development and supply relationships for key technologies*. However, in the future, procurement policies should not be built around traditional keiretsu-style practices, which make the bidding process opaque, or on monopsonistic buying tactics such as those that set standards that are unrelated to performance. As telecommunications negotiations continued to break new ground related to trade policy, a seemingly endless stream of restrictive Japanese competitive practices were unearthed. Agreements on standards are meaningless unless they translate into sales. Even after Japan reluctantly agreed that the NTT monopoly to provide terminal equipment should be broken, many issues remained. In 1990, for example, the United States called Japan back to the table because NTT continued to claim network channel terminating equipment as part of the network, not as terminal equipment. NTT, of course, relied on Japanese firms to supply this equipment.[23]

Decisions get still messier when it becomes necessary to determine what constitutes local supply for the purposes of government procurement. EC government procurement expenditures amount to about 15 percent of gross domestic product. Before the 1992 effort began, member states, not the European Community, had jurisdiction over most of this spending. (The GATT Procurement Code was amended in 1988, at the same time that the European Community was drafting directives aimed at achieving a unified internal market by 1992.) As a first step, EC officials tried to bring all but explicitly excluded sectors—such as public utilities, transport, and telecommunications—under EC jurisdiction. Subsequently, the European Community moved to establish its sway over the excluded sectors. The United States has played the role of active critic, posing many questions as the program progresses.

However, it was not too difficult for the European Community to deflect many U.S. criticisms because the EC's program was deliberately modeled on the U.S. "Buy America" policy. All firms with local EC subsidiaries and 50 percent EC content are treated as local. Ownership per se means nothing. If a firm does not qualify as local, it may be excluded from a project or may have a 3 percent price penalty added to its bid.

Not surprisingly, the local content rule is ambiguous. It is not clear whether local content must be satisfied on a project-by-project basis (such as half the value of telephone switching equipment including software must be added locally) or on a company-by-company basis (such as AT&T must meet 50 percent EC local content for all of its telecommunications equipment sales). Moreover, spending on R&D and software as a percentage of total development costs of high-technology products from computers to aircraft has increased sharply since 1970. Since neither of these items is easily apportioned, it is not evident how to compute local content. However, we can safely say that the January 1992 decision by Los Angeles County to require that mass transit vehicles purchased by the county be produced at a particular plant in the county would not be permitted under any of these criteria. Ironically, in October 1992 the Los Angeles County Transportation Commission voted unanimously to buy fifteen metro lines cars from Sumitomo, but more than 60 percent of the value of the vehicles will consist of components made in the United States, and the cars will be shipped semifinished from Japan and completed in Los Angeles.[24]

Research and Development and Technical Standards

If companies are excluded from participating in R&D consortia in critical sectors or in the process of setting technical standards, they are likely to find themselves at a competitive disadvantage. Therefore governments likely will scrutinize national, regional, and global efforts to develop new breakthroughs and to set key standards to make certain that their firms are treated fairly in these activities.[25]

Research and Development Research and development accounts for an increasing share of the fixed costs of industry. Firms therefore are eager to amortize it on a global basis and, where possible, to share the R&D costs with each other through joint consortia and with governments. R&D also provides firms with clues about the possible directions of their competitors and key supplier industries. Both Japan and the European Community industrial policy efforts tried to use R&D for this purpose, with differing degrees of success. Governments also use shared R&D programs among firms as guides for setting technical standards and other market regulations. Complex issues remain to be resolved.

To make progress toward competition, the European Commission tried to use its R&D policies to construct an industrial policy. It has identified numerous strategic industries and is using research and collaborative cross-national efforts to try to foster a more unified European market. President Jacques Delors has indicated a desire for even more focused and product-related efforts. But these programs have had, at best, mixed results (as noted in Chapters 6 and 7). Still, they pose questions about who may join them. U.S. firms with EC-based research facilities may join Esprit. But what constitutes a legitimate research facility? And should the United States encourage the migration of R&D overseas?

Technical Standards Other EC programs, notably RACE, were designed to help Europe define its policy goals concerning technical standards. The European Community has made progress in setting technical standards internally. Using the principle of mutual recognition, EC members must recognize the standards of other members in the absence of a binding EC-wide standard. Should trade rules concerning transparency and access to the decision-making processes apply? Similarly, if DG-IV succeeds in bringing strict antitrust scrutiny to the setting of EC-wide standards, the market will be stimulated as many hidden trade barriers are removed. But how can antitrust policies be applied consistently to R&D consortia that include the European Community as a partner?[26]

During the Tokyo Round an Agreement on Technical Barriers to Trade—the Standards Code—was crafted. Uruguay Round negotiators aimed to strengthen this code. The draft Uruguay Round agreement endorses the principle of proportionality by requiring parties to adopt rules that are not "more trade-restrictive than necessary to fulfill a legitimate objective."[27]

One reason foreign firms enter ICAs is to improve their access to the European (and Japanese) standards process and to tap their experience in preparing for variations on global technologies. (As noted in Chapter 7, specialized consultative bodies are setting standards for processes that in the past were not transparent or easily accessible to foreigners.) One problem for foreign firms after entry is that consortia often have elaborate terms and conditions concerning the sharing of technology, which poses the question of whether the individual firm's intentions about sharing technology are consistent with those of the country's firms in general.[28] This issue moved to the top of the trade agenda when the U.S. government insisted on convening the U.S.-Japan Commission on High Technology to scrutinize Japanese terms for foreign entry into its Intelligent Manufacturing Initiative at the start of the 1990s. Washington wanted to assure itself that U.S. firms would be able to sign technology-sharing agreements with balanced benefits for both sides. The European Community also joined the talks.

International Principles Although principles for the international system are less evident with regard to R&D and technical standards, two stand out: (1) foreign companies should be granted access to the deliberations of R&D and standard-setting consortia if these consortia are used to make trade-related polices, such as the early development of technical standards; and (2) foreign companies can be required to maintain substantial "local" R&D facilities before being eligible to join the consortia.

But should it be compulsory to accept foreign companies if they meet these tests? ICAs could help resolve such diplomatic problems. The IBM purchase of a minority share of the French computer maker Bull in early 1992 and its ties with Siemens on semiconductors open channels for back-door diplomacy. Bull and Siemens will participate in a Texas-based computer chip project with IBM and Motorola that is separate from, but near to, Sematech and MCC. When ICAs do not resolve such problems, entry into R&D consortia may need to be negotiated. Governments are likely to consider whether there is equivalent access to R&D consortia in the complaining country. If the European Community still wanted to prevent entry, perhaps it should "pay" by extending other trade concessions.

Governments will need to decide under what conditions an exclusive national R&D program is acceptable. Japan kept satellite systems off the negotiating table as long as possible by insisting that as a part of its national aerospace research effort, they were not subject to trade liberalization. The United States countered that Japanese satellite restrictions were a procurement ploy, not an R&D development issue. In 1985 the controversy was eased on an ad hoc basis when Japan allowed the new Japanese satellite ventures (but not NTT) to form ICAs with Ford (now Loral) and Hughes for joint development of the new communications networks. U.S. satellite makers, which held a clear technological lead, were permitted to share the risks of building new satellites while their Japanese partners soaked up their technology. At the same time NTT continued to bankroll a new Japanese satellite as a crucial R&D effort. In 1989 under the "Super 301" provisions of Trade Act of 1988, U.S. Trade Representative Carla Hills cited this practice as one of three Japanese restrictions that would lead to U.S. retaliation unless they were resolved. In March 1990 Japan reluctantly agreed that NTT's purchase of the system for its network would no longer be exempted as an R&D project. Once this barrier was removed, NTT withdrew its support, leading to the cancellation of the project. This case suggests a provocative new principle that also might be applied to future NASA projects: R&D projects should be subject to GATT review if they are being developed for the commercial market.

WORLD TRADE DIPLOMACY
IN THE TWENTY-FIRST CENTURY

We asked three questions at the beginning of this book: Can the open world economy resist protectionism and thereby avoid breaking into warring regional economic blocs? Can the traditional relationships between firms and governments assumed under the GATT continue? And, can the old tools for managing the world economy continue to serve policymakers effectively in the future? Our answers are yes, no, and no.

A false dichotomy has plagued discussions of domestic economic policy. The growth of activist government policies does not doom the competitive, integrated market inside a country, but it does demand careful consideration of the effects of government intervention on markets. The same is true internationally, as the United States long has acknowledged with regard to macroeconomic policies. (See Chapter 2.) For forty years governments did not make the hard choices to reconcile activist government at the microeconomic level with free trade. Trade negotiators just hoped that conventional liberalization of major manufacturing markets would provide enough impetus to advance global integration. This is no longer sufficient.

As the examination of trade and investment dynamics in Chapter 3 showed, despite various indicators of rising protectionism, trade and foreign investment are deepening. Firms believe they need to be global. They are developing new tools such as ICAs to acquire new markets and resources abroad. ICAs are one way that globalization has gone beyond international production and sales. They are the investment-led complement to intraindustry trade, long the lubricant of the traditional system for managing the world economy. They permit refocusing of specialized competitive resources, speed innovation, and share risks. Although firms also are demanding protection and specialized help from governments at the same time, their broader interests are pushing them to prefer pinpoint contingent protectionism.

As long as the United States keeps its markets reasonably open, this pattern is likely to be maintained, which is one reason that the United States retains considerable influence over the agenda of economic diplomacy. That position is reinforced because both European and Asian business interests want a strong U.S. core to the world economy. The strategic problem for the United States is that although its interests are global, many of the most pressing negotiations need to be bilateral or regional. The United States needs multilateralism to ensure that the playing field is level and to safeguard against becoming entangled in its own web of contradictory bilateral deals. At issue, then, is how to reconcile global arrangements with bilateral, regional, and industry-specific initiatives.

Despite all the pressures toward global integration, painful adjustment still is necessary. Countries need to develop mutually acceptable practices for open industrial policies. We call the emerging lexicon of international responses to this problem a "market-access regime."

The politics and economics of Japan and the European Community doom the old GATT assumptions about the relationships between firms and governments. Once it is acknowledged that Europe is both interventionist and open to world commerce, it is evident that activist governments and global integration can coexist. The government and firms of Japan, always more protectionist than Europe, are slowly accepting that foreign firms will have to play a larger role in the Japanese economy. This was a result of pressure from trade negotiation and the growing realization that the logic of globalization applied to Japanese firms. Trade negotiators were forced to move beyond GATT rules and principles to redefine what should constitute an acceptable Japanese model within the context of the international economic community. Japan still has a way to go, but so too does the United States, which has stubbornly refused to acknowledge that its well-worn trade policy must also bear the brunt of adjustment. The United States has obligations to the international community to fix its budget deficit, boost savings and investment, and find more flexible ways to assist its industries.

The international policy community has ways to successfully oversee open industrial policies, but some new tools are needed. As we advocated in Chapter 9, close attention needs to be paid to process because experience at the domestic level suggests that there should be less emphasis on lengthy codes and more on general principles of accountability and review. Governments do not seek trade wars, but pernicious incentives, short-run opportunism, and ineffective bargaining in ill-chosen forums still could lead to economic conflict. ICAs could help ease tensions.

Government intervention needs to be reconciled with effective foreign access to markets, and accountability needs to be shifted to the level of the firm (by pinpointing remedies on the basis of individual accountability). To accomplish this governments need to pay more attention to global antitrust policies and to rules of conduct for firms. We envision a world economy in which firms are cosmopolitan and held accountable for their actions.

We live in an untidy world, one neither blessed by the beauty of a classic free-trade regime nor cursed by fragmentation and protectionist trade wars. Many crucial experiments are underway to discover how to manage this messy mix. But wistful proponents of the classic GATT or old-fashioned government regulation of markets are oblivious to the fact that world trade diplomacy has diverged from their world views. The proliferation of new developments—including alliances, bilateral diplomacy, new GATT codes for services, and the 1992 program of Europe—are leading policymakers around the world to the realization that they are witnessing the birth of a new market-access regime for world commerce.

The breakup of the Soviet Union and the death of the cold war buried the old bipolar world dominated by security issues. If we nurture the emerging market-access regime, the frictions that will accompany the refocusing of foreign policy attention on international economic issues may be eased. To paraphrase Mikhail Bulgakov's devilish stranger in the frontispiece of this book, to govern the situation here on earth we need to have a plan for at least a fairly decent period of time. We have presented the building blocks from which such a plan might emerge and assembled a few pieces of a complicated puzzle. The ad hoc experiments of governments and companies could become the foundations of a new world economic order.

Notes

CHAPTER 1

1. Jagdish Bhagwati, *Protectionism* (Cambridge, MA: MIT Press, 1988); Jan Tumlir, *Protectionism* (Washington, DC: American Enterprise Institute, 1985).
2. Paul Kennedy, *The Rise and Fall of the Great Powers* (New York: Random House, 1987), is the leading voice of the decline theory. Two differently argued opposing views are Joseph S. Nye, Jr., *Bound to Lead: The Changing Nature of American Power* (New York: Basic Books, 1990), and Henry R. Nau, *The Myth of America's Decline* (New York: Oxford University Press, 1990).
3. The relationship between the public and private sectors is straightforward: corporations exist and operate on terms set by governments. Firms must address broad, long-term problems (such as how to continue to innovate) and make short-term decisions (such as how to distribute new investment among projects and regions). If governments do not like the way firms behave, governments change the rules. Knowing this, firms seek strategies that maximize their advantages under existing rules or prod governments to alter the rules in ways that will help them.
4. Local partners often provided political contacts for the foreign TNC as well. Sometimes, as in Iran, these partners could become liabilities if the old leaders were suddenly replaced by a new government. Farok J. Contractor, "Ownership Patterns of U.S. Joint Ventures Abroad and the Liberalization of Foreign Government Regulations in the 1980s," *Journal of International Business Studies* 21:1 (1st quarter 1990), pp. 55–73, found a broad trend toward liberalization of restrictions on foreign direct investment. But he also discovered that many ICAs invest in large countries to obtain complementary partners, acquire skills, or achieve economies of scale.
5. Koji Kobayashi, *The Rise of NEC* (Cambridge, MA: Blackwell, 1991), pp. xvii–xx.
6. The automobile industry is examined in more depth in Chapter 5.
7. There were exceptions. See "Are Foreign Partners Good for U.S. Companies?," *Business Week*, May 28, 1984, pp. 58–60. For a balanced look at this phenomenon from the business press, see Louis Kraar, "Your Rivals Can Be Your Allies," *Fortune*, March 27, 1989, pp. 66–76. Business International Corporation even issued a detailed manual, *Competitive Alliances: How to Succeed at Cross-Regional Collaboration* (New York: Business International Corporation, July 1987).
8. Robert B. Reich and Eric D. Mankin, "Joint Ventures with the Japanese Give Away Our Future," *Harvard Business Review* 64 (March-April 1986), pp. 78–86.

9. Tom Peters, *Thriving on Chaos* (New York: Harper & Row, 1987). James C. Abegglen notes that in the late 1980s only 50 percent of U.S. firms investing in Japan joined with Japanese partners. In the mid-1980s about 70 percent took partners. "Japanese Technology" (Survey), *Economist*, December 2, 1989, p. 4.

10. Jonathan David Aronson, "Politics and the International Consortium Banks," *Stanford Journal of International Studies* 11 (Spring 1976), p. 46. But the club approach to banking ultimately failed: the last major banking consortia closed in 1990. "The Last of the Consortium Banks: Bad Day for Librans," *Economist*, March 17, 1990, p. 76.

11. Michael Porter, *The Competitive Advantage of Nations* (New York: Free Press, 1990).

12. For this line of thinking we are indebted to Alexis Jacquemin, "Strategic Competition in a Global Environment," in OECD, *Trade, Investment and Technology in the 1990s* (Paris: OECD, 1991), pp. 13–33.

CHAPTER 2

1. Stephen Krasner, ed., *International Regimes* (New York: Cornell University Press, 1983).

2. In *The Political Economy of International Relations* (Princeton: Princeton University Press, 1987), Robert Gilpin notes similar consequences of these changes.

3. This was a case of "embedded liberalism," a phrase coined by John Gerard Ruggie in his seminal article "International Regimes, Transactions, and Change: Embedded Liberalism in the Postwar Economic Order," *International Organization* 36:2 (Spring 1982), pp. 379–416.

4. See Richard N. Gardner, *Sterling-Dollar Diplomacy in Current Perspective: The Origins and the Prospects of Our International Economic Order* (New York: Columbia University Press, 1980), particularly pp. 369–380. Also see John H. Jackson, *World Trade and the Law of GATT* (Charlottesville, VA: Michie, 1969).

5. See particularly Alfred D. Chandler, Jr., *Scale and Scope: The Dynamics of Industrial Capitalism* (Cambridge, MA: Harvard University Press, 1990), and *The Visible Hand* (Cambridge, MA: Harvard University Press, 1977), and also Raymond Vernon, *Sovereignty at Bay* (New York: Basic Books, 1971).

6. See David C. Mowery and Nathan Rosenberg, *Technology and the Pursuit of Economic Growth* (New York: Cambridge University Press, 1989), pp. 123–168.

7. James Abegglen estimates that Japan acquired all of its key technology from 1950 to 1980 for just $10 billion, an incredible bargain. "Japanese Technology" (Survey), *Economist*, December 2, 1989, p. 4.

8. See William Brock, "Trade and Debt: The Vital Linkage," *Foreign Affairs* 62:5 (Summer 1984), pp. 1037–1057.

9. The Charter of the ITO explicitly recognized this problem. We thank William Diebold, Jr. for this observation.

10. Jackson, *World Trade and the Law of GATT*, pp. 293–294.

11. See Ronald Kent Shelp, *Beyond Industrialization* (Boulder: Praeger, 1981).

12. Jackson, *World Trade and the Law of GATT*, p. 164.

13. Michael Gilligan, "The Institutionalization of International Trade Policy: Laying the Micro-Foundations of International Cooperation," Paper presented to the American Political Science Association, September 1991. Although the GATT does not restrict most-favored-nation (MFN) treatment to contracting parties, permitting members to give a free ride to outsiders, negotiators generally tried to keep free riding to a minimum. The United States originally favored restricting MFN status to contracting parties, but the Czechs pointed out that they could not treat the Soviet Union that way. William Diebold, Jr., suggests that this may be the greatest influence the USSR ever had on the GATT.

14. Models of the GATT rounds suggest that past agreements emphasized fairness (benefits in proportion to contributions) more than efficiency. Even the notion of contingent multilateral liberalization undermines many of the efficiency gains assumed under programs of unilateral liberalization championed prior to 1945. Kenneth S. Chan, "The International Negotiation Game: Some Evidence from the Tokyo Round," *Review of Economics and Statistics* 67 (Spring 1985), pp. 456–464.

15. See Donald L. Guertin and John M. Kline, "Building an International Investment Accord" (Washington, DC: Atlantic Council, July 1989).

16. Charles Lipson has pointed out that there was substantial agreement among industrial countries but substantial disagreement between industrial and developing nations. Charles Lipson, *Standing Guard* (Berkeley: University of California Press, 1985). Dennis J. Encarnation and Mark Mason, "Neither MITI nor America: The Political Economy of Capital Liberalization in Japan," *International Organization* 44:1 (Winter 1990), pp. 25–54, show that even after Japan began to admit it was a developed economy, it deviated from the rules until recent years.

17. The newest exposition of this approach is exemplified by Michael Porter, *The Competitive Advantage of Nations* (New York: Free Press, 1990).

18. See Chandler, *The Visible Hand*, for the rise of the modern business enterprises in the mid-nineteenth century. On the rise of TNCs see Mira Wilkins, *The Emergence of Multinational Enterprise* (Cambridge, MA: Harvard University Press, 1970).

19. Vernon, *Sovereignty at Bay.*

20. The multination domestic firm is an idea suggested by Michael Porter. The first generation of TNCs was depicted in Raymond Vernon's early work on the product cycle. Porter described the multinational strategies of contemporary firms as networking strategies. Pankaj Ghemawat, Michael E. Porter, and Richard A. Rawlinson, "Patterns of International Coalition Activity," in Michael E. Porter, ed., *Competition in Global Industries* (Cambridge, MA: Harvard Business School Press, 1986), pp. 345–365. See also the work of Promethee on networking: "Deregulation in the 1990s," *Project Prométhée Perspectives*, No. 5 (Paris: Promethee, March 1988).

CHAPTER 3

1. *GATT Focus*, No. 86, November–December 1991, p. 2.

2. See the classic work by Herbert Feis, *Europe, the World's Banker, 1870–1914* (New York: Norton, 1965).
3. "The Impact of 1992," *CTC Reporter*, no. 27 (Spring 1989), p. 22.
4. These conclusions are based on tables in Derek Healey, *Japanese Capital Exports and Asian Economic Development* (Paris: OECD, 1991), pp. 78–87.
5. We thank Harry Freeman for his helpful observations.
6. Disagreement about how to formulate the argument about international power persists. An intriguing approach to international power that dovetails with our arguments about transaction costs and globalization of the firm is Beth V. Yarbrough and Robert M. Yarbrough, "Cooperation in the Liberalization of International Trade: After Hegemony, What?," *International Organization* 41:1 (Winter 1987), pp. 1–26. Also see Robert O. Keohane, *After Hegemony: Cooperation and Discord in the World Political Economy* (Princeton: Princeton University Press, 1984), on cooperation among a small group of powers and the difficulties imposed by opportunism. On the positive side, successful international regimes often have inertia because of the transaction costs facing governments that wish to alter them in major ways.
7. This shift in preferences is documented in Helen V. Milner, *Resisting Protectionism: Global Industries and the Politics of International Trade* (Princeton: Princeton University Press, 1988); Jeffrey Frieden, "Invested Interests: The Politics of National Economic Policies in a World of Global Finance," *International Organization* 45:4 (Autumn 1991), pp. 425–451.
8. In this light the Super 301 provision of the 1988 Trade Act can be seen as a tool to open foreign markets. Helen V. Milner and David B. Yoffie, "Between Free Trade and Protectionism: Trade Policy and a Theory of Corporate Trade Demands," *International Organization* 43:2 (Spring 1989), pp. 239–272.
9. I. M. Destler and John S. Odell, *Anti-Protectionism* (Washington, DC: Institute for International Economics, 1987), make this argument at the national level.
10. An insightful discussion of levels of effective protection is Judith Goldstein, "The Political Economy of Trade: The Institutions of Protection," *American Political Science Review* 80:2 (April 1986), pp. 161–184.
11. International Chamber of Commerce, Position Paper No. 17, "Toward Greater Competition in Telecommunications: Basic Services and Network Infrastructure" (Paris: ICC, December, 1991).
12. Frieden, "Invested Interests"; Kenneth A. Froot and David B. Yoffie, "Strategic Trade Policies in a Tripolar World," Paper prepared for a conference on "International Political Economy in a Tripolar World," January 12–13, 1991, argue that mobility of capital is rising even in industries where increasing returns to scale discourage it. Increased mobility via foreign investment reduces the credibility of improved market return from protectionist trade policies and thus negates much of the benefit derived from protectionism.
13. This deal had many critics. Arguably, a different U.S. policy might have provided greater confidence that this partnership would not lead to the decline of McDonnell Douglas. The European Community questioned whether the deal might introduce an Airbus-style subsidies via the Taiwanese government role in Taiwan Aerospace. Ralph Vartabedian, "Douglas Sale to Taiwanese Firm Isn't a Done Deal," *Los Angeles Times*, January 10, 1992, p. D1. Boeing officials also worried about unfair subsidies and union officials feared the loss

of jobs and technology. *Seattle Times*, February 27, 1992, pp. C1, C5. Taiwanese legislators also were concerned that they were not getting enough for their money. *Business Week*, March 9, 1992, p. 49. It appears that Taiwan would build the wings and fuselage of the new MD-12, McDonnell's competitor to the Boeing 747. However, so far there are few orders for this jumbo jet. David Holley and Ralph Vartabedian, "McDonnell Deal Faces New Doubt," *Los Angeles Times*, April 27, 1992, p. D1. In May 1992, Taiwan Aerospace withdrew its equity offer and promised to buy MD-12s if it could build the wings and fuselage and if McDonnell Douglas had other orders.

14. Beth V. Yarbrough and Robert M. Yarbrough, *Cooperation and Governance in International Trade: The Strategic Organizational Approach* (Princeton: Princeton University Press, 1992).

15. Lawrence Krause, "Managed Trade: The Regime of Today and Tomorrow," *Journal of Asian Economics* 13 (Fall 1992), pp. 301–314.

16. DeAnne Julius, *Global Companies and Public Policy* (New York: Council on Foreign Relations, 1990), p. 23, makes the comparison. Foreign direct investment data are from J. Saul Lizondo, "Foreign Direct Investment," in IMF, *Determinants and Systemic Consequences of International Capital Flows* (IMF Occasional Paper No. 77, March 1991), p. 68. Also see United Nations, *The Trend in Foreign Direct Investment, 1991 World Investment Report* (New York: United Nations, 1991).

17. Estimates of trade shares reported by the U.N. Centre on Transnational Corporations are more cautious. *CTC Reporter*, no. 26 (Autumn 1988). McKeown estimates that intrafirm trade constituted 30 percent of U.S. exports and 40 percent of imports in 1985 and accounted for roughly 30 percent of Japanese exports and imports. Japanese authorities stated that 10 percent of U.S. exports in 1991 were accounted for by Japanese subsidiaries in the United States. Timothy J. McKeown, "A Liberal Trade Order? The Long-Run Pattern of Imports to the Advanced Capitalist States," *International Studies Quarterly* 35:2 (June 1991), pp. 151–171.

18. The accelerated flow of investment into the United States created new worries, which are discussed throughout the book. Two points are of less consequence. First, the United States did not become a major debtor with regard to the private balance on foreign investment. Mahnaz Fahim-Nader, "Business Enterprises Acquired or Established by Foreign Direct Investors in 1990," *Survey of Current Business* (May 1991), pp. 31–39, showed that previous fears on this count were mainly due to accounting problems. Second, the share of Japanese holdings is increasing, but the levels in themselves are not worrisome. See the BEA data and Edward M. Graham and Paul R. Krugman, *Foreign Direct Investment in the United States* (Washington, DC: Institute for International Economics, 1989).

19. Based on Julius, *Global Companies*, pp. 24, 75.

20. But see Dennis J. Encarnation, *Rivals beyond Trade: America versus Japan in Global Competition* (Ithaca: Cornell University Press, 1992).

21. Contrast the situation today, for example, with the Asian-dominated investment strategy Japan employed until the mid-1970s. Kiyoshi Kojima, *Japan and a New Economic Order* (Boulder, CO: Westview Press, 1977).

22. *CTC Reporter*, no. 26 (Autumn 1988), p. 14. JETRO estimates are reported in Louis Emmerij, "International Investments and Rising Protectionism," *Asian*

Development Review 8:2 (1990), p. 113. Also see Yutaka Fujiwara, "Cross-Border M&A between Japan and the U.S.: Increasing Interdependence," *Pacific Rim Digest* (February 1991), pp. 18–19.

23. Encarnation, *Rivals beyond Trade*. Graham and Krugman, *Foreign Direct Investment*, pp. 60–63, appear optimistic that Japanese firms will change as a result of the well-established learning curve for conducting foreign production operations. Japan lags in matching the U.S. mix of trade and investment in Europe. European imports are almost twice as much from the United States as from Japan, but the stock of Japanese direct investment was only about a quarter of the U.S. level. Stephen Thomsen and Phedon Nicolaides, *The Evolution of Japanese Direct Investment in Europe* (London: Harvester Wheatsheaf, 1990).

24. Siji Naya and Eric D. Ramstetter, "Policy Interactions and Direct Foreign Investment in East and Southeast Asia," *Journal of World Trade* 22 (April 1988), pp. 57–71.

25. Also see Lynn Krieger Mytelka, ed., *Strategic Partnerships and the World Economy* (London: Pinter, 1991).

26. Global firms also try to benefit from sectoral policies of many countries. However, sectoral policy has received so much attention that there is little need to elaborate here. The Berkeley Roundtable on the International Economy (BRIE) has developed a body of examples on creating comparative advantage. Laura D'Andrea Tyson, *Who's Bashing Whom? Trade Conflict in High-Technology Industries* (Washington, D.C.: Institute for International Economics, 1992).

27. David C. Mowery and Nathan Rosenberg, "Competition and Cooperation: The U.S. and Japanese Commercial Aircraft Industries," *California Management Review* 27 (1985), pp. 70–92; David C. Mowery, "Collaborative Ventures between U.S. and Foreign Manufacturing Firms: An Overview," and "Joint Ventures in the U.S. Commercial Aircraft Industry," in David C. Mowery, ed., *International Collaborative Ventures in U.S. Manufacturing* (Cambridge, MA: Ballinger, 1988), pp. 1–22, 71–110. The seminal treatment of user-interactive technological innovation is E. Von Hippel, "The Dominant Role of Users in the Scientific Investment Innovation Process," *Research Policy* 5 (1976), pp. 212–239.

28. This book does not discuss trade in raw materials or commodities. Our overview of technology and complementary assets as being critical for globalization follows the approach of Gary P. Pisano, Michael V. Russo, and David J. Teece in Mowery, ed., *International Collaborative Ventures*, pp. 23–70.

29. David Friedman, *The Misunderstood Miracle: Industrial Development and Political Change in Japan* (Ithaca: Cornell University Press, 1988); Michael J. Piore and Charles F. Sabel, *The Second Industrial Divide: Possibilities for Prosperity* (New York: Basic Books, 1984).

30. See Gregory H. Feldberg, "Joint Ventures in Japan Suffering Wedding Bell Blues," *Japan Economic Journal*, August 25, 1990, pp. 1, 7. To sample the theoretical literature see Oliver Williamson, *The Economic Institutions of Capitalism* (New York: Free Press, 1988); R. E. Caves, H. Crookell, and J. P. Killing, "The Imperfect Market for Technology Licenses," *Oxford Bulletin of Economics and Statistics* 45 (1983), pp. 249–268.

31. Dorothy B. Christelow, "International Joint Ventures: How Important Are They?," *Columbia Journal of World Business* 22 (Summer 1987), p. 7.
32. *New York Times*, April 30, 1992.
33. See David D. Friedman, William M. Landes, and Richard A. Posner, "Some Economics of Trade Secret Law," *Journal of Economic Perspectives* 5:1 (Winter 1991), pp. 61–72.
34. James Risen, "Town Car Odyssey," *Los Angeles Times*, October 8, 1989, p. IV-1.
35. "Automatic Financial Markets," *Economist*, March 10, 1990, pp. 19–20, 24. Promethee, a Paris-based research institute, has been a leader in developing thinking about "networked" economies.
36. Ellen R. Auster, "International Corporate Linkages: Dynamic Forms in Changing Environments," *Columbia Journal of World Business* 22 (Summer 1987), p. 4.
37. See Joan Spero, "Guiding Global Finance," *Foreign Policy* 73 (Winter 1988–89), pp. 114–135.
38. United Airlines owns 51 percent of Covia, which owns and operates the Apollo computer reservation system. *International Herald Tribune*, March 4, 1992, p. C1. There are two major European-based computer reservation systems: Amadeus was founded in 1987 by Lufthansa, Air France, SAS, and Iberia airlines; Galileo was formed by their European rivals, including British Airways, Swiss Air, and KLM. "Amadeus Plot Global Networking," *Communications Week International*, July 15, 1991, p. 31.
39. Rob Van Thulder and Gerd Junne, *European Multinationals in Core Technologies* (Chichester: John Wiley, 1988), pp. 126–130, 177–185.
40. Lawrence G. Franko, "New Forms of Investment in Developing Countries by U.S. Companies: A Five-Industry Comparison," *Columbia Journal of World Business* 22 (Summer 1987), pp. 39–55.
41. See the discussion of economies of scale in Lacy Glenn Thomas, "Multifirm Strategies in the U.S. Pharmaceutical Industry," in Mowery, ed., *International Collaborative Ventures*, pp. 147–182. On the basis of a small sample, Bruce Kogut suggests that new technologies encourage successful ICAs but high rates of growth may slowly undermine their stability. Distribution systems also depend increasingly on brand name advertising and sophisticated customer services (including customization) that selling from abroad cannot satisfy. Karen J. Hladik, *International Joint Ventures* (Lexington, MA: Lexington Books, 1985); Kathryn Harrigan Rudie, *Managing for Joint Venture Success* (Lexington, MA: Lexington Books, 1986).
42. Artemis March, "The U.S. Commercial Aircraft Industry and Its Foreign Competitors," in MIT Commission on Industrial Productivity, *The Working Papers of the MIT Commission on Industrial Productivity*, vol. 1 (Cambridge, MA: MIT Press, 1989), pp. 33, 44.
43. This appears to have occurred in the Mitsubishi–Daimler Benz project, discussed in Chapter 5.
44. See the discussion of telecommunications services alliances in Chapter 7.
45. Bruce Kogut, "The Stability of Joint Ventures: Reciprocity and Competitive Rivalry," *Journal of Industrial Economics* 38:2 (December 1989), pp. 183–198; and Claude d'Aspremont and Alexis Jacquemin, "Cooperative and Noncooperative R&D in Duopoly with Spillover," *American Economic Re-*

view 78:5 (December 1988), pp. 1133–1137, agree that R&D ventures are safer than large-scale manufacturing ventures. Kogut notes that a broader total relationship improves the chances of effective mutual controls on behavior. Paul W. Beamish and John C. Banks, "Equity Joint Ventures and the Theory of the Multinational Enterprise," *Journal of International Business Studies* 9:2 (Summer 1987), pp. 1–16, stress the need for careful fits between objectives and contracting formats for ICAs.

46. Kirkor Bozdogan, "The Transformation of the U.S. Chemicals Industry," in MIT Commission on Industrial Productivity, *The Working Papers of the MIT Commission on Industrial Productivity*, vol. 1, p. 4.

47. Interview, Tokyo, November 1988.

CHAPTER 4

1. Peter J. Katzenstein, *Small States in World Markets* (Ithaca: Cornell University Press, 1985); Robert Bates, Philip Brock, and Jill Tiefenthaler, "Risk and Trade Regimes: Another Exploration," *International Organization* 45:1 (Winter 1991), pp. 1–18.

2. The best known appeal to European cooperation in the face of the U.S. onslaught was Jean-Jacques Servan-Schreiber, *The American Challenge* (New York: Avon Books, 1968). Canada also fretted about U.S. domination. See Kari Levitt, *The Silent Surrender* (New York: Liveright, 1970).

3. See Thomas Pepper, Merit E. Janow, and Jimmy W. Wheeler, *The Competition: Dealing with the Japanese* (New York: Praeger, 1985); Ira Magaziner and Mark Patinkin, *The Silent War: Inside the Global Business Battles Shaping America's Future* (New York: Random House, 1989); and Martin Tolchin and Susan J. Tolchin, *Buying into America: How Foreign Money Is Changing the Face of Our Nation* (New York: Random House, 1988).

4. On the rise of the Japanese and European markets to parity with the North American market see Kenichi Ohmae, *Triad Power: The Coming Shape of Global Competition* (New York: Free Press, 1985).

5. See Helen V. Milner and David B. Yoffie, "Between Free Trade and Protectionism: Strategic Trade Policy and a Theory of Corporate Trade Demands," *International Organization* 43:2 (Spring 1989), pp. 239–272.

6. See Kent E. Calder, *Crisis and Compensation: Public Policy and Political Stability in Japan, 1949–1986* (Princeton: Princeton University Press, 1988); and Michael Mochizuki, *Ruling Japan: Conservative Dominance in the Postwar Era* (Berkeley: University of California Press, forthcoming 1993).

7. Samuel Kernell, "The Primacy of Politics in Economic Policy in Samuel Kernell, ed., *Parallel Politics* (Washington, DC: Brookings Institution, 1991), and Peter F. Cowhey, "Elect Locally, Order Globally: Domestic Politics and Multilateral Cooperation," in John Ruggie, ed., *Multilateralism* (New York: Columbia University Press, 1992).

8. Charles H. Ferguson, "Computers and the Coming of the U.S. Keiretsu," *Harvard Business Review* (July-August 1990), pp. 55–70; Masahiko Aoki, *The Cooperative Game Theory of the Firm* (New York: Oxford University Press, 1984); Takeo Hoshi, Anil Kashup, and David Scharfstein, "The Role of Banks in Reducing the Costs of Financial Distress in Japan," *Journal of*

Financial Economics 27 (1990), pp. 67–88. Even in Japan there is some criticism of these practices. See "Cross-Shareholding in Japan Comes under Fire," *Nikkei Weekly*, November 11, 1989, p. 7.

9. Kenneth Flamm, "Semiconductors," in Gary Clyde Hufbauer, ed., *Europe 1992: An American Perspective* (Washington, DC: Brookings Institution, 1990), pp. 225–292.

10. This is one of the few points of agreement between Masaru Yoshitomi and Chalmers Johnson in their pointed discussions of keiretsu in *International Economic Insights* 1:2 (September-October 1990), pp. 10–17.

11. Edward J. Lincoln, *Japan's Unequal Trade* (Washington, DC: Brookings Institution, 1990).

12. Martin Fransman, *The Market and Beyond: Cooperation and Competition in Information Technology in the Japanese System* (New York: Cambridge University Press, 1990).

13. See Wayne Sandholtz and John Zysman, "1992: Recasting the European Bargain," *World Politics* 42:1 (October 1989), pp. 95–128.

14. Esprit and other programs initiated by Étienne Davignon depended on the European Roundtable group of companies, particularly GEC, ICL, Plessey, Thomson-Brandt, CIT-Alcatel (CGE), Bull, Siemens, AEG, Nixdorf, Olivetti, Stet, and Philips. These companies received the bulk of Esprit's funding in the early days and even today receive a large portion of Esprit funding. Eureka involves 295 R&D projects in nine areas of advanced technology. Major programs include the Joint European Semiconductor Silicon Project (JESSI), an eight-year, $4 billion campaign to keep Europe's semiconductor industry alive, and an $800 million project to counter Japan in HDTV. Esprit sponsors 406 programs within the European Community to bolster Europe's information technologies, including creating a European multiprocessor computer. RACE is a collection of 88 projects to develop a powerful, fiber optics–based data communications system across Europe by 1995. BRITE sponsors research to integrate new advanced materials and manufacturing technologies into key industries such as shipbuilding and aerospace.

15. Malcolm Laws, "RACE Phase II Ready to Go," *Communications Week International*, November 18, 1991, p. 25.

16. Much of the analysis that follows is based on interviews conducted by one of the authors with Commission officials in March 1992.

17. *Computer Week*, September 27, 1990, p. 91. The Motorola figure was offered by a company official at the National Research Council conference in November 1990.

18. The new literature on openness and domestic politics stresses that smaller states with greater dependence on trade usually create political institutions to restrain interests opposed to openness. Powerful countries with less dependence on trade have to cope with the problem that there is always a constituency for protectionism. Ronald Rogowski, "Trade and the Variety of Democratic Institutions," *International Organization* 41:2 (Spring 1987), pp. 203–224. Domestic and international explanations often are viewed as mutually exclusive, but see the analysis of power and factor movements in David Lake and Scott James, "The Second Face of Hegemony," *International Organization* 43:1 (Winter 1989), pp. 1–29. Also see Cowhey, "Elect Locally, Order Globally."

19. See Frances McCall Rosenbluth, *Financial Politics in Contemporary Japan* (Ithaca, NY: Cornell University Press, 1989).

20. See Daniel M. Kasper, *Deregulation and Globalization: Liberalizing International Trade in Air Services* (Cambridge, MA: Ballinger, 1988).

21. The new literature concerning strategic trade suggests that high-technology markets are especially likely to be imperfect and dominated by oligopolies. See particularly James A. Brander, "Rationalities for Strategic Trade and Industrial Policy," pp. 23–46, and Barbara J. Spencer, "What Should Trade Policies Target?," pp. 69–89, in Paul Krugman, ed., *Strategic Trade and the New International Economics* (Cambridge, MA: MIT Press, 1986). An excellent review of the literature that demonstrates that qualifications are more abundant than propositions is J. David Richardson, "Strategic Trade Policy," *International Organization* 44:1 (Winter 1990), pp. 107–135.

22. See Ryutaro Komiya, ed., *Industrial Policy of Japan* (Tokyo: Academic Press, 1988).

23. See Rob Paarlberg, *Fixing Farm Trade* (Cambridge, MA: Ballinger, 1988).

24. See Vinod Aggarwal and Stephan Haggard, "Politics of Protection in U.S. Textile and Apparel Industries," pp. 249–312, and David B. Yoffie, "Adjustment in the Footwear Industry," pp. 313–349, in John Zysman and Laura Tyson, eds., *American Industry in International Competition* (Ithaca: Cornell University Press, 1983).

25. See Krugman, ed., *Strategic Trade*, and Richardson, "Strategic Trade Policy." However, as sentiment for protectionism increases, groups that benefit from open markets are more likely to organize and lobby for free trade. See Helen Milner, *Resisting Protectionism* (Princeton: Princeton University Press, 1989). Also see I. M. Destler and John S. Odell, *Anti-Protectionism* (Washington, DC: Institute for International Economics, September 1987).

26. See Sylvia Maxfield and James H. Nolt, "Protectionism and the Internationalization of Capital," *International Studies Quarterly* 34:1 (March 1990), pp. 49–82.

27. See John Fayerweather, *The Mercantile Bank Affair* (New York: New York University Press, 1974).

28. For a brief overview of MCC see "This Research Consortium Gets Its Research to Market," *Business Week*, January 27, 1992, p. 58.

29. Joel Davidow and Paul Schott Stevens, "Antitrust Merger Control and National Security Review of Foreign Acquisitions in the United States," *Journal of World Trade* 24:1 (February 1990), pp. 39–56.

30. "Guiding Hand: In Asia, the Japanese Hope to 'Coordinate' What Nations Produce," *Wall Street Journal*, August 20, 1990, pp. A1, A4.

31. According to Rod Schwartz, chief London banking analyst for Shearson Lehman Hutton, cited in "Banking on the Future," *Europe*, March 1990, p. 9.

32. *Seattle Times*, August 25, 1990, p. D1.

33. Goals such as a better educated work force or increased savings are important, but there are other, possibly more important factors as well. See Robert B. Reich, *The Work of Nations: Preparing Ourselves for 21st-Century Capitalism* (New York: Alfred Knopf, 1991). An argument that it is possible and even desirable for countries to create comparative advantage is found in Stephen S. Cohen and John Zysman, *Manufacturing Matters: The Myth of the Post-Industrial Economy* (New York: Basic Books, 1987).

34. Paul Krugman, *Has the Adjustment Process Worked?* (Washington, DC: Institute for International Economics, 1991).
35. *Economist*, April 18, 1992, p. 68. U.S. firms worried about European restrictions on Japanese-sourced semiconductors because of the growth of Japanese production in the United States for shipment to Europe. Edwin Vermulst and Paul Waer, "European Community Rules of Origin as Commercial Policy Instruments?," *Journal of World Trade* (June 1990), p. 80. Similarly, statisticians regard Dupont as a Canadian firm because Seagram's holds 20 percent of its common shares. Hufbauer, ed., *Europe 1992*, p. 48.
36. *Los Angeles Times*, November 30, 1990, p. D2/SD.
37. See Ingo Walter, *Global Competition in Financial Services: Market Structure, Protection, and Trade Liberalization* (Cambridge, MA: Ballinger, 1988), pp. 60–69. Nonetheless, governments did arrive at least a partial answer. In the aftermath of the financial unrest of the mid-1970s, the Basle Concordat made parent banks (and indirectly their central banks) responsible on a pro rata basis. If a British bank operating in the United States failed, the Bank of England was obligated to help clean up the mess. Ethan Kapstein, "Resolving the Regulator's Dilemma: International Coordination of Banking Regulations," *International Organization* 45:2 (Spring 1989), pp. 323–347.
38. Richardson, "Strategic Trade Policy."
39. William M. Evan and Paul Olk, "R&D Consortia: A New U.S. Organizational Form," *Sloan Management Review* 37 (Spring 1990), p. 42.

CHAPTER 5

1. Peter F. Cowhey and Edward Long, "Testing Theories of Regime Change: Hegemonic Decline or Surplus Capacity?," *International Organization* 37:2 (Spring 1983), pp. 157–183. Based on 1983 data in James A. Dunn, "Automobiles in International Trade," *International Organization* 41:2 (Spring 1987), pp. 225–252, intra-EC trade accounted for roughly 40 percent of exports, the U.S.-Canada automobile agreement covered almost 13 percent, Japanese and European exports to the United States were responsible for 24 percent, and Japanese exports to Europe for 10 percent.
2. We draw on James Womack, "Multinational Joint Ventures in Motor Vehicles," in David C. Mowery, ed., *International Collaborative Ventures in U.S. Manufacturing* (Cambridge, MA: Ballinger, 1988), pp. 301–347. See also James P. Womack, Daniel T. Jones, and Daniel Roos, *The Machine That Changed the World* (New York: Rawson Associates, 1990).
3. No persuasive economic argument exists that voluntary export restraints aimed against Japan are the best way to organize a market. Even antidumping actions (legal under the GATT) are efficient only under a limited range of circumstances. The real issue is whether, judged on political and economic criteria, such policies constitute a sound, second-best approach in an imperfect world. As in U.S. regulation of traditional public utilities or the oil market from the 1930s through the 1960s, major technological advances were achieved even though market distortions occurred. See the exchange of views among Laura Tyson, Avinash Dixit, and Robert Baldwin in Robert Z. Lawrence and Charles L. Schultze, eds., *An American Trade Strategy: Options for the 1990s*

(Washington, DC: Brookings Institution, 1990), pp. 142–207; Leonard Waverman, "Strategic Trade Policy and 1992," in B. Burgenmeier and J. L. Mucchielli, eds., *Multinationals and Europe 1992: Strategies for the Future* (London: Routledge, 1992), pp. 59–77.

4. Leslie Helm and Donald Woutat, "Angry Reaction to Japan's Auto Quota Renewal," *Los Angeles Times*, January 12, 1991, p. D2.

5. Cowhey and Long, "Testing Theories of Regime Change," p. 159. This formula allowed countries to shield their national champions in the automobile industry from foreign purchase. Thus, West Germany maintained an open industrial policy while protecting Volkswagen from foreign investors. France was more restrictive, but complaints by U.S. firms were limited because they had access to the EC as a whole. See Simon Reich, "Roads to Follow: Regulating Direct Foreign Investment," *International Organization* 43:4 (Autumn 1989), pp. 543–584. Sometimes U.S. firms were indifferent about exports, even supporting import-substituting industrialization in larger developing markets because they were the beneficiaries of protectionism. See Sylvia Maxfield and James H. Nolt, "Protectionism and the Internationalization of Capital," *International Studies Quarterly* 34:1 (March 1990), pp. 49–82.

6. Gary C. Hufbauer and Jeffrey J. Schott assisted by Jay Magnus Lambsdorff, "Options for a Hemispheric Trade Order," *Inter-American Law Review* 22 (Spring-Summer 1991), pp. 261–296.

7. *Wall Street Journal*, June 9, 1992, p. A15.

8. This discussion relies on Womack, Jones, and Roos, *The Machine That Changed the World* and on Kim B. Clark and Takahiro Fujimoto, *Product Development Performance* (Boston: Harvard Business School Press, 1991).

9. Michael Piore and Charles Sabel use automobiles as the paradigmatic industry in their study of U.S. political economy, *The Second Industrial Divide: Possibilities for Prosperity* (New York: Basic Books, 1984).

10. Alasdair Smith and Anthony J. Venables, "Automobiles," in Gary Hufbauer, ed., *Europe 1992: An American Perspective* (Washington, DC: Brookings Institution, 1990), pp. 119–158.

11. See Hurmut Berg, "Motor-Cars: Between Growth and Protectionism," in H. W. de Jong, ed., *The Structure of European Industry* (Dordrecht: Kluwer, 1988), pp. 245–265.

12. General Motors resisted changing the trade rules but supported pollution emission requirements that were engineered to hamper Volkswagen. We thank Mathew McCubbins for this point.

13. Clark and Fujimoto, *Product Development Performance*.

14. There is some evidence that Japanese firms benefit from their more or less simultaneous entry in a foreign market. Dominique Matlanssens and Johny K. Johansson, "Rivalry as Synergy? The Japanese Automobile Companies' Export Expansion," *Journal of International Business Studies* 22 (Third Quarter 1991), pp. 503–526.

15. In 1984 the first VRA called for 1.68 million vehicles per year but included the expectation that this figure could increase by about 16.5 percent of the growth in the U.S. market. It reached 1.85 million units by 1985. In 1991 Japan offered to retain its 1990 limit of 2.3 million vehicles. In March 1992 MITI announced it would reduce its self-imposed quota on automobile exports to the United States to 1.65 million in fiscal 1992. This represents a real cut of

about 5 percent from the approximately 1.73 million units that were shipped in the fiscal year ending March 31, 1992. *Los Angeles Times*, March 19, 1992, p. D1. Although the limit long appeared toothless, it poses problems for second-tier producers like Isuzu, which wants to sell more cars independently in the United States and cannot get a larger share of the VRA to do so. James A. Dunn, Jr., "The Asian Auto Imbroglio: Patterns of Trade Policy and Business Strategy," in Stephen Haggard and Chung-In Moon, eds., *Pacific Dynamics: The International Politics of Industrial Change* (Boulder, CO: Westview, 1989), pp. 155–184.

16. Hiromichi Mutoh, "The Automotive Industry," in Ryutaro Komiya, Masahiro Okuno, and Kotaro Suzumura, eds., *Industrial Policy of Japan* (Tokyo: Academic Press, 1988). In 1974, in response to antidumping complaints, the U.S. Treasury asked five foreign automobile manufacturers to increase prices. The International Trade Commission rejected limits on imported automobiles in 1980, but the Reagan administration negotiated a VRA in 1981 that was renewed in 1984. The formal VRA has lapsed, but Japan renews a unilateral limit each year. Nonetheless, Detroit initiated other actions, including an antidumping case against Japanese minivans, which led to a finding of dumping in 1991.

17. The Japanese companies have begun to follow their U.S. counterparts into the rental business. We thank Peter Pestillo for bringing these developments to our attention.

18. The most provocative work on costs has been published by the Economic Strategy Institute. It argues that Chrysler and Ford would be the lowest-cost producers in the world if health costs, pension benefits, and idle plant capacity were omitted from the calculations. See Clyde Prestowitz, Paul S. Willen, and Lawrence Chimerine, *The Future of the Auto Industry: It Can Compete, Can It Survive?* (Washington, DC: ESI, 1992). Their approach to disaggregating costs is controversial because it is not comprehensive. Should, for example, higher costs of land for plants in Japan due to Japanese public policy be subtracted? And the cost of capacity usually is considered one of the core costs that companies manage. Subtracting idle capacity costs is like subtracting the costs of a failed product model. Still, these studies show clearly that U.S. firms are more competitive and labor costs are no longer a crippling burden. In 1991 Japan had the highest gross hourly wages in the automobile industry, slightly exceeding those in Germany, Sweden, and the United States. Kevin Done, "Japanese Earn Highest Motor Industry Wages," *Financial Times*, February 20, 1992, p. 4.

19. "Honda: Is It an American Car?," *Business Week*, November 18, 1991, pp. 105–112, reports the nuances of the debate.

20. Leslie Helm and Donald Woutat, "Angry Reaction to Japan's Auto Quota Renewal," *Los Angeles Times*, January 12, 1991, p. D2; George A. Patterson, "Rep. Dingell Joins Washington Backlash against Inroads by Japanese Car Firms," *Wall Street Journal*, October 31, 1991, p. A6.

21. Smith and Venables suspect that there was an informal export restriction enforced on sales to Germany by MITI. Weiss noted that former West German Minister of Commerce and Industry Count Otto von Lambsdorf used a weak VRA deal in 1981 to preempt and kill a much tougher proposed EC-wide VRA. Hiromichi Mutoh, "The Automotive Industry," and Frank D. Weiss,

"Will the Automobile Industry Go the Way of the Steel Industry?," in Claude
E. Barfield and Mark Perlman, eds., *Industry, Services, Agriculture: The
United States Faces a United Europe* (Washington, DC: American Enterprise
Institute, 1992), pp. 73–92.

22. Our discussion relies on *New York Times*, October 8, 1990, p. 1, and March 5,
1991, p. C5; *Financial Times*, December 20, 1990, p. 12; *Economist*, September 29, 1990, pp. 79–80; and *Nikkei Weekly*, August 17, 1991, p. 7. The
annexes to the agreement were disclosed in Kevin Done, "Car Sales Accord
Light on Consensus," *Financial Times*, September 23, 1991, p. 4; Kevin Done,
"Car Sales Quotas Divide EC and Japan," *Financial Times*, September 23,
1991, p. 16.

23. France pushed to limit the Japanese automobiles in France to 5.7 percent from
imports and 5.4 percent from transplants. Japanese sources say the final
agreement set import limits at 190,000 for Britain, 150,000 for France,
130,000 for Italy, 79,000 for Spain, and 23,000 for Portugal. *Nikkei Weekly*,
August 10, 1991, p. 9.

24. Smith and Venables state that announced Japanese plants will reach 4 percent
of EC productive capacity by the late 1990s. Guy de Jonquières, "Car Quotas
Cause Friction," *Financial Times*, December 20, 1990, p. 13.

25. "Sir Leon Outgunned," *Economist*, May 2, 1992, p. 88, and *Wall Street
Journal* (European edition), April 30, 1992.

26. According to "The Automotive Industry in Korea," *KDB Report* 14 (December 1990), pp. 1–6, Korea is willing to do "knockdown" kits for assembly of
automobiles in developing countries.

27. *Automotive News*, December 16, 1991, pp. 1, 45.

28. "The Heartbeat of America Is Imported," *Economist*, September 8, 1990, p.
81. This will change when Isuzu leaves the passenger car business.

29. General Motors bought 5.2 percent of Suzuki, the largest maker of minicars in
Japan, in 1981. Suzuki wanted General Motors technology and marketing
help. It sells 46 percent of its output as exports. When Isuzu had financial
difficulties in 1987, it asked General Motors to help define new options in the
global market. One result was a 40 percent share in a U.K. truck plant. *Japan
Economic Journal*, March 25, 1989, p. 35. After recovering Isuzu set a sales
target of 600,000 vehicles in 1990, with 380,000 destined for export. In 1989
General Motors cut its equity share from 40.2 to 38 percent, realizing a pretax
profit of $125 million. *Japan Economic Journal*, February 17, 1990, p. 17.

30. "GM Venture in Korea Nears End, Betraying Firm's Fond Hope," *Wall Street
Journal*, January 16, 1992, pp. A1, A4.

31. *New York Times*, November 8, 1990, p. C5; *Wall Street Journal*, January 16,
1992, p. 1.

32. Maryann Keller, *Rude Awakening: The Rise, Fall and Struggle for Recovery of
General Motors* (New York: HarperCollins, 1990), is a sharply critical account of the decline of General Motors by a leading financial analyst. Keller
argues that most problems of General Motors were self-inflicted due to an
inappropriate incentive system within the organization. It even used its ICAs
badly. Keller points out that since 1971 General Motors owned almost 50
percent of Isuzu but that it never asked its partner for help in evaluating
Japanese cost performance. When it finally did so in 1980, General Motors
discovered that Isuzu could build the next subcompact planned by General

Motors for $2,857, as opposed to GM's target of $5,731 in costs (p. 83). Besides having inappropriate understanding of its NUMMI venture with Toyota, General Motors then failed to consult with Toyota when it bought 48 percent of the famed British automobile designers, Lotus, in which Toyota held a 22 percent share (pp. 175–176). General Motors is not alone. Former Xerox executives have confirmed that Xerox often ignored warnings from Fuji, its major Japanese partner.

33. An in-depth discussion of this alliance is found in "The Partners," *Business Week*, February 10, 1992, pp. 102–107. Ford and Mazda plan to produce 120,000 automobiles per year, which will be divided equally among them. By drawing on Ford component suppliers, they will have an 80 percent local content. *Japan Economic Journal*, February 3, 1990, p. 13.

34. *Automotive News*, December 16, 1991, p. 1.

35. Wolfgang Streeck, "Successful Adjustment to Turbulent Markets: The Automobile Tale," in Peter J. Katzenstein, ed., *Industry and Politics in West Germany* (Ithaca: Cornell University Press, 1989), pp. 113–156.

36. *Los Angeles Times*, March 18, 1991, p. D1; *New York Times*, February 17, 1992, p. C3.

37. *Nikkei Weekly*, August 27, 1991, p. 7.

38. *Economist*, April 14, 1990, pp. 79–82; *Wall Street Journal*, November 20, 1990, p. A13.

39. See Karen Hladick, in Frank J. Contractor and Peter Lorange, eds., *Cooperative Strategies in International Business* (New York: Free Press, 1987), p. 193. Ford subsequently sold off its farm equipment venture to Fiat in part to pay for its upgrading of Jaguar. *Wall Street Journal*, August 1, 1990, p. A12. But so far Ford's $2.5 billion investment in Jaguar is not paying off: Jaguar lost $431 million in 1990 and 1991. *New York Times*, April 21, 1992, p. C1.

40. Some analysts argue that Chrysler lost $400 million on Diamond Star during a three-year period. *Automotive News*, December 16, 1991, pp. 1, 4.

41. "Lee's Yen," *Economist*, April 20, 1991, p. 69; "Mitsubishi, Chrysler Reach Model Accord," *Japan Economic Journal*, November 10, 1990, p. 13.

42. The Chrysler data is in Keith Bradsher, "Return of an Issue: Protectionism," *New York Times*, June 16, 1992, p. C1.

43. After a proposed alliance with Ford fell apart, Fiat considered taking on Chrysler as a junior partner. Neither Fiat nor Peugeot have a substantial presence in Japan or the United States. Their future growth depends mostly on their future success in Eastern Europe, developing countries (such as Asia), and the European Community. Indeed, although its Russian venture has had trouble, Fiat is taking over 90 percent of the largest automobile firm in Poland. *Financial Times*, May 22, 1992, p. 18.

44. The original Volvo-Renault deal gave Renault 25 percent of Volvo cars and 45 percent equity in Volvo trucks plus another 10 percent of the parent holding company (whose shares were bought on the open market). Volvo bought 20 percent of Renault cars with an option of acquiring another 5 percent, plus 45 percent of the equity in Renault's truck and bus subsidiary. The deal features various agreements on sourcing, such as Renault engines for Volvo cars. *New York Times*, November 8, 1990, p. C5. The Volvo-Mitsubishi venture will use an existing Volvo plant in the Netherlands that is owned 70 percent by the government and 30 percent by Volvo. Mitsubishi cited differences with Daim-

ler Benz about production and technology preferences as a reason for its deal with Volvo. *Nikkei Weekly*, June 1, 1991, pp. 1, 8. But when the Japanese market slumped and Renault made a stronger than expected turnaround, Volvo, which is half the size of Renault, got interested again. The current joint venture has projected 1995 cost savings through joint product development of $670 million per year, which greatly exceeded the original forecast. It already is yielding about $67 million per company. Renault and Volvo already have agreed on a joint schedule for new product launches in the 1990s. *Wall Street Journal* (European edition), April 30, 1992; *Financial Times*, May 7, 1992, p. 18.

45. *Automotive News*, April 29, 1991, p. 3.
46. *New York Times*, September 23, 1990, p. F1.
47. Ferdinand Protzman, "South Carolina Plant Is Planned for BMW," *New York Times*, June 23, 1992, pp. C1, C5.
48. Hiroshi Kakazu, "Industrial Technology Capabilities and Policies in Asian Developing Countries," *Asian Development Review* 8:2 (1990), pp. 46–76; Richard Doner, *Driving a Bargain* (Ithaca: Cornell University Press, 1991), esp. pp. 78–85.
49. *Japan Economic Journal*, September 15, 1990, p. 12.
50. See Harvard Business School, "Note on the World Auto Industry in Transition," No. 9-385-332, Rev. 1/86.
51. *Automotive News*, December 23, 1991, p. 25.
52. General Motors expects to boost Japanese sales by 250 percent by 1995 (to $350 to $450 million in items like engine controls and brakes), while Ford projects Japan will be 15 to 25 percent of its global parts sales market (up from 8 percent). *Nikkei Weekly*, July 13, 1991, p. 8. The export goal for Japanese plants in the U.S. is equal to the total exports of the Big 3 in the United States. *Economist*, December 1989, p. 7, and April 14, 1990, pp. 79–82. The rest of our discussion draws on "Lean, Mean and through the Windscreen," *Economist*, February 23, 1991, pp. 68–70; Sumihiko Nonoichi, "Japan's Exports to EC 'Made in USA,' " *Nikkei Weekly*, August 10, 1991, p. 9; Kevin Done, "The Global Network," *Financial Times*, December 12, 1990, p. 9; "Toyota Talks of Car Imports," *New York Times*, May 23, 1991, p. C17; Leslie Helm and Donald Woutat, "Angry Reaction to Japan's Auto Quota Renewal," *Los Angeles Times*, January 12, 1991, p. D2. In response to a 1985 law that requires consolidation of the automobile industry into five groups, Toyota and General Motors have agreed to merge their Australian subsidiaries for design, engineering, and model sharing. But this cooperative effort fell short of rumors that Toyota and General Motors would form a joint corporation in Australia. *International Herald Tribune*, March 18, 1992, p. 22.
53. *Automotive News*, December 23, 1991, p. 28; *Nikkei Weekly*, January 11, 1991, p. 3.
54. "European Car Goals for Japan," *New York Times*, January 15, 1992, p. C2. For more on European worries see: *Nikkei Weekly*, February 2, 1992, p. 3.
55. *Japan Economic Journal*, July 21, 1990, p. 12, March 24, 1990, p. 23.
56. *Automotive News*, December 2, 1991, p. 1.
57. *Nikkei Weekly*, July 13, 1991, pp. 3, 8.
58. Kozo Yamamura has produced the most responsible review of the issues. Ulrike Wassmann and Kozo Yamamura, "Do Japanese Firms Behave Differ-

ently? The Effects of Keiretsu in the United States," in Kozo Yamamura, *Japanese Investment in the United States: Should We Be Concerned?* (Seattle: Society for Japanese Studies, 1989), pp. 119–150. Japanese component firms are responding to trade criticisms, trying to spread risks by multisourcing, and responding to Japanese labor markets by starting to source parts for Japan from joint ventures in the United States (e.g., Akebono with General Motors). "Joint Ventures May Be in Sight," *Financial Times*, December 20, 1990, p. 10. There is some irony to U.S. charges that Japanese firms resist providing local content. A study of the Mexican automobile industry found Volkswagen and Nissan far more disposed to meeting Mexican targets for content and exports than U.S. firms. Barbara Samuels, *Managing Risk in Developing Countries* (Princeton: Princeton University Press, 1991).

59. *Computer World*, September 10, 1990, p. 76.

60. "Trade Issues Over Honda," *New York Times*, August 15, 1991; Letter from Marina von N. Whitman, Vice President of General Motors, to the *Wall Street Journal*, August 14, 1991, p. A11. However, in early March 1992, the U.S. Customs Service ruled against Honda. *New York Times*, March 8, 1992, p. E3. Canada has protested the U.S. ruling.

61. Fusae Ohta, "Multiple Alliances Key to Auto Success," *Nikkei Weekly*, November 2, 1991, p. 6. But this strategy will work only if foreign components firms open shop in Japan.

62. Robert Baldwin, "Commentary," in Lawrence and Schultze, *An American Trade Strategy*, pp. 195–214.

63. James Dunn, "The Asian Auto Imbroglio," in Haggard and Moon, eds., *Pacific Dynamics*, takes a similar view.

CHAPTER 6

1. This chapter draws extensively on an unpublished paper coauthored by David Hytha, who is not responsible for interpretations in this chapter, and Peter Cowhey.

2. Dynamic random-access memory (DRAM), the standard memory chip, accounts for about 30 percent of the market, and application-specific integration circuits (ASICs) account for 11 percent of the market. (Customized metal oxide on silicon (CMOS) chips are one type of ASIC technology.) Erasable programmable read-only memory (EPROM) is a more expensive chip, and microprocessors are the high-end "computers on a chip" that are at the heart of computers (the reduced instruction set chip (RISC) is a new microprocessor technology).

3. J. Nicholas Ziegler, "Semiconductors," *Daedalus* 120:4 (Fall 1991), pp. 155–182.

4. John Alic, "From Weakness to Strength: American Firms and Policies in a Global Economy," in Lynn K. Mytelka, ed., *Strategic Partnerships and the World Economy* (London: Pinter Publishers, 1991), pp. 152–156, compares joint ventures in the automobile and microelectronics sectors.

5. One of the first and best examinations of U.S.-Japanese semiconductor rivalry is Daniel I. Okimoto, Takuo Sugano, and Franklin B. Weinstein, eds., *Compet-*

itive Edge: The Semiconductor Industry in the U.S. and Japan (Stanford: Stanford University Press, 1984).

6. William G. Ouichi and Michael Kremen Bolton, "The Logic of Joint Research and Development," *California Management Review* 30:3 (Spring 1988), pp. 9–33; Janet J. Barron, "Consortia: High Tech Co-ops," *Byte*, June 1990, pp. 269–276.

7. Michael G. Borrus, *Competing for Control: America's Stake in Microelectronics* (Cambridge, MA: Ballinger, 1988).

8. Valerie Rice, "Losing the High-Tech Lead," *Infoworld*, September 23, 1991, p. 40. A DRAM plant may now require a 6 percent share of the world market to be cost effective. Kenneth A. Froot and David B. Yoffie, "Strategic Trade Policies in a Tripolar World," Paper prepared for a conference on "International Political Economy in a Tripolar World," January 12–13, 1991.

9. Froot and Yoffie cite estimates that costs can decline 30 to 40 percent every time production doubles. Overall Japanese spending on semiconductor manufacturing in 1990 was about $4.36 billion. *Economist*, July 8, 1990, p. 65, July 14, 1990, pp. 71–72.

10. LSI Logic even allows customers to specify their own choice of circuits to combine with Sun and Mips microprocessors on an LSI-designed and -produced chip. *Wall Street Journal*, February 18, 1992, p. B8.

11. Andrew Pollack, "U.S. Makers of Chips in Alliance," *New York Times*, July 14, 1992, p. C1.

12. *New York Times*, January 20, 1992, p. C2. The U.S. Air Force also has a proposal to fund a factory for flat-panel displays. *Computerworld*, February 10, 1992, p. 31.

13. *New York Times*, September 2, 1990, p. C1.

14. We thank Richard Solomon for this observation.

15. This view is held by some electronics firms and by analysts like Charles Ferguson, "Computers and the Coming of the U.S. Keiretsu," *Harvard Business Review* (July–August, 1990), pp. 55–70.

16. Representatives of this camp include George Gilder and Michael Porter.

17. We thank Lawrence Krause for suggesting this possibility.

18. See the research tradition following the work of Masahiko Aoki, *The Cooperative Game Theory of the Firm* (Oxford: Oxford University Press, 1984).

19. Borrus, *Competing for Control*, p. 18.

20. The industrial engineers' information was made available to us in 1990 interviews with a major semiconductor company. Two factors that help explain the large number of projects in Japan are secrecy (relatively little research is conducted in universities) and the immobility of technical personnel, which hampered the exchange of information among Japanese firms. Michael Borrus, "Chip Wars: Can the U.S. Regain Its Advantage in Microelectronics?" *California Management Journal* 30:4 (Summer 1988), pp. 64–79, emphasizes the reduced risk faced by Japanese manufacturing-process suppliers and innovative research efforts on generic technologies.

21. John Kingery, "The U.S.-Japan Semiconductor Agreement and the GATT: Operating in a Legal Vacuum," *Stanford Journal of International Law* 25 (Spring 1989), pp. 467–497.

22. Also see Jeffrey A. Hart, "The Origins of the U.S.-Japan Semiconductor Dispute," in Stephan Haggard and Chung-In Moon, eds., *Pacific Dynamics:*

The International Politics of Industrial Change (Boulder: Westview, 1989), pp. 129–153.

23. *Japan Economic Journal*, July 14, 1990, pp. 1, 15.

24. We thank William Finan for this insight. David Lammers, "New Deal, Old Debate," *Electronic Engineering Times*, August 5, 1991. Honda has pledged to buy 20 percent of its semiconductors in fiscal 1993 from foreign producers. *Nikkei Weekly*, November 9, 1991, p. 8.

25. Kingery, "The U.S.–Japan Semiconductor Agreement," p. 479.

26. Ibid., p. 480. The European Community objected that any side agreement would discriminate in practice against EC firms.

27. *Nikkei Weekly*, June 8, 1991, p. 3.

28. "European Observer" *Electronics*, June 1991, p. 33. On Japanese firms' views see David Lammers, "New Deal, Old Debate," *Electronic Engineering Times*, August 5, 1991.

29. An example of the muted Japanese suggestions was the address of senior Hitachi executive Kazuo Kimbara to the 1988 Tokyo Semiconductor Round-table, (no title), October 5, 1988 (mimeo). The evidence on shares was in *Electronic Business*, January 8, 1990, p. 60. The U.S. share was 33 percent versus 35 percent for the Far East in the 1990s global market of $733 billion (in 1988 dollars).

30. The need for restructuring and alliances was a central theme of a Texas Instrument presentation at a major Tokyo conference. William P. Weber, "Issues for the Future of the Semiconductor Industry," October 5, 1988, Tokyo Semiconductor Roundtable (mimeo). The emphasis on alliances and services infrastructure can be found in National Advisory Committee on Semiconductors, *Second Annual Report: Towards a National Semiconductor Strategy—Regaining Markets in High-Volume Electronics* (Washington, DC: February 1991).

31. See particularly W. Edward Steinmueller, "International Joint Ventures in the Integrated Circuit Industry," in David C. Mowery, ed., *International Collaborative Ventures in U.S. Manufacturing* (Cambridge, MA: Ballinger, 1988), pp. 111–145.

32. Ibid., p. 127.

33. Michel M. Kostecki, "Electronics Trade Policy in the 1980s," *Journal of World Trade* 23 (February 1989), pp. 17–35. Ironically, if the Korean or IBM entry into the market does not succeed in the long term, the most economically efficient strategy may be to subsidize the competitive fringe through a price guarantee and let open market prices prevail. Using trade pacts to control pricing and production capacity is not the way to go. Antidumping laws can be streamlined (U.S. antidumping actions in 1986 covered both current and future generations of DRAMs) and at least have the virtue of dealing with the average costs of individual firms rather than a general price floor. Subsidies are unpopular in an era of fiscal constraints because they require taxes to support them.

34. Mitch Betts, "A Boost for Advanced Technology R&D," *Computer World*, August 20, 1990, p. 81.

35. Patrick Burnson, "Vendors Debate Failure of U.S. Memories," *Infoworld*, January 22, 1990, p. 41.

36. Tom Redburn, "White House Seeks to Loosen Antitrust Rules," *Los Angeles Times*, May 8, 1990, p. 1.
37. "Perkin-Elmer Majority Stake in Chip Unit," *Los Angeles Times*, May 16, 1990, p. D3. Also see *Infoworld*, October 30, 1989, p. 6.
38. *Electronic Components*, December 1991, pp. 44–45.
39. See Borrus, *Competing for Control*, for a pointed review of the dangers.
40. Yasuko Yoshimi, "U.S., Japan Venture into Fifth-Generation Computer," *Computerworld*, June 4, 1990, p. 17.
41. Stephen Kreider Yoder, "Intel, Ensuring Chip Supply, Allies with Japanese Firm," *Wall Street Journal*, January 23, 1990, p. 1.
42. *Nikkei Weekly*, February 15, 1992, p. 1.
43. Valerie Rice, "Why Teaming Up Is So Hard to Do," *Electronic Business*, April 18, 1991, pp. 30–34.
44. James Daly, "Sun Contracts with Philips to Make RISC Chips," and J. A. Savage, "HP Taps Samsung for RISC-based PCs," both in *Computer World*, August 14, 1989, p. 12. Sun has an alliance also with Fuji Xerox to launch a work station venture in Japan. *Computer World*, February 20, 1989, p. 86.
45. Michiyo Nakamoto, "Foreign Chip Makers Advance into Europe," *Financial Times*, May 12, 1992, p. 6.
46. *Wall Street Journal*, April 1, 1986.
47. *New York Times*, September 16, 1990, p. C1.
48. "Japanese Purchases in Europe Could Throw the EC's Joint Research Projects into Disarray," *Wall Street Journal*, September 5, 1990, p. A10. In June 1991 the Fujitsu-controlled ICL bought Nokia Data Systems from Finland's leading high-technology firm. It was rumored, but denied, that ICL also sought to merge with Italy's Olivetti. *Computerworld*, June 17, 1991, p. 74.
49. Rob Van Tulder and Gerd Junne, *European Multinationals in Core Technologies* (Chichester: John Wiley, 1988), pp. 36–38.
50. Ralph Bancroft, "U.S., Europe Firms Call for Toughness on Chip Dumping," *Communication Week*, November 20, 1989, p. 18.
51. *Economist*, February 1, 1992, pp. 76–77.
52. *Electronics Components*, December 1991, p. 422.
53. Michael Borrus first suggested this idea for U.S. firms.
54. *New York Times*, June 11, 1991, p. C4.
55. Firms also may use intercorporate ventures instead of resorting to government action to address externality problems (for example, when crucial R&D is so easy to duplicate that it is unprofitable to undertake).

CHAPTER 7

1. Peter F. Cowhey, "Telecommunications," in Gary Hufbauer, ed., *Europe 1992: An American Perspective* (Washington, DC: Brookings Institution, 1990), pp. 217–218.
2. This chapter draws on our previous work, particularly Jonathan David Aronson and Peter F. Cowhey, *When Countries Talk: International Trade in Telecommunications Services* (Cambridge, MA: Ballinger, 1988), and Peter F. Cowhey, Jonathan D. Aronson, and Gabriel Székely, eds., *Changing Net-*

works: Mexico's Telecommunications Options (La Jolla: Center for U.S.-Mexican Studies, University of California, San Diego, 1989).

3. Estimates are by Michael Kennedy of Arthur D. Little as cited in *Wall Street Journal*, October 4, 1991, p. R1.

4. The emergence and evolution of pressure for liberalization in trade in services is documented in William J. Drake and Kalypso Nicolaides, "Ideas, Interests, and Institutionalization: Trade in Services and the Uruguay Round," *International Organization* 46:1 (Winter 1992), pp. 37–100.

5. According to data published by the International Institute of Communications in London in 1990 traffic between the United States and Canada, Mexico, and the United Kingdom exceeded 1 billion minutes of international traffic. Traffic between the United States and Japan and Germany exceeded 500 million minutes of international traffic. Germany also shared more than 500 million minutes of traffic with Austria and Switzerland. We thank J. P. Singh for bringing these statistics to our attention.

6. In 1990 the five largest international carriers were AT&T, the Deutsche Bundespost, British Telecom, France Telecom, and Telecom Canada, but from 1986 to 1990 the five fastest-growing international carriers were Sprint, MCI, the Communication Authority of Thailand, Cable & Wireless, and Embratel (Brazil). Ibid.

7. See Henry Ergas and Paul Paterson, "The Joint Provision of International Telecommunications Services: An Economic Analysis of Alternative Settlement Arrangements." Paper prepared for the eighth ITS International Conference, Venice, March 18–21, 1990; Robert M. Frieden, "Accounting Rates: The Business of International Telecommunications and the Incentive to Cheat," *Federal Communications Law Journal* 43:2 (April 1991), pp. 111–139.

8. For measured accounts of the breakup of AT&T and its consequences see Peter Temin with Louis Galambos, *The Fall of the Bell System* (New York: Cambridge University Press, 1987); Robert W. Crandall, ed., *After the Breakup: U.S. Telecommunications in a More Competitive Era* (Washington, DC: Brookings Institution, 1991).

9. PTT Telecom Netherlands, however, which is involved in a fifteen-year plan with AT&T to modernize and extend the Ukrainian telecommunications system, found that many of the switches currently in operation are older than most exhibits in the Dutch telephone museum. In early 1992 the Ukraine became the third former Soviet republic to open its telecommunications infrastructure to foreign ownership. In late 1991 the Swedish operator Televerket signed separate agreements to help modernize telecommunications in Latvia and Estonia. "Ukraine Opens Its Network" *Communications Week International*, January 20, 1992, p. 8.

10. Henry Geller, "Fiber Optics: An Opportunity for a New Policy?" Report prepared for the Annenberg Washington Program (Washington, DC: Annenberg Washington Program, 1991).

11. Jonathan Solomon, "Telecommunications and the New World Order." Speech to the Networked Economy Conference sponsored by *Communications Week International* and Blenheim Online, Paris, March 4, 1992.

12. Richard H. Vietor and David B. Yoffie distinguish among equipment manufacturers that are evolving into more broadly integrated firms (AT&T, NEC,

Siemens), those that are remaining focused firms (Ericsson, Alcatel, Northern Telecom), and large niche players (Toshiba, Bosch). "International Trade and Competition in Global Telecommunications," May 23, 1991, mimeo, pp. 37–53. Soon many of these equipment manufacturers as well as large electronics manufacturers may have to decide whether to emulate AT&T and enter into the business of providing both new telecommunications services and equipment. So far, for example, Northern Telecom has indicated that it does not choose to enter the services market. By contrast, Philips, which was squeezed out of the network equipment market, announced in late 1991 a deal to team with Sears to offer IBM-compatible data services over their corporate networks. *Communications Week International*, December 16, 1991, p. 10.

13. Solomon, "Telecommunications and the New World Order."
14. *New York Times*, April 23, 1992, pp. C1, C6.
15. "The Wiring of Wall Street," *Economist*, February 22, 1992, pp. 69–70.
16. Interview with representatives of large customers, Washington DC, February 1991.
17. Eli Noam, *Telecommunications in Europe* (New York: Oxford University Press, 1992).
18. For example, the United States usually defines universal public service as the provision of basic household telephone services. Some countries believe that the next generation of innovation in electronics, software, and information services will occur only if smaller businesses and households fully participate in tapping new technologies. The development of the VCR suggests a useful analogy. The United States pioneered the technology, but U.S. companies thought it would mostly be used to record television programs for large production studios. After some stumbling, Japanese companies brought the technology to households so viewers could watch movies at home. James Lardner, *Fast Forward: Hollywood, the Japanese, and the VCR Wars* (New York: Norton, 1987).
19. A positive picture of Minitel is painted in Marie Marchand, *A French Success Story: The Minitel Saga* (Paris: Larousse, 1988). For a contrary view on the high cost of Minitel see Henry Ergas, "France Telecom: Has the Model Worked?" Paper prepared for a seminar on "The Interplay of Government, Industry and Research in France," Royal Norwegian Council for Scientific and Industrial Research, Oslo, January 29, 1992. In addition, *Communication Week International* reported that by the year 2000, according to a report by Coopers & Lybrand, France Telecom will have spent $9 billion on Minitel and that it is unlikely to break even on its investment until 1996 or 1998, eighteen years after the program was launched. September 2, 1991, p. 1. Francois Bar, Michael Borrus, and Benjamin Coriat, *Information Networks and Competitive Advantage*, vol. 1 (Paris: OECD, 1989).
20. Peter Cowhey and J. D. Aronson, "The ITU in Transition," *Telecommunications Policy* 15:4 (August 1991), pp. 298–310.
21. Arend Lijphart, *Democracies* (New Haven: Yale University Press, 1984).
22. For an elaboration of our views about competing models for the future see Peter Cowhey and Jonathan D. Aronson, "Trade in Services and Changes in the World Telecommunications System," in Cowhey, Aronson, and Székely, eds., *Changing Networks*, pp. 5–47.

23. Charles F. Mason, "Cellular Carriers Join Hands for Wireless Standard," *Telephony*, April 27, 1992, pp. 8–9.
24. *Wall Street Journal*, September 10, 1990, p. B6.
25. This point was explicitly made about HDTV in a letter by Ronald Blunden of Thomson Consumer Electronics in the letters page of the *Economist*, September 1, 1990, p. 8.
26. Interviews, November 1988, Tokyo.
27. For a historical analogy see Paul A. David, "The Dynamo and the Computer: An Historical Perspective on the Modern Productivity Paradox," *American Economic Review* 80:2 (May 1990), pp. 355–362.
28. In late November 1991 the Working Party on Telecommunications and Information Services Policies of the Committee for Information, Computer, and Communication Policy of the Directorate for Science, Technology, and Industry of the OECD issued a Note by the Secretariat, "Mobile and PSTN Communications Services: Competition or Complementarity." The note examined the extent to which mobile communications services eventually will "compete with, or substitute for, fixed linked telecommunications services in terms of tariffs, traffic and subscribers" and asked "for how long will mobile communications continue to be regarded as a complementary service to the traditional telephony?" How these questions are answered will influence the way telecommunications is regulated in the future.
29. *Communications Week International*, May 11, 1992, p. 1.
30. Peter Cowhey and John Zysman, "Telecom Policy at Crossroads: Stalemate or Starting Point?," draft, April 2, 1992.
31. Ergas and Paterson, "Joint Provision."
32. See "F.C.C. Acts to Cut Rates Up to 50 percent on Calls Abroad," *New York Times*, July 17, 1990, pp. A1, C7, and the insightful discussion reported in *Forum Notes, A Quarterly Bulletin of the IIC Telecommunications Forum* (October 1990), and Leonard Waverman, "Pricing Principles and International Telecommunications." Paper presented to the OECD Working Party on Telecommunications and Information Services Policies of the Committee for Information, Computers, and Communications Policy of the OECD, April 1991. In 1991 efforts were under way in Study Group III of the CCITT in the ITU to try to reduce accounting rates by about 10 percent per year for the next several years. If this is all that occurs, European monopolists will stay in control. The United States government, however, pushed in other forums, including the OECD, for more transparency and for more rapid change. After breakthroughs in May 1992, ratified by the CCITT in June 1992, accounting rates are likely to be made far more transparent and tariffs could fall even more rapidly.
33. "Rome to Bonn via New Jersey," *Business Week*, April 13, 1992, pp. 84–85.
34. See J. D. Aronson and P. F. Cowhey, "Bilateral Telecommunications Negotiations," in Albert Bressand and Kalypso Nicolaidis, eds., *Strategic Trends in Services: An Inquiry into the Global Service Economy* (New York: Harper & Row, 1989), pp. 207–222; P. Cowhey and J. D. Aronson, "Telecommunications Networks: Can They Save Europe's Computer and Microelectronics Industries?," in Alfred Pfaller, ed., *Der Kampf um den Wohlstand von morgen—Internationaler Strukturwandel und neuer Merkantilismus* (Bonn: Friedrich Ebert Stiftung, 1986), pp. 131–147 (in German); J. D. Aronson and

P. F. Cowhey, *When Countries Talk: International Trade in Telecommunications Services* (Cambridge, MA: Ballinger [for the American Enterprise Institute], 1988).

35. *Telephony*, November 18, 1991, p. 3, and April 27, 1992, pp. 16–17.
36. U.S. data, which exclude traffic to Canada and Mexico, are from the FCC. Oftel and industry sources provided the information on the United Kingdom (which excludes traffic to Ireland). The Japanese Ministry of Posts and Telecommunications and industry sources provided the Japanese data. The International Institute of Communications assembled the data in 1991.
37. *Transnational Data and Communication Report*, August-September 1988, p. 4.
38. *New York Times*, April 22, 1992, pp. C1, C7.
39. Interview with a former AT&T official.
40. Richard Vietor and David Yoffie, "International Trade and Competition in Global Telecommunications: Japan's Telephone Colossus Takes Its First Baby Steps Overseas," *Business Week*, March 13, 1989, p. 144; "NTT Unit to Vie with U.S. Firms in Data Communications Services," *Wall Street Journal*, February 21, 1990, p. B4; "NTT to Shift into Global Telecom Market," *Nikkei Weekly*, February 15, 1992, p. 9.
41. *Economist*, March 28, 1992, p. 69.
42. *Wall Street Journal*, April 22, 1992, p. B7; *Communications Week International*, May 11, 1992, pp. 1, 4.
43. "Questions Linger Over Unicom," *Communications Week International*, November 4, 1991, p. 4; "Outsourcing Alliances Forge Ahead," *Telephony*, September 28, 1992, p. 16.
44. *Communications Week International*, May 11, 1992, p. 12.
45. Anne C. Dibble, "Telecommunications Deregulation in Brazil Rings Up Sales for U.S. firms," *Telephony*, April 6, 1992, p. 28. On the European situation see John Williamson, "European Mobile Communications Is Hot, Hot, Hot," *Telephony*, May 28, 1990, pp. 32–38; OECD, "Mobile and PSTN Communications Services," November 1991.
46. Kas Kalba, "Identifying the Competition: Lessons from Telecommunications," February 1991, mimeo.
47. *Computer Weekly*, July 22, 1991, p. 83.
48. Although demand cannot be foretold, Henry Geller, "Fiber Optics," pp. 29–30, suggests that a *Field of Dreams* approach may not be unreasonable: "If you build it, they will come."
49. Anthony Ramirez, "Lifetime Telephone Numbers That Ring Anywhere You Go," *New York Times*, April 29, 1992, pp. A1, C2; Richard Karpinski, "AT&T Unveils Number-for-Life," *Telephony*, May 4, 1992, pp. 9, 12.
50. "Telefonica of Spain Bidding in Puerto Rico Privatization," *Telecommunications Reports International*, January 25, 1991, p. 1; *Communications Week International*, May 11, 1992, p. 12. This deal did not go through when bidders were unwilling to meet the price demanded by the Governor of Puerto Rico.
51. Keith Bradsher, "Allure of Spain's Phone Company," *New York Times*, March 29, 1990, p. C8.
52. Fascinating historical material about the early efforts to tie together continents with submarine cables can be found in Daniel Headrick, *The Invisible Weapon: Telecommunications and International Politics 1851–1945* (New York: Cambridge University Press, 1991).

53. Interview with a senior planner at a regional Bell operating company, January 1992.

54. "Cable & Wireless in Russian Joint Venture," *Financial Times*, April 15, 1992, p. 18.

55. "BT Rethinks Mobile Plans," *Communications Week International*, December 16, 1991, p. 3.

56. John J. Keller, "British Telecom Plans Billion-Dollar Global Network," *Wall Street Journal*, August 18, 1992, p. B1.

57. "Small Players Plug into Telecom Niches," *Financial Times*, April 23, 1992, p. 19. However, Sir Brian Carsberg, the outgoing director of Oftel, urged the British Telecom be split into a local and a long-distance company. *Communications Week International*, April 11, 1992.

58. For an account of the politics of the decision to allow separate satellite systems see Peter Cowhey and Jonathan D. Aronson, "The Great Satellite Shootout," *Regulation* (May-June, 1985), pp. 27–35.

59. "Iridium Plan Altered," *Communications Week International*, January 24, 1992, p. 6.

60. Bernard Simon, "Taking a Provincial Telecom into the World Market," *Financial Times*, May 11, 1992, p. 21.

61. Pekka J. Tarjanne, "Open Frameworks for Telecommunications in the 1990s: Access to Networks and Markets," *Telecommunications*, April 1990, pp. 22–24, 48. Tarjanne is the Secretary General of the ITU.

62. Richard E. Butler, "The Changing Environment: Multidimensional Issues," *Telecommunications Policy* 14:4 (August 1990), pp. 275–278. Richard Butler was Secretary General of the ITU during the 1980s.

CHAPTER 8

1. Jean-Claude Paye, "The Role of the OECD in the Age of Globalization and Networks," *Project Promethee Perspectives*, No. 18-19 (Paris: Promethee, December 1991), pp. 6–7.

2. For an overview of what was expected to emerge from the Uruguay Round see C. Michael Aho and Jonathan D. Aronson, *Trade Talks: America Better Listen!* (New York: Council on Foreign Relations, 1985).

3. Alan Oxley, *The Challenge of Free Trade* (New York: St. Martin's Press, 1990), p. 222. Oxley, the Australian negotiator for most of the Uruguay Round, published this first insider account of the round just before the unsuccessful December 1990 ministerial meeting in Brussels.

4. *Coalition of Service Industries Reports*, December 1990, p. 3.

5. "German Grain Blamed for GATT Stalemate," *Financial Times*, May 7, 1992, p. 4.

6. Keith Bradsher, "Bush and Europe Fail to Bridge Gap on Trade Barriers," *New York Times*, April 23, 1992, pp. A1, C6.

7. Ian Goldin and Dominique van der Mensbrugghe, "Trade Liberalisation: What's at Stake?" (Paris: OECD Development Centre, 1992), cited in *Financial Times*, April 22, 1992, p. 6.

8. Robert Kuttner, *The End of Laissez-Faire: National Purpose and the Global Economy After the Cold War* (New York: Knopf, 1991).

9. Fumio Kodama, "High Time to Review High-Tech Transfer," *Nikkei Weekly*, May 30, 1992, p. 6.
10. Philip G. Cerny, "The 'Little Big Bang' in Paris: Financial Market Deregulation in a Dirigiste System," *European Journal of Political Research* 17:2 (1989), pp. 169–192.
11. See Daniel M. Kasper, *Deregulation and Globalization: Liberalizing International Trade in Air Services* (Cambridge, MA: Ballinger, 1988).
12. Vinod K. Aggarwal, Robert O. Keohane, and David B. Yoffie, "The Dynamics of Negotiated Protectionism," *American Political Science Review* 81 (June 1987), pp. 345–366, argue that this is particularly true for industries with low barriers to entry.
13. See the essays in Ryutaro Komiya, ed., *Industrial Policy of Japan* (Tokyo: Academic Press, 1988).
14. Lawrence B. Krause, "Japanese Capitalism: A Model for Others?," *International Economic Insights* (November/December 1991), pp. 6–10.
15. See Paul Krugman, ed., *Trade with Japan: Has the Door Opened Wider?* (Chicago: University of Chicago Press, 1991).
16. This point is subject to many qualifications. Bernard M. Hoekman, "Determining the Need for Issue Linkages in Multilateral Trade Negotiations," *International Organization* 43 (Autumn 1989), pp. 693–714. Also see Robert Lawrence's essay in Richard O'Brien, ed., *Finance and the International Economy*, vol. 5 (Oxford: Oxford University Press, 1991).
17. The structure of negotiations at the ITU's world administrative radio conferences has been more successful. Representatives gather for a set period of time and focus on relatively narrow, technical issues, and negotiators often try to achieve consensus through exhaustion rather than return home without agreement. Still, in the future the ITU wants to hold biannual mini-WARCs that would cover a narrower range of topics; this would allow for a quicker response to technological change and less opportunity to trade off concessions among unrelated services. *Economist*, March 7, 1992, pp. 89–90.
18. Walter Russell Mead, "Bushism, Found—A Second Term Agenda Hidden in Trade Agreements," *Harper's*, September 1992, pp. 37–45.

CHAPTER 9

1. A strong defense of multilateralism is Jagdish Bhagwati, "Multilateralism at Risk: The GATT Is Dead, Long Live the GATT," *World Economy*, June 1990, pp. 149–169. On the dangers of regional trading blocs see C. Michael Aho, "A Recipe for RIBS: Resentment, Inefficiency, Bureaucracy and Stupid Signals," and Richard V. L. Cooper, "Blocs: Making the Best of a 'Second-Best' Solution," both in Richard S. Belous and Rebecca S. Hartley, eds., *The Growth of Regional Trading Blocs in the Global Economy* (Washington, DC: National Planning Association, 1990), pp. 22–29, 30–35.
2. Sylvia Ostry, *Governments and Corporations in a Shrinking World: Trade and Innovation Policies in the United States, Europe and Japan* (New York: Council on Foreign Relations, 1990), p. 1. By the same token Geza Feketekuty, a senior U.S. trade adviser, agreed that the current GATT rules were outdated and needed to be systematically reformed. *IMF Survey*, July 15, 1991, pp. 209,

216–217. A more vehement attack on the GATT as an institution and a call for an entirely new U.S. economic strategy is Clyde V. Prestowitz, Jr., Alan Tonelson, and Robert W. Jerome, "The Last Gasp of GATTism," *Harvard Business Review* (March-April 1991), pp. 130–138.

3. See the editorial by former German Economics Minister Otto Lambsdorff, "Regional Alliances Should Serve Global Market," *Japan Economic Journal*, February 18, 1989, p. 11. Although he is more pessimistic than we are, this is the spirit of Jeffery E. Garten, *A Cold Peace: America, Japan, Germany and the Struggle for Supremacy* (New York: Times Books, 1992).

4. William Diebold, Jr., notes the big differences between bilateralism today and in the 1930s in "The New Bilateralism?" in William Diebold, Jr., ed., *Bilateralism, Multilateralism and Canada in U.S. Trade Policy* (Cambridge, MA: Ballinger, 1988), pp. 128–188.

5. Paul Milgrom, "Employment Contracts, Influence Activities, and Efficient Organizational Design," *Journal of Political Economy* (February 1989), pp. 42–60. Similarly, private markets work better than government fiat when there is little private information and urgency is not vital. Patrick Bolton and Joseph Farrell, "Decentralization, Duplication, and Delay," *Journal of Political Economy* (August 1990).

6. Robert Hudec, *The GATT Legal System and World Trade Diplomacy* (New York: Praeger, 1975), p. 152.

7. *New York Times*, December 2, 1991, p. A15.

8. See Geza Feketekuty, *International Trade in Services: An Overview and Blueprint for Negotiations* (Cambridge, MA: Ballinger, 1988), pp. 175–187. Also see Diebold, ed., *Bilateralism, Multilateralism and Canada in U.S. Trade Policy*.

9. On the U.S.-Japanese textile negotiations during the early Nixon administration see I. M. Destler, Haruhiro Fukui, and Hideo Sato, *The Textile Wrangle: Conflict in Japanese-American Relations, 1969–1971* (Ithaca: Cornell University Press, 1979).

10. L. Jerold Adams, "The Law of United States–Japan Trade Relations," *Journal of World Trade* 24:2 (April 1990), p. 46.

11. Dennis J. Encarnation and Mark Mason, "Neither MITI nor America: The Political Economy of Capital Liberalization in Japan," *International Organization* 44:1 (Winter 1990), pp. 25–54.

12. Alan B. Smith, "The Japanese Foreign Exchange and Foreign Trade Control Law and Administrative Guidance: The Labyrinth and the Castle," *Law and Policy in International Business* 16 (1984), p. 423, quoted in Adams, "The Law of United States–Japan Trade Relations," p. 47.

13. See Louis W. Pauly, *Opening Financial Markets: Banking Politics on the Pacific Rim* (Ithaca: Cornell University Press, 1988).

14. We thank Miles Kahler for his observation that the counterpart to these talks was the steady U.S. pressure on Japan to increase foreign aid, yet another way to alter the fundamentals of Japanese savings and payments dynamics.

15. John Kingery, "The U.S.-Japan Semiconductor Arrangement and the GATT: Operating in a Legal Vacuum," *Stanford Journal of International Law* 25 (Spring 1989), p. 479.

16. See for example James W. Prendergast, "The European Economic Community's Challenge to the U.S.-Japan Semiconductor Arrangement," *Law and Policy in International Business* 19:3 (1987), pp. 579–602.

17. Beth V. Yarbrough and Robert M. Yarbrough, "Reciprocity, Bilateralism and Economic 'Hostages': Self-Enforcing Agreements in International Trade," *International Studies Quarterly* 30 (March 1986), pp. 7–22; Beth V. Yarbrough and Robert M. Yarbrough, *Cooperation and Governance in International Trade: The Strategic Organization Approach* (Princeton: Princeton University Press, 1992).

18. Paul Krugman, "Regional Blocs: The Good, the Bad and the Ugly," *International Economy* (November-December 1991), pp. 54–56. See the essays by Robert Lawrence and Jeffrey Frankel in Richard O'Brien, ed., *Finance and the International Economy*, vol. 5 (Oxford: Oxford University Press, 1991).

19. Former French foreign minister Jean François-Poncet has called for an "intercontinental directorate" for coordination among regional centers. *Project Promethee Perspectives*, No. 16 (Paris: Prométhée, March 1991), p. 14.

20. McMillan notes that theory has shown that any group of countries could set up a block in a way that would meet his test. He suggests that disaggregation of trade flows into groups of products and services, and adjustments for changes in gross domestic product on trade flows would be desirable. John McMillan, "Does Regional Integration Foster Open Trade? Economic Theory and GATT's Article XXIV," in Kym Anderson and Richard Blockhurst, eds., *Regional Integration and the Global Trading System* (London: Harvester Wheatshead, 1993).

21. Stephen Woolcock, Michael Hodges, and Kristin Schreiber, *Britain, Germany and 1992: The Limits of Deregulation* (New York: Council on Foreign Relations, 1991). The classic paper on oversight is Mathew McCubbins, Roger Noll, and Barry Weingast, "Administrative Procedures as an Instrument of Political Control," *Journal of Law, Economics and Organization* 3 (1987), pp. 243–277.

22. *GATT Focus*, No. 69, June 1989.

23. See Yoichi Funibashi, *Managing the Dollar: From the Plaza to the Louvre* (Washington, DC: Institute for International Economics, 1988).

24. The USTR argues that it is getting harder to block adoption of GATT dispute settlement panels even under the current rules, but MTO will reinforce this trend. USTR talking points on the MTO, 1992. We thank Jane Bradley for her comments.

25. Stephen L. Lande and Craig Van Grasstek, *The Trade and Tariff Act of 1984: Trade Policy in the Reagan Administration* (Lexington, MA: Lexington Books, 1986).

26. Andreas F. Lowenfeld, "What the GATT Says (or Does Not Say)," in William Diebold, Jr., *Bilateralism, Multilateralism and Canada in U.S. Trade Policy* (Cambridge, MA: Ballinger, 1988), pp. 55–68.

27. Jonathan D. Aronson and Peter F. Cowhey, *When Countries Talk: International Trade in Telecommunications Services* (Cambridge, MA: Ballinger, 1988). We consider these proposals consistent with the spirit of those of Graham and Krugman, *Foreign Investment in the U.S.*, pp. 125–131.

28. Kenneth Flamm, "Managing New Rules: High-Tech Trade Friction and the Semiconductor Industry," *Brookings Review* (Spring 1991), pp. 22–29.

29. Clyde V. Prestowitz, Jr., *Trading Places: How We Allowed Japan to Take the Lead* (New York: Basic Books, 1988), p. 99.
30. Kent E. Calder, *Crisis and Compensation: Public Policy and Political Stability in Japan, 1949–1986* (Princeton: Princeton University Press, 1988), points out that bureaucratic discretion opens endless opportunities for political leadership to collect "rent" by arbitrating disputes.
31. For an overview see Geza Feketekuty, *International Trade in Services* (Cambridge, MA: Ballinger, 1988), and Phedon Nicolaides, *Liberalizing Trade in Services: Strategies for Success* (New York: Council on Foreign Relations, 1989).
32. On tariffication see Robert Z. Lawrence and Robert E. Litan, *Saving Free Trade: A Pragmatic Approach* (Washington, DC: Brookings Institution, 1986).
33. For a review see John H. Jackson and Edwin A. Vermulst, eds., *Antidumping Law and Practice: A Comparative Study* (Ann Arbor: University of Michigan Press, 1990).
34. CSPP, *Perspectives on Market Access and Antidumping Law Reform* (Washington, DC: CSPP, 1991).
35. Brian Hindley, "Trade in Services within the European Community," in Herbert Giersch, ed., *Free Trade in the World Economy* (Tübingen, Germany: Mohr, 1987). An excellent treatment of GATT rules on dumping is John H. Barton and Bart S. Fisher, *International Trade and Investment: Regulating International Business* (Boston: Little, Brown, 1986), Chapter 5.
36. We feel that the exporter should have the option of demanding consultations when faced by conflicting restraints. Our other suggestions are drawn from Kingery, "The U.S.-Japan Semiconductor Arrangement and the GATT."
37. For a discussion of additional problems involving safeguards in the context of the Free Trade Agreement see J. David Richardson, "Adjustments and Safeguards," in Peter Morici, ed., *Making Free Trade Work: The Canada-U.S. Agreement* (New York: Council on Foreign Relations, 1990), pp. 60–83.
38. Lande and Van Grasstek, *The Trade and Tariff Act of 1984.*
39. Several proposals have contained elements of these thoughts. We relied especially on the reasoning of Gary N. Horlick and Debra P. Steger, "Subsidies and Countervailing Duties," in Morici, ed., *Making Free Trade Work*, pp. 84–101.

CHAPTER 10

1. Trade and investment usually are substitutable in any given case, but they are complementary in aggregate over the long-term. For a useful demonstration of the dynamics in the context of North American free trade see Alan M. Rugman, *Multinationals and Canada–United States Free Trade* (Columbia, SC: University of South Carolina Press, 1990).
2. David Leyton-Brown, "Implementing the Agreement," in Peter Morici, ed., *Making Free Trade Work: The Canada-U.S. Agreement* (New York: Council on Foreign Relations, 1990), pp. 48–49.
3. See Edwin Vermulst and Paul Waer, "European Community Rules of Origin as Commercial Policy Instruments," *Journal of World Trade* 24:3 (June 1990), pp. 55–99; and N. David Palmeter, "The U.S. Rules of Origin Proposal to GATT: Monotheism or Polytheism?," *Journal of World Trade Law* 24:2 (April 1990), pp. 25–36.

4. See Vermulst and Waer, "European Community Rules of Origin as Commercial Policy Instruments," pp. 55–99.

5. See David Yoffie in Thomas K. McCraw, ed., *America vs. Japan* (Boston: Harvard Business Review Press, 1986), p. 66.

6. The European Community insisted on 60 percent European Free Trade Area content for any automobile imported under the special tariff terms granted to the European Free Trade Area. *Economist*, "Europe's Internal Market: A Survey," July 8, 1989, p. 36. As Vermulst and Waer note, this requirement is typical of the distinctions made in all countries between rules of origin for goods under preferential and nonpreferential trading arrangements. For example, the U.S.-Canada Free Trade Agreement set up special value-added tests on third-party suppliers for textiles, steel, and automobiles in the free-trade area. Joseph Greenwald, "Negotiating Strategy," in Hufbauer, ed., *Europe 1992*, p. 372. Our analysis of semiconductors relies on Kenneth Flamm, "Semiconductors," in Hufbauer, ed., *Europe 1992*. While the European Community tackled VERs and local production by foreign firms, the GATT tried to negotiate a new code on subsidies for exporting. The GATT is following the principle of describing some subsidies as forbidden, others as permitted, and still others as conditionally acceptable depending on their impact on the market.

7. Our interpretation is based on facts presented by Vermulst and Waer, "European Community Rules of Origin as Commercial Policy Instruments."

8. Ibid., p. 90.

9. Ibid.

10. Barry E. Hawk, "European Economic Community Merger Regulation," *Antitrust Law Journal* 59:2 (1990), pp. 457–464.

11. "Joint Comments of the ABA Section of Antitrust Law and the Section of International Law and Practice on Japan Fair Trade Commission Antimonopoly Act Enforcement Guidelines," *Antitrust Law Journal* 60:1 (1991), pp. 291–326. The need to address the keiretsu issue is urged by the American Chamber of Commerce in Japan even though it does not endorse specific antitrust measures. *Trade and Investment in Japan: The Current Environment* (Tokyo: American Chamber of Commerce, 1992).

12. Clyde H. Farnsworth, "Antitrust Extension Is Weighed," *New York Times*, April 16, 1990, p. C1. The 1982 Export Trading Company Act directs the Justice Department to apply the Sherman Act to such problems. The Department of Justice cites numerous problems but does not believe that comity (respect for another country's sovereign laws) is an absolute bar to action. "60 Minutes with the Hon. James F. Rill, Assistant Attorney General, U.S. Department of Justice, Antitrust Division," *Antitrust Law Journal* 60:1 (1991), pp. 217–242.

13. Kozo Yamamura, ed., *Japanese Investment in the United States: Should We Be Concerned?* (Seattle: Society for Japanese Studies, University of Washington, 1989).

14. Douglas Rosenthal, "Competition Policy," in Hufbauer, ed., *Europe 1992*, p. 323.

15. Alasdair Smith and Anthony Venables, "Automobiles," in Hufbauer, ed., *Europe 1992*, pp. 119–158.

16. EC-wide tests of concentration may prove more powerful than national ones, but there is no agreement on this standard at the policy level. Smith and

Venables, p. 134. Hawk points out that U.S. analysts find the Commission's distinctions between cooperative and concentrative joint ventures (drawn from German cartel law) to be "metaphysical." Hawk, "European Economic Community Merger Regulation," p. 460.

17. Michael Calingaert, *The 1992 Challenge from Europe: Development of the European Community's Internal Market* (New York: National Planning Association, 1988).

18. See Simon Reich, "Roads to Follow: Regulating Direct Foreign Investment," *International Organization* 43:4 (Autumn 1989), pp. 543–584. However, Wolfgang Kartte, the president of the German Cartel Office, has begun to move against strategic alliances when there is no access for third parties. In April 1992 he threatened to take Allianz, Europe's largest insurer, to court unless it voluntarily cut back its holdings of Dresdner Bank, Germany's second-largest financial institution, from 22.3 percent to 19.1 percent. *Financial Times*, April 22, 1992, p. 3.

19. This quotation is cited in Catherine Distler, "Convergence and Conflicts over Competition Law," *Project Promethee Perspective*, No. 15 (Paris: Promethee, January 1991), p. 26.

20. The Japanese equivalent of the Federal Trade Commission has unsuccessfully sought higher levels of fines, but it has raised the punitive surcharges for collusion. The U.S. desires the FTC to use its power to bring criminal complaints more actively. Al Nakajima, "FTC Chief Says LDP Stymied Plan to Hike Monopoly Fines," *Nikkei Weekly*, December 28, 1991, and January 14, 1992 (double issue), p. 4.

21. *The Age of Diminished Expectations* (Cambridge, MA: MIT Press, 1990), p. 131.

22. Even in an era of floating rates, the exchange rates of the principal trading currencies remain controversial because they impact trade flows. The adjustment of exchange rates remains an effective influence on balance-of-payments swings. Paul Krugman, *Has the Adjustment Process Worked?* (Washington, DC: Institute of International Economics, October 1991).

23. Clyde H. Farnsworth, "U.S.-Japan Telecommunications Accord," *New York Times*, March 3, 1990, p. Y19.

24. "County to Buy 15 Rail Cars from Sumitomo," *Los Angeles Times*, October 6, 1992, p. A1.

25. Under the rubric of innovation policy, Ostry, *Governments and Corporations in a Shrinking World*, pp. 53–78, explores some of these same issues.

26. On RACE, see Peter Cowhey, "Telecommunications"; on the others see Kenneth Flamm, "Semiconductors," both in Hufbauer, ed., *Europe 1992*, pp. 208–209, 225–292.

27. *GATT Focus*, No. 85, October 1991, p. 5.

28. In the fall of 1991 the International Telecommunications Union, as an experiment, made many of its standards available on-line through a file server in Boulder, Colorado. Many large users, especially European firms that previously found it difficult and expensive to obtain technical standards, kept the transatlantic lines busy as they downloaded the standards. Their own telecommunications operators had little incentive to make it easy for them to know and understand international communications standards; they might, after all, decide to become competitors.

INDEX

Abegglen, James C., 294n7 (Ch. 2), 294n9 (Ch. 1)
ACE (Advanced Computing Environment), 149
Acquisitions, 63, 280
Administrative Procedures Act of 1946, 18
Advanced Battery Consortium, 118
Advanced Micro Devices, 151
Advanced Order Entry system, 173
Advanced Technology Program, 150
Advertising, 71
Aeroflot, 173
Aerospace industry, 106, 111; and global strategies of suppliers, 35, 36; and the joint development of common products, 54; and the telecommunications sector, 209–10
Agriculture, 33, 36, 75, 218–21, 250
AIG (American International Group), 21
Airbus, 6, 54, 85, 268
Aircraft industry, 68, 71, 85, 223
Air freight, 52–53, 154
Airline industry, 52, 173, 198, 201, 222; discounting of tickets in, and airline agreements, 230; and open industrial policies, 229; and restructuring the world economy, 241

Alcatel, 169, 172, 284
Alfa Romeo, 110
Allied Bank International, 8
Amadeus, 52
AMD (Advanced Micro Devices), 129, 132, 148, 155
Amdahl, 84
American Airlines, 173
American Express, 21, 85
American National Standards Institute, 180
Ameritech, 202
Antidumping policy, 237, 248, 263–67, 271–82, 291; and the automobile sector, 120–21; and increasing local content concerns, 78; and open industrial policies, 231; and the semiconductor industry, 136, 140–41, 143, 144–45; and subsidies, 269
Antitrust policy, 61, 237, 287, 291; and the automobile sector, 94, 113, 119, 120, 122, 279, 280; and concerns about fair competition raised by alliances, 79–80; and Department of Justice "enforcement guidelines," 257; and the global counterpart to free trade, 15; and global strategies of suppliers, 36;

Liberalization, 14, 15, 87, 289–90; and antitrust policy, 280; and the automobile sector, 91, 93, 120; and global services and global goods, resemblance of, 72; and national treatment, principle of, 260; and the OECD Capital Liberalization Code, 243–44; and open industrial policies, 227, 231; and promoting the free movement of goods and investment, 22–23; and restructuring the world economy, 243, 246, 247; and the semiconductor industry, 139–40, 162; and the telecommunications sector, 165, 170, 174, 179, 181, 183, 185–87, 190, 214; and tiered reciprocity, 261–62; and the Uruguay Round, 217, 221

Licensing, 44, 45; and antitrust laws, 244; and complementary resources, 47; and the globalization of commerce, 57; and government procurement, 284; and intellectual property issues, 49–50; and the telecommunications sector, 191, 201–4

Life cycles, product, 26–27, 53, 125, 130, 140, 265

Lincoln Town Car, 51

Lipson, Charles, 295n16

Liquid crystal display technology, 49, 160

Lithography, 151–52

Lobbying, 18, 198

Local content rules, 78–79, 112, 114, 116, 121, 122, 274, 275, 284–86

Los Angeles, 286

Lowenfeld, Andreas, 255–56

LSI Logic, 50, 56, 132, 149, 151, 152

LTV, 154

Lyonnaise Communications, 202

Maastricht Treaty, 213

McCaw, 179, 193, 208

McDonnell Douglas, 35, 54

McFadden Act, 260

McKeown, Timothy J., 297n17

McMillan, John, 250, 320n20

Major, John, 209

Malaysia, 112, 206

Mannesmann Mobilfunk, 202

Matsushita, 129, 280

Mazda, 7, 53, 83, 97, 106, 107, 113–18

MCA, 281

MCC (Microelectronics Computer and Electronic Corporation), 8, 79, 87, 150, 288

MCI, 192, 194, 195, 199, 208–9

Mercantile Bank, 77

Mercedes Benz, 98, 103, 111, 113

Mercury, 192, 194, 196, 208, 209

Mergers, 280

Merrill Lynch, 173

Mexico, 110, 202, 206, 219. See also NAFTA (North American Free-Trade Agreement)

MFN (most-favored-nation) status, 143, 189–90, 214, 248

Michigan, 83

Micron Technology, 132, 134

Microprocessors, 128, 133, 140, 156

Microsoft, 134, 160

Military technology, 85, 128, 135

Miniaturization, 72

Minilateral relations, 75, 163, 235–36, 240–42, 251, 256, 257

Minitel, 178

Minolta, 84

MIPS, 149

MITI (Ministry of International Trade and Industry, Japan), 8, 97, 101, 103, 108, 112, 153, 178, 227–28, 244, 257, 263; and the Japanese model of industrial organization, 62–63; and redeployment of the Japanese manufacturing structure, 43; and rules of origin, 275; and the semiconductor industry, 121–22, 126, 135, 136, 139, 141, 144, 149–50

Mitsubishi, 113–14, 115

Mitsubishi Electric, 155

Mitsubishi Heavy Industries, 108

ABOUT THE AUTHORS

Peter F. Cowhey is a Professor of International Relations and Political Science at the University of California, San Diego. Jonathan D. Aronson is Professor of International Relations at the University of Southern California. Their jointly authored books on international trade and investment include *When Countries Talk: International Trade in Telecommunications Services* (Ballinger, 1988) and *Changing Networks: Mexico's Telecommunications Options* (Center for U.S.–Mexico Studies, 1989). Their individual books and articles have covered the politics of trade policy and the regulation of the world markets for automobiles, banking, energy, and services.